No. 1203
$14.95

HANDBOOK OF MICROPROCESSOR APPLICATIONS

BY JOHN A. KUECKEN

T2-DXK-354

TAB BOOKS Inc.

BLUE RIDGE SUMMIT, PA. 17214

FIRST EDITION

FIRST PRINTING—JULY 1980

Copyright © 1980 by TAB BOOKS Inc.

Printed in the United States of America

Library of Congress Cataloging in Publication Data

Kuecken, John A
  Handbook of microprocessor applications.

  Includes index.
  1. Microprocessors. I. Title.
QA76.5.K778   001.64'04   80-14549
ISBN 0-8306-9935-X
ISBN 0-8306-1203-3 (pbk.)

Other TAB books by the author:

No.   929   *Solid-State Motor Controls*
No. 1128   *How To Make Home Electricity From Wind, Water & Sunshine*
No. 1236   *Fiberoptics*

Contents

Introduction

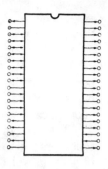

Compared to most inventions, the microprocessor has come to commercial maturity at a dizzying pace. The automobile can be described as having been invented in about 1880 and it did not attain a significant commercial stature until about 1911. The airplane was invented in 1903 and it was not until 1916, during World War I combat, that its use became widespread. The transistor was invented in 1948 and did not begin to significantly penetrate the electronics markets until about 1958. The integrated circuit (IC) was invented in 1958 and did not come into widespread use until about 1968. By comparison, the microprocessor was invented in 1974 and was in widespread use by 1977; a scant three years later!

The various reasons for the very rapid and widespread acceptance of this device are covered in this book. The rapid acceptance of the microprocessor has taken place so fast that a great many of the instructors and practicing engineers have not had the time to keep pace with new development. The proliferation of seminars and courses offered by non-traditional education sources such as consulting firms, semiconductor manufacturers and other sources is testimony to the desire of a great many firms and individuals to acquire the requisite skills to keep up with the changes.

At the outset, the microprocessor was a relatively difficult beast to handle. It usually required the use of some relatively expensive teleprinters, storage devices and other items which brought the entry level cost to approximately $20,000. This investment was required before any significant amount of development work could be accomplished to determine whether the microprocessor would be a viable addition. The investment had to made on sheer faith. This tended to restrict the acquisition of microcomputer skills to firms large or adventurous enough to accept the initial investment.

About 1977, this picture changed sharply with the introduction of entry level microcomputer kits in the $20 to $600 price range. These units made possible the development of stand-alone products. With no tools other than these evaluation kits, it became possible for the engineer to develop microprocessor based products and to demonstrate the operation of these products at a very economical level.

It is the object of this book to show the principles of microprocessors and to demonstrate some of the nearly infinite numbers of ways in which the microprocessor can be applied to measurement, process sequencing, "smart" instruments and some of the more traditional computer applications.

Emphasis is placed upon the use of the microprocessor in the control, sequencing and measurement functions and the manipulation of bits and bytes at the machine or assembly language level in which most of the simple evaluation kits operate. It will not be assumed that any of the extensive "development systems" are available to the reader.

It has been argued that machine language development of software is very slow, difficult to do, and incomprehensible to anyone other than the developer or programmer. I will attempt to demonstrate that machine or assembler language development can be fast, cost effective and easily followed by others if proper documentation is kept. To this end a system of documentation is introduced which makes it possible to analyze a program and locate any given step in short order.

In order to avoid vague generalities, I will deal with two microprocessors with significantly different architecture: the Motorola 6800 family and the RCA Cosmac (1802) family. The contrasts between the architectures and the manipulation techniques for these machines are sufficient for the reader to have a "feel" for the usage of nearly any microprocessor once the operation of these two types has been mastered. Specific subroutines, programs and manipulation techniques will be given for these machines.

The dealings of the microprocessor with the real world are also extensively covered. This treatment extends to the inclusion of specific circuit diagrams which show techniques of interfacing, external device switching and sensing. Circuits and software techniques for multiplexing are also shown since these form a large and very necessary part of the use of microprocessors.

In keeping with the basic philosophy of making the text as

simple and understandable as possible, the section on Boolean algebra is treated in terms of ladder diagrams which can be easily visualized by even an untrained eye. These diagrams are commonly used in the control industry and are usually accepted as the simplest way of presenting relatively complex Boolean relationships.

This book is written with the assumption that the reader has no familiarity with binary arithmetic, BCD, hexadecimal or octal notation and these are treated early in the discussion. Algorithms in machine or assembler language are given for number base conversion as well as for addition, subtraction, multiplication and division for long string numbers. Basic treatment of transcendental functions, logarithms and trig functions is also presented. The use of these mathematical manipulations in data messaging and reduction is discussed at length.

The basic aim of the text is to render the use of microprocessors as simple as possible in the widest possible span of applications. At the risk of being repetitious, the same subjects have been treated in different locations in the text from different viewpoints. This has been done with the hope that a second and perhaps third encounter with the same topic will generate greater familiarity and understanding of some of the less familiar concepts.

John A. Kuecken

Microprocessor Functions 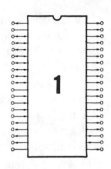 1

What can a microprocessor *not* be used for? It will not mend a broken heart. It will not ensure justice among all men. It will not bring happiness to the lonely. It will not perform its functions instantaneously.

Outside of those constraints, there is very little that it cannot do or assist in doing. Nearly all physical measurements can be reduced to electrical measurements through the use of one or another form of transducer. As a general rule, anything that can be measured can be controlled through the use of one form or another of actuator. It follows then that nearly any physical phenomenon can be measured by a transducer of some form. The data might be digested and perhaps manipulated by a microprocessor and the phenomenon can then be controlled by actuators operating on commands issued by the microprocessor.

As an example, consider the process of baking bread. The oven might be equipped with a set of thermocouples which translate temperature into a non-linear electrical voltage. An analog to digital converter converts this voltage into digital format which is fed to the microcomputer. Since the voltage is non-linear, the microcomputer must convert this digital reading into a temperature reading. On the basis of preset limits, the microcomputer can then determine whether the oven is too hot or not hot enough and operate the gas valves which control the oven temperature accordingly. If the oven is a flow-through affair, in which the bread enters one end unbaked and emerges on a conveyor belt fully baked at the other end, the unit might be equipped with an infrared sensor or a color sensor to determine the state of the actual baking of the bread at some point part way through the tunnel. If the bread is baking slowly, the microprocessor could slow the conveyor so that the loaves are in the tunnel for a longer time. Conversely, if the bread is baking too rapidly, the processor could speed up the conveyor so that the bread emerges faster. Since the unit senses the passage of each loaf, it could keep a tally of the number of loaves in the run and issue instructions to other machinery to make more dough or to stop the dough making process.

You might question why the acceleration and slowdown process is required since the temperature of the oven is being controlled by the processor. The answer is that the oven has a substantial amount of inertia. Simply turning the gas up does not instantaneously change the temperature within the oven. Also, the mixing of the bread dough is a batch process which is somewhat variable. From one batch to the next, there are variations in the amount of moisture in the dough. For this reason, some of the batches will tend to bake slightly faster than others. As an overview, it can be said that the processor in this example is exercising the same judgement over the baking process that the skilled baker would. It would, of course, be necessary that a skilled baker initially adjust the machine so that the baking process proceeds properly. Thereafter the machine could proceed without much guidance and the process could be said to be fully automated.

In the example of the baking control, notice that the machine requires few of the usual accourtrements of a computer. In place of the teletype keyboard for the entry of programs or data, a machine of this type is more likely to be equipped with a small calculator-type keyboard with only 16 or 20 keys. This keyboard can even be located behind a locked door or in a separate pocket-size package to be carried by the foreman or master baker. This prevents unauthorized entries to the control process.

Another familiar item is missing. The unit is very unlikely to be equipped with the familiar TV screen. If there is a display at all, it will probably consist of a small window showing a few numeric characters. Again the similarity to a pocket calculator is evident. If there are any messages to be displayed such as "enter batch size" or "oven not up to temperature" they will usually be printed on the back of a glass or plastic window and will become readable only when the lamp behind the designated message is illuminated. Cathode ray TV tubes are expensive and bulky to include in an electronic machine. The inclusion of the tube to display a very limited number of messages would represent an unnecessary expense in a single purpose machine such as this. If the number of possible messages exceeds a dozen or so, the machine could employ one of the alphanumeric displays for one or two lines of 12 to 30 characters. Only when the number of characters to be displayed exceeds 40 or so does the cathode-ray tube begin to be economically attractive.

A very low cost approach is one in which all of the possible messages are silk-screened or printed on the front panel of the machine. A single lamp alongside each message will light to indicate which messages apply:

Lamp	Message
0	ENTER PRODUCT TYPE
0	ENTER BATCH SIZE
0	ENTER BAKE TEMPERATURE
☼	OVEN NOT UP TO TEMPERATURE
0	. . . . . .
0	. . .
0	PRESS "RUN" TO START BAKING

In this example, the product type has been entered along the batch size and the bake temperature and the operator is waiting for the oven to reach the proper temperature. The display has been organized to prompt the operator through a step-by-step sequence to load the required data into the machine. This is an approach which seems to be highly favored by "Human Engineering" groups. The operator sees the lighted lamp walk down the column of messages prompting him to take the required actions in sequence. If he is interrupted or distracted, he still knows exactly where the process left off and where he should resume.

You can see that the average user would not even know that a microcomputer was doing the work inside the machine if the machine builder did not design the machine with apperance and marketing appeal in mind. The user is not required to know anything about computer programming or to learn any very sophisticated things about the machine. To the user the machine is simply a remarkable automatic control over the baking process.

DEDICATED APPLICATIONS

When confronted with the word *microprocessor* the average electronics enthusiast who has not worked with these devices will usually conjure up visions of a TV game, or one of the home/hobby stored program general purpose computers. These items can be built using one of the available microprocessor chips and this book will cover those applications as well. However, the hidden, dedicated microprocessor or microcomputer will surely dominate the market within the immediate future.

The use of microcomputers in automobile engine controls alone is predicted to run at a level in excess of 7 million units per year by 1982. Added to this are the microcomputers being incorporated into home laundrys, microwave ovens, sewing machines, heating controls and energy management devices. It is not difficult to see the reasons for this proliferation in the marketplace. Even if the average American home contains a home/hobby computer and a few TV games by 1982, the few microprocessors in these units are likely to be grossly outnumbered by the dedicated and hidden units in other appliances and automobiles.

The chips used in these high volume dedicated applications are very special units indeed. They will mostly belong to the computer-on-a-chip variety as represented by the Motorola 6801, the RCA 1801 or the Intel 8081. These devices contain within the single package all of the clock circuitry, the read/write memory, input/output circuitry in both serial and parallel format and programmable counter/time circuitry. In short, all of the functions required for the operation of a full-grown computer are deposited upon a single silicon chip and housed within the single integrated circuit package.

When these devices are purchased by the auto or appliance manufacturer, they will leave the shipping dock of the semiconductor house with all of the operating instructions or the program required to make the device an auto engine control or a sewing machine masked into the read-only-memory (ROM) built onto the chip. The chip will be identified by a special number for that product alone. When the chip arrives at an auto or appliance plant, that manufacturer need only plug it into the socket. Aside from incoming inspection, the manufacturer need only install and then pay for the device. In 10,000 lots, the price of these devices is already down to levels of a few dollars and the price can be expected to go even lower.

Above all, low price is the source of the widespread appeal of the microprocessor. Since the beginning of mass production, inventors have dreamed of a universal device that could, by means of some minor adjustment, be made to do anything. The microprocomputer comes closer to this goal than any other device developed by man. The same basic microprocessor chip can be run off by the millions with the final masking process determining whether the device is an engine control or a sewing machine control, etc. The full economics of scale can be realized with the product since the widest possible spectrum of useage is accommodated. The microprocessor is just about the universal component. Furthermore, it is itself amendable to fully automated fabrication techniques for most of the operations needed to produce a finished unit. Because of the very large product volume involved and the relative freedom from design change, very large expenditures can be justified to automate the production. Changes in what the product does can be incorporated by simply changing the program which, in itself, involves only a change in the ROM mask.

There is a catch hidden in this game, particularly for the small firm or the firm which anticipates only a small volume for a given product. The masking of the operating program into the ROM carries a one-time charge of several thousand dollars. Where product is to be made in the thousands, this charge is insignificant since it would cost far less in the aggregate than the cost of individually programmed ROM chips—including testing, installation and board real estate. For small volume application, this masking charge can represent a very significant overhead item. This is especially true in view of the fact that *any* change in the operating program will incur a second masking charge. This represents a significant financial risk with any untried program. If the unit is taken directly to the masked-ROM stage the designer is betting that the program is perfect and will not require any changes at all.

A few of the chips such as the Intel 8083 are offered in an ultraviolet (UV) erasable version for program development. In this case the unit can be programmed and tried. If some changes are desired, the ROM can be erased by exposure to UV light in an inexpensive eraser and then reprogrammed with alterations until a satisfactory operating program is attained. The UV erasure unit is many times as expensive as the mask programmed unit. Therefore, this approach carries a penalty in applications where the product volume does not carry the expectation that it will ever reach the break even point for masking. The product will simply remain more expensive.

Some of the semiconductor houses offer a multi-chip set for program development. In this case these special (and therefore very expensive) chips are constructed so that the final performance is identical to the performance of the eventual masked Rom version.

This kind of approach is usually justifiable only in products where the volume projections clearly indicate a product level which fully justifies an early jump into the masked ROM unit.

For product developments where a more cautious entry into the market is indicated, the development can be accomplished using the general purpose chips of the generic family in a board constructed to represent the final product. A few manufacturers present a spectrum of family products which are generally compatible with one another so that the transition from the general purpose development unit to the final dedicated masked ROM microcomputer can be made in several stages.

As a case in point, consider the Motorola 6800 family. The 6800 proper is a general purpose chip which started the family. It requires an external clock chip, external memory for both read/write and ROM and external input/output devices. This chip is offered in the Motorola Evaluation Kit: MEK-D2. The kit sells for approximately $200 without power supply (single 5V). It is supplied and comes equipped with the J Bug operating PROM which permits various types of operation. It has a keyboard and display of six digits.

It is also equipped with a user peripheral interface adapter (PIA) which offers 20 input/output lines and two interrupt lines. The J Bug places the unit in an operating mode in which it services the keyboard and the display. It also permits the operator to read, modify or write into any memory location. It can handle breakpoints and quasi-single step operations so that the operator can go through a program one step at a time to see what the machine is doing. The J Bug also services the Kansas City input/output whereby programs can be stored on an ordinary audio cassette and reloaded to the machine on command.

Within the limitations of the read/write memory size and the number of input/output lines, this two-board microcomputer can be used to simulate a proposed product. The program can be written into the read/write memory and the unit interfaced to the product devices through the PIA. The program can be edited at will from the keyboard until the product performs as desired. Alternate programs can be stored on tape for later retrieval. The processor board is also flexible enough so that additional memory in either read/write or ROM can be constructed and added. Additional input/output capability is also easily accommodated. This MEK-D2 unit represents the extreme low end approach to development of a 6800 family based product.

The Motorola 6802 represents another step in this product spectrum. The 6802 is slightly less of a general purpose chip. However, for accommodation into a product, it offers certain advantages. First of all, it has the clock circuitry built on-chip. If a precision clock is required, it is only necessary to add an external crystal. If clock precision is not required, the clock function can be implemented in a single outboard (off of the chip) resistor and capacitor. A clock output driver is also provided for supplying the clock to other chips which might require it.

The 6802 also has 64 bytes of onboard read/write memory. For a surprising number of small product applications, this represents a fully adequate scratchpad and no external read/write memory chips are required. The lower 36 bytes of this memory are protectable with a low power battery backup so that some of the scratchpad data can be preserved through a power failure.

The 6802 is still provided with a full set of 16 address lines and 8 data lines. It is intended for use with external ROM and external input/output and timer functions in the form of other chips. The 6800 family treats all input/output just as external memory is treated. Therefore, extreme flexibility in input/output operations is provided. An output can be accomplished with a single write-to-address XXXX instruction and an input becomes a single read-from-address YYYY instruction. With the 16 address lines, a total of 65,536 locations can be directly addressed. Any of these can be either read/write memory, ROM or an input/output device.

By contrast, the Motorola 6801 has no external address or data lines and therefore is not really intended to handle external memory or input/output devices. Like the 6802 it has an onboard clock oscillator so that the requirement for an external clock chip is eliminated. However, the 6801 also incorporates circuitry equivalent to about 1½ PIA chips for input and output in parallel format. It also incorporates the circuitry for a serial input/output arrangement. In addition to this, it has the circuitry for a programmable counter timer chip. It also has bytes of onboard read/write memory and 2K bytes of onboard masked ROM.

Referring to the bake oven controller example, you can see that the development of this product could proceed in a three-step sequence:

■ At the outset, the entire control process can be implemented with the MEK-D2 kit. The program can be written into the read/write memory and stored on tape. When the product is functioning properly, the next step can be taken.

■ At the second stage of development, you might like to have a design which is suitable for a deliverable product. The product will still need a keyboard and a display. However, the keyboard will not require the capability to program the machine. Since only data is to be entered, a number of keys on the keyboard can be dispensed with. In addition, the MEK-D2 contains a fairly substantial number of chips associated with writing to and reading from tape in Kansas City format. These can also be eliminated from the deliverable product.

For this stage, a board can be developed which carries the 6802 microprocessor, an UV erasable ROM chip and the necessary input/output chips to service the bakign machine as well as the limited keyboard and display. The keyboard and display can also be designed in formal and final style.

When this step is completed, the microcomputer board will have been reduced from about 20 chips to about five chips. The UV erasable ROM will be the most expensive chip at perhaps $30. The parts cost, including the smaller board, will be under $200 in quantities of 100 units or so. You now have a finished and working product that can be sold to customers. If customer acceptance is good, you are in a position to proceed to step three.

■ In step three of the program, the product which has by now had the benefit of customer acceptance and experience can be reduced to the 6801 microcomputer. A program, a *modus operandi* in which you have confidence and a market have been established for the product. There is definite indication that you can sell enough to recover the masking charges. The program is sent to Motorola with the few necessary address changes and a custom-masked part is produced which can be bought in quantity for less than $10. The board and the incoming inspection and the power supply also fall in cost. You can probably reduce the price to the customer and at the same time increase profit.

This type of stepped evolution has a number of advantages in risk and investment minimization. First of all, the language of the chips is common. Therefore, the program written to accommodate the original 6800 will also run on the later versions. There are a few exceptions to this however. These include the matter of addresses. The J Bug ROM in the MEK-D2 kit occupies the address which must be filled by the ROM in the second version. However, the operating program in the MEK must be written into read/write memory. This means that at least some of the addresses in the program must change before the program will run in the second unit. Since the second unit is programmed with electrically programmable read only memory (EPROM), an error in transposition is not a major catastrophy. The PROM need only be erased and correctly reprogrammed. However, from the second to the third stage, an error in address transposition can be expensive. There are certain advantages, therefore, in giving the second unit the same input/output and memory addresses as the final microcomputer version.

Programming errors are not the only reasons why a program might have to be changed. The customer might also decide that certain changes are desirable after he has had some experience with the product. For example, he might decide that it would be more practical to enter the baking temperature first and then enter all of the other parameters so that he did not have to wait for the oven to rise to the proper temperature before entering the remaining data. He might like to have the process start as soon as it is ready or he might insist upon human intervention before starting. For the small firm, the incorporation of additions or customer changes-of-mind would seem to be a fact of life.

One of the large advantages of the three-step approach is the fact that such changes in philosophy can be fairly inexpensive to incorporate in the second step whereas they become considerably more expensive to incorporate in the third step. It should be noted that in some cases, certain manufacturers will offer an instruction set which is translatable from the general purpose microprocessor to the single chip microcomputer. In this case, the assembly language or mnemonic commands can be identical for the two devices whereas the exact machine language commands cannot be. In these cases, an exact machine language translation can be made by another computer without error.

As new microprocessors are introduced into a family, they can also bring new and useful instructions with them. In this case, most manufacturers will attempt to ensure that the new chip will run on all of the old programs. The old programs cannot, of course, take advantage of the power of the new instructions. The Motorola 6809 is a case in point. It can be made to run 6800 programs but the use of the power of the new instructions is lost unless the programs are rewritten especially to take advantage of them.

HIGHER LEVEL LANGUAGES

It is the purpose of this book to teach the usage of the very compact machine or assembler language programming for the general purpose chips. This programming technique is appropriate for either direct usage or for translation into small dedicated programs. Because of the prevalence of discussion on the topic of higher level language programming, a few words on the subject are in order here.

One of the best articles on the subject of higher level language programming which has come to my attention is: Kenneth Wickham, "Pascal is a 'natural,' " *IEEE Spectrum*, Vol. 16. No. 3 (March 1979), 35-41. In the article, Wickham states that after a consideration of Pascal, Fortran, BASIC, PL/M and Cobol on 15 different attributes, Pascal emerged as the language of choice for programming at Texas Instruments and that Texas Instruments has decided to use Pascal for in-house programming. Mr Wickham notes that:

—The use of the high level language creates machine language instructions that permit the programmer to solve the problems at an abstract level rather than having to be concerned with machine architecture.

—A structured high-level language (HLL) like Pascal allows problems to be solved "top down" the way natural thought processes work.

—Because Pascal is easier to read, it is easier to modify.

On the other hand, Wickham concedes that even Pascal programs require more memory space and more running time than machine language coding, and that critical portions of the program should be hand coded in machine language for "fine tuning."

In an editorial box on the same article, several people from Tektronix (a leading instrument builder) were also quoted. Stephen Dum, new product research manager, notes that where a number of constants must be used, Pascal ends up using two and a half to three times the space to do the job. If memory space is inexpensive and available this might not be a problem. However, for small, single chip applications, memory space is sharply limited. If the capacity of the chip is exceeded, the hardware price for the product doubles.

It is also noted that the high level generated programs tend to run slower, and factors of two or three are mentioned by some. Wickham notes that Texas Instruments "fine tunes" Pascal generated programs wherever running times are critical by rewriting in hand-coded machine language. Lynn Saunders, a hardware engineer at Tektronics, notes: "It's difficult to mix Pascal and assembly code. Fast program execution is vital for real-time instruments like a multimeter. The number of sales that multimeter is going to make is inversely proportional to the number of milliseconds the program takes to get around the operating loop. He (the programmer) can do 80 percent of his job with a high level language but there's 20 percent where he has to worry about the nitty-gritty dirty stuff to get the multimeter to running at top speed."

Wickham notes that Texas Instruments has experienced an increase in programming efficiency of two and one-half to three times and that maintenance time has been reduced by a factor of two by replacing hand coding with Pascal.

In response I would like to put forward the following propositions:

■ Hand coding in machine language need not result in "spaghetti" code which is incomprehensible to anyone but the writer. The system of documentation to be set forth shortly will make any given step in a hand-coded program easily accessible to any skilled programmer.

■ "Top-down" logical approaches to a problem can be maintained as easily in machine coding as in a HLL approach.

■ The running time and memory requirements of a HLL program can make the difference between the success or failure of a small product. A basic knowledge of the device is imperative to development of a truly competitive product.

■ Even in products where maximum memory and running time efficiency are not always crucial, the programmer should be capable of this approach to be able to know how close the program has come in critical areas.

■ There are a great many places in the input/output operations of a typical controller where the use of a high level language is no help whatever and it might be an actual hindrance.

The last point cited is worthy of a little amplification. In control applications where the microprocessor addresses the input and output as memory, each output—such as the lamps on the prompting menu shown previously—is represented as one bit in the output word. To be specific, this menu is repeated with the control word added.

In this example the identifying number is shown but the condition of the lamp is not given. The control word represents the data which must be written to the output port or address in order to light that lamp. With a 1 in that position, the lamp lights. With a

Lamp #	Message	Control
0	ENTER PRODUCT TYPE	0000 000I
1	ENTER BATCH SIZE	0000 00I0
2	ENTER BAKE TEMPERATURE	0000 0I00
3	OVEN NOT UP TO TEMPERATURE	0000 I000
4	....	
5	.....	
6	..	
7	PRESS "RUN" TO START	I000 0000

zero, the lamp goes out. The number of the lamp is actually the power of two which represents the lamp position in the control word. If you wanted to light both lamp 3 and lamp 7 simultaneously with all of the other lamps out, the control word would be I000 I000. To light all of the lamps at the same time, the control word would be IIII IIII. For all of the lamps to be out the word would be 0000 0000. To actually effect such a control simply write the control word into the memory address representing the output device. The sequence would be:

The machine code is shown here mainly as an example of how simple the machine coding for this action is. The data 04 represents the binary code 0000 0I00 which would light the lamp #2 for the legend ENTER BAKE TEMPERATURE. The two bytes 80 06

	Machine Code Command	Data
Load the accumulator	86	
with the control word		04
Write the accumulator	B7	
to the output device		80
		06

represent the address of the output device which runs the lamps. The notation is hexadecimal and the coding is for 6800 family devices.

The point of this exercise is simply to show that a high level language would be of very little assistance in writing this routine. After having to use the routine a few times—note that the bake oven routine would require at least 8 repetitions of this routine—the programmer will be able write it from memory just as he remembers the office telephone number. The high level routine to call up the same action would be considerably longer.

There is no question that a high level language is helpful if the instruction requires the determination of the logarithm of N if the language contains a simple statement for the operation. However, the standard version of Pascal does not now contain a statement for raising a number to the N'th power therefore a routine would have to be written in machine language in any event. Routines such as Sin, Cos, Multiply, Divide, etc. do come out simpler when pre-written in the high level language.

In most control applications, the requirement for precision is relatively limited since most of the measurements are not accurate to better than 0.1 percent and many are no more than 1 percent. Many of the transcendental functions can be implemented with sufficient accuracy with a lookup-table-and-interpolate routine.

Wickham notes that Pascal programs can be executed (but not compiled) on machines with as little as 8 K of memory. The shortest version of BASIC (which does not include logs and tangents) runs 4K bytes and a reasonably full BASIC requires 16K. The typical one chip microcomputer has only one or two K of ROM. Therefore, not too many of the longer routines from either of the languages could be accommodated along with the housekeeping necessary for the operation of the device in the particular application.

Actually, compact subroutines for such things as servicing a seven segment display, servicing a keyboard or a 10 decimal digit by 10 decimal digit multiply, can usually be transported from one application to another in the same microprocessor family with minimal changes. This is a cumulative situation. As more products have been developed, the library of useful routines grows and the programming becomes simpler—provided only that the routines were well and clearly documented in the first place. In the same manner, the machine language algorithms from the high level languages can be lifted and used where required.

In summary, I believe that level language programming can be used to save a considerable amount of programming effort if running time and memory use is not critical. At the very least, critical areas should probably be re-coded by hand. This might be more difficult than starting out with hand coding. Control applications obtain less benefit from HLL programming and the use of single chip microcomputers might require hand coding just because of the limitations on memory size and the requirement for fastest running time. In any event, the programmer should be capable of writing native machine code if he or she intends to produce competitive products.

Binary, Hexadecimal And Octal Notation

2

All digital computers operate in the binary system of numbers since this number system can be fully represented by the simple on/off, low/high or true/false condition of switches, relay contacts, transistors, etc. There is a great advantage in this. Analog computers were designed to output a voltage to represent a given quantity. Therefore, output of 9.05 volts could represent the quantity 905 in decimal notation. However, these computers were always limited in accuracy. If the voltage driver were to drift slightly with age or temperature and the voltage reader were to suffer a similar drift, the drift would be present as a reading error. The units had to be continuously adjusted and calibrated if results as accurate as 1 percent were to be obtained. By comparison, the cheapest $5 pocket calculator will infallibly solve problems like $1,000,000_{10} - 2_{10} = 999,998_{10}$; a problem which the finest analog computer could never have solved because of accuracy limitations. The subscript 10 is used in the above example to indicate that the numeric notation is in the base 10.

This advantage in accuracy in digital devices is because the interpreting device has only to distinguish whether the voltage on a given wire is low or high. In the commonly used transistor-transistor (TTL) standard, any voltage less than 0.8 volts is low and any voltage higher than 1.8 volts is high. Anything in between is an illegal level and is subject to ambiguous interpretation. However, it is relatively simple to make devices using transistors which when operated from a 5 volt supply, will pull the load below 0.8v for a low and will pull it above 1.8v for a high. It is not difficult to transfer digital information in an essentially error-free manner in the binary system. A given number can be replicated, transmitted, stored and retrieved any number of times with essentially no degradation in accuracy.

BINARY NOTATION

Binary notation simply refers to numbers written in the number base two. Most of us learned numbers in the base 10. We were taught in grade school to add, subtract, multiply and divide in the decimal system. In any number base, you count up to the number that is one less than the base and then start with a count in the next most significant place. In the number base 10, the number following nine is 10, the number following 99 is 100 and the number following 999 is 1000. The step to the next most significant number takes place at integral (whole number) powers of the base. Therefore:

$10^0 = 1$ (any number to the zero power is equal to 1)
$10^1 = 10$
$10^2 = 100$
$10^3 = 1000$

Since there are only two numbers smaller than two, a binary number can contain only the digits zero and one. In computer useage, a group of eight zeros and ones is usually referred to as a byte. This is usually written in two groups of four, which are sometime called a nibble. The individual slot which always contains either a zero or a one is referred to as a bit. Binary numbers like decimal numbers, are written with the least significant bit on the right and the most significant bit on the left. These are usually abreviated as LSB and MSB. Each bit slot represents the next highest power of 2. Therefore:

power of 2	binary	decimal value
2^0	0000 000I	1
2^1	0000 00I0	2
2^2	0000 0I00	4
2^3	0000 I000	8
2^4	000I 0000	16
2^5	00I0 0000	32
2^6	0I00 0000	64
2^7	I000 0000	128

As with any number system, the total value of a number is the sum of the values of the individual powers. Therefore:

$$(0000\ IIII)_2 = 2^3 + 2^2 + 2^1 + 2^0 = (8 + 4 + 2 + 1)_{10} = 15_{10}$$

The next highest binary number is:

$$(0000\ IIII) + (0000\ 000I) = (000I\ 0000)$$
$$15_{10}\ +\ 1_{10}\ =\ 16_{10}$$

This sets forth some of the rules for binary arithmetic:

$$0 + 0 = 0 \qquad 0 + I = I \qquad I + 0 = I$$
$$I + I = I0 \text{ (Carry to next MSD)}$$
$$I + I + \text{carry} = II$$

Decimal	Binary	
3	0000 00II	
+ 4	+ 0000 0I00	
= 7	= 0000 0III	ADDITION
8	0000 I000	
+ 9	+ 0000 I00I	
= 17	= 000I 000I	
15	0000 IIII	
+ 15	+ 0000 IIII	
= 30	= 000I III0	

Subtraction is somewhat different in the binary system. Because of the requirement for some form of hardware implementation for addition operations at high speed, subtraction operations are usually performed by addition. In the decimal subtraction $9 - 3 = 6$ you can obtain the same result by adding $9 + 7 = 16$ and discarding the carry to obtain 6. Note that $7 = 10 - 3$. In other words, subtraction can be performed subtracting the number to be subtracted from the number base and adding the result. Subtracting from the number base in binary can be accomplished by complementing and adding one. Complementing simply means substituting 0 for I and I for 0 on a bit by bit basis. The complement of 0000 00II (decimal 3) is IIII II00. Therefore:

Decimal	Binary/Complement	
9	0000 I00I	
− 3	+ IIII II00	
	+ 0000 000I	
= 6	= 0000 0II0	COMPLEMENTARY
30		SUBTRACTION
− 15	000I III0	
	+ IIII 0000	
= 15	+ 0000 000I	
	= 0000 IIII	

Note that the number being subtracted from is *not* complemented and that the carry from the operation is simply discarded. While this might seem a bit roundabout, the speed of the operation and the simplicity of implementing subtraction at high speed by using the high speed adder has made this the generally used technique in microprocessors. An alternative technique, where the number to be subtracted from is simply decremented (reduced by one) a number of times equal to the number being subtracted, will also work but it is very slow by comparison. For example, to subtract 255 from 255 would require 255 iterations of: decrement the minuend, increment the count, test the count for equality with the subtrahend loop. This routine would probably require 500 to 1000 times the running time of: complement the subtrahend, add to the minuend, add one routine.

MULTIPLICATION

It usually comes as a profound shock to people during their first contact with microprocessors to find that most of the four- and eight-bit units do not have a multiply or a divide command in the repertoire. A few of the latest generation eight-bit machines do include a multiply and divide. Most of the new generation 16-bit machines do, but most of the 8-bit one-chip microcomputers do not.

This is because it is a bit difficult to do a meaningful multiply in an eight-bit register. The largest number that can be accomodated in an eight-bit register is: $IIII\ IIII_2 = 255_{10}$.

The largest numbers which can be multipled without overrunning the eight-bit register are $15_{10} \times 15_{10} = 225$. If either of the multipliers is larger than 15, the other would have to be smaller to avoid overrunning the register: $255_{10} \times 255_{10} = 65,025_{10} = (IIII\ III0\ 0000\ 000I)_2$. The product of an 8-bit by 8-bit multiply would require a 16-bit register to contain the result. The typical second generation 8-bit machine does not have a 16-bit register to contain the results of calculations. A few of the new machines, such as the Motorola 6809, are configured internally to permit certain 16-bit manipulations—including multiply and divide. However, notice that a limit of 255 on a multiplication severely restricts the use of the instruction. It could not be used directly for most financial transactions except as a part of a bigger routine. A four-bit by four-bit multiply would be still less useful.

Multiplication is usually performed by successive addition. For the decimal multiplication $4 \times 3 = 12$, you would actually do $4 + 4 + 4 = 12$. The main problem with this approach is that it is time consuming. The larger the number by which you multiply, the longer it is liable to take. For numbers more than one byte long, the routine gets slower and slower and slower to run. This makes it important that an efficient algorithm be found for the multiplication. An extended arithmetic multiply routine is explained in Chapter 5.

DIVISION

If multiplication is slow, division is even worse. Division can be performed by subtraction, which is inherently about three times as slow as addition. For example, suppose that you want to divide 255 by 7. You could subtract seven a total of 37 times and note that on the last subtraction the result went negative. At this point, you could add seven back in and decrement the count to 36. Then insert a decimal point, multiply the remainder by 10 and start subtracting again. It is obvious that this proceedure would get very, very slow if you tried dividing a very large number by a very small number. On a typical 8-bit microprocessor, the division of 10,000,000 by .2 could occupy the machine fully for a time on the order of 20 minutes. An alternate technique will reduce the running time for this division to a fraction of a second. An erroneous entry, which would try to divide by zero, would leave the machine chewing on the problem for eternity.

The long division problem is one in which running time is particularly important. One of the distinctions between what you can do and what you cannot do with a microcomputer hinges upon the problem of running time. It is surprisingly easy to write a program in such a manner that it can take the machine impractical lengths of time to solve. Although microprocessor chips have improved dramatically in recent years, they are not particularly fast as computers go and it is no great challenge to design problems in such a manner that it takes the unit seconds, minutes, days or even years to get through the loop. As a matter of fact, one of the chief errors made by beginning programmers is to write a program in such manner that the machine would never finish.

OTHER NUMBER BASES

The binary system is very convenient to use in digital machinery since it requires only yes/no or low/high or input-output decisions to be made by the recipient on the far end of the wire. Addition, subtraction, multiplication and division can all be performed in the binary system with relatively simple hardware requiring no calibration. It is evident that the binary system is the right way to do arithmetic within the computer.

If you study computers and calculators, you will find that within the computer itself, all arithmetic is indeed done in the binary system; or at least most arithmetic is done in the binary system.

THE OCTAL SYSTEM

Sometimes a certain chip is referred to as an octal chip and another one is a hexadecimal. In general, both machines operate in binary. They have different names because octal and hexadecimal systems are easier for people to use.

While the binary system might be ideally suited to being read and manipulated by a machine, it is ill suited to being read and manipulated by the human beings who use the machine. For example, there are very few people, even among those who have worked with digital equipment for years, who could instantly tell whether the statement $(000I\ III0)_2 = 30_{10}$ is true. The statement is true. The point seems to be that binary notation is just too unwieldy and strung out for the human eye to comprehend with any ease and grace. A number that is trivial to read in decimal notation requires the use of pencil and paper when noted in binary.

The difficulty in reading the long strings of O's and I's proved to be a significant stumbling block in programming. For a good many years, minicomputers were equipped with a long row of lamps and a long row of switches. Using these facilities, the operator would laboriously load and attempt to read, one bit at a time, enough program into read/write memory so that the machine could recognize the input from a tape reader or some other non-volatile source in order to load an operating program into read/write memory. Every time the power to the machine was turned off, the entire contents of the read/write memory was lost and this process had to be repeated.

Two developments removed this curse from the lot of the programmer. The first was the read-only memory which could be preprogrammed with an operating systems so that the first time the power hit the machine it was ready to accept an input from a teletype or keyboard and to print memory contents on request. The second was the concept of applying octal coding.

The octal (base 8 numbering system) like any other numbering system employs digits from zero to the number one less than the base. In octal, you would count:

Decimal Value	Octal Number
1	1
2	2
3	3
4	4
5	5
6	6
7	7
8	10
9	11
10	12

Note that in any numbering system there is no single symbol for base. In the decimal system you must write *two* symbols; 10 for the base. Similarly, in binary you must write *two* symbols for the base; $10_2 = 2_{10}$. For octal you write two symbols: $10_8 = 8_{10}$. The more significant symbol (the one to the left) represents the base number to the first power. The third place to the left represents the base to the second or squared power. The fourth place to the left represents the base number to third or cubed power. Therefore, you would read the octal number:

$$377_8 = (3 \times 8^2) + (7 \times 8^1) + (7 \times 8^0)$$
$$= (3 \times 64) + (7 \times 8) + (7 \times 1) = 255_{10}$$

Note: *Any* number to the zero power is equal to one. *Any* number to the one power is equal to itself.

If all of us, like Mickey Mouse, had been born with only three fingers and a thumb on each hand, the chances are good that we would have learned all of our counting and arithmetic in octal. We would know at a glance that the number following 7_8 was 10_8 and that the number following 17_8 was 20_8 and that the number following 77_8 was 100_8. Under such circumstances, the learning of machine language programming would seem to be much more straightforward at the start.

But alas! Such was not the case. Our four fingers and thumb on each hand have firmly entrenched the concept of counting to the base ten and we learn our system of numerals accordingly. The mathemetician makes a distinction between a number and a numeral. The *number* of cows in a given field is the same regardless of whether that number is written in Arabic numerals to the base 10, Arabic numerals to the to the base 8, Roman numerals, Cunieaform symbols or German script. The changing of the base does not change the number—only the representation.

Not all base and numbering systems are equally familiar or easy to use in arithmetic. For example try this subtraction problem:

Decimal	Roman
55	LV
− 23	− XXIII
= 32	= XXXII

It is fairly easy to see that there would be a great deal more to learn about addition, subtraction, multiplication and division if we had to do all our arithmetic in the Roman system of numerals. To most of us, the problem of learning this sort of thing would be similar to having to learn a foreign language.

The real problem with directly reading binary lies in the fact that we are used to reading numbers in powers of 10 and 10 is not an integral power of two: ($2^3 = 8$ and $2^4 = 16$). The number 101 written in binary is $(1010)_2$ and the number 9 is (1001). There is simply no place for a smooth break into the familiar powers of 10.

The real advantage of the octal system is that eight is an even power of two. In earlier examples, the eight-bit byte is separated two four-bit nibbles. They could just as easily have been separated into groups of three bits—three bits and two bits going from least to most significant. Table 2-1 shows this. When one of the triads fills up, one simply carries over to the next and clears the first.

The octal representation presents a number of advantages over the presentation of binary:

■ It is more compact. A modest valued number does not spread all across the page.

■ It is easy to memorize the binary representation for numbers zero through seven. a long binary "word" can be broken into triads and translated to octal notation by inspection.

■ Since octal uses only the Arabic numerals zero through seven, the required characters are available on existing typewriters and printers.

■ Because of the ease of reading binary into octal, the machine can be allowed to continue to operate in the most efficient manner: binary. Only the instruction manual and the operator interpret what is done in octal.

■ Since it is written entirely in familiar characters, octal does not look so frightening and "foreign."

30

Table 2-1. The Octal System.

Decimal Value	Binary representation	Octal representation
1	00 000 00l	001
2	00 000 0l0	002
3	00 000 0ll	003
4	00 000 l00	004
5	00 000 l0l	005
6	00 000 ll0	006
7	00 000 lll	007
8	00 00l 000	010
9	00 00l 00l	011
10	00 00l 0l0	012
.		
.		
.		
255	ll lll lll	377

There is, to the best of my knowledge, no machine or computer currently being used in which the data or address wires attain eight stable states. In other words, there is no such thing as a truly octal machine. However, there are a large number of machines in which the addresses, the data, and the instruction codes are interpreted and printed in octal for the convenience of the operator.

HEXADECIMAL NOTATION

The same advantages that make the use of the number base eight also apply to the use of the number base 16, which is the next higher power of two. A few additional advantages are gained as well. Since 16 is larger than 10, the hexadecimal system of numerals is even more compact than the decimal system. It is considerably more compact than octal. The most significant problem with the hexadecimal system is that you get all the way to the numeric value of fifteen before moving out of single numerals. This means that some new numerals must be invented to cover the values: 10, 11, 12, 13, 14, and 15. While several people have suggested designs for a new numeral system for hexadecimal applications—including one design consisting of a triangle and dot which looked rather like a cunieform symbol—there has been no widespread acceptance of such symbols.

In practice, most microcomputer or minicomputer applications will use either a printer or a seven-segment display to show the contents of memory, addresses, etc. In general, these do not have any new characters available to use for the extra single character numerals. Furthermore, it would generally be prohibitively expensive to redesign a printer to incorporate the extra characters. For this reason, the letters A thru F have been generally employed as shown in Table 2-2. The characters on the right have been shaped to look like the characters in a seven-segment display.

There are several things worthy of note about Table 2-2. First of all you will notice that it is necessary to present both "b" and "d" in the lower case whereas all of the rest of the letters are upper case. This is because the seven segment display for an upper case B would be indistinguishable from an eight and the seven-segment presentation for an upper case D would be indistinguishable from a zero. Secondly, note that it is necessary to put the leg on top of the numeral six so that it is distinguishable.

Also notice the compactness of the notation. The numeric value of 255 can be presented with only two characters. Many of the eight-bit microprocessors have a 16-bit address bus. When all 16 of the bits are set high, this corresponds to the top address of the machine. This has a numeric value of 65,535 which can be written:

$$65,535_{10} = 177777_8 = (\text{IIII IIII IIII IIII})_2 = FFFF_{16}$$

Binary notation requires 16 places to write this number, octal requires six, decimal requires five and hexadecimal requires only four.

There are obviously some problems involved with the use of the same symbols to mean different things. For example, the set of characters FACE could be either an English word or the hexadecimal number 64,178. In order to avoid misinterpretation, printed texts will frequently preceded an octal number with a pound sign (#) and a hexadecimal number with a dollar sign ($).

Henceforth in this book any:

—Numerals without a prefix will be assumed to be decimal.

—Character string preceded by the sign # will be presumed to be octal.

—Character string preceded by a dollar sign will be presumed to be hexadecimal.

—Character string consisting only of 0's and I's which is broken into sets of four will be presumed to be binary.

There is a tendency on the part of a number of people to "freeze up" on their first contact with the hexadecimal number system. The hexadecimal system really should not be so frightening for several reasons. The decimal value of a hexadecimal number is very easily calculated with the pocket calculator routine

Table 2-2. Hexadecimal Notation.

Decimal Value	Binary representation	Hexadecimal representation
1	0000 0001	01
2	0000 0010	02
3	0000 0011	03
4	0000 0100	04
5	0000 0101	05
6	0000 0110	06
7	0000 0111	07
8	0000 1000	08
9	0000 1001	09
10	0000 1010	0A
11	0000 1011	0b
12	0000 1100	0C
13	0000 1101	0d
14	0000 1110	0E
15	0000 1111	0F
16	00p1 000	10
17	0001 0001	11
255	1111 1111	FF

used in the Chapter on flow charting. Secondly the actual decimal value of a hexadecimal number is often of no particular interest. If the starting address of ROM in your computer is $FC00, the programmer usually need only know this. Knowing the actual numeric value of the address is of little interest.

A third point of interest that binary-based or hexadecimal-based divisions are very common in the English Measurement system. It is always relatively easy to divide a given distance, weight, volume, etc. into two equal portions without any precision apparatus. Each of these halves may then itself be halved, etc.

We commonly think of the American monetary system as being decimal and money is commonly written in decimal form. However, note that the coinage system is actually divided into half-dollars, quarter dollars, dimes, nickels and pennys. Of these, only the dime and the penny are decimal. The half-dollar and the quarter are binary and the nickel is half of a dime. Stock prices are commonly quoted on the stock exchange in eighths, which is half of a quarter.

The gallon is commonly divided into the half-gallon, the quart, the pint (one-eighth gallon) and the half-pint (one-sixteenth gallon). Furthermore, the pint is divided into fluid ounces (one-sixteenth pint). The pound is divided into 16 ounces. The inch is divided into halves, quarters, eighths, sixteenths, thirty-seconds, and sixty-fourths. Modern engineering practice frequently is to write fractional inches in decimal form, however one-sixteenth inch is easier to read than 0.0625 inches.

There are some who would argue that the present push to convert to the metric system represents a rather considerable inconvenience. There was a time when we counted on our fingers and the ability to multiply or divide by 10 simply by moving the decimal point was a considerable advantage. However, that time has passed. Now, all but the simplest counting and arithmetic is done on computers and calculators—which are fundamentally binary machines. To be pushing even further away from a fundamentally binary-based system of weights and measures toward a decimal-based system is a step in the wrong direction. A fully binary-based system would have considerable saving in terms of computer running time and memory useage. This would be reflected in savings in costs of nearly everything we use. If the dime were replaced with the shilling worth one-eighth of a dollar and the nickel were replaced by the half-shilling or one-sixteenth of a dollar, then only one place behind the binary point would be required to print prices. A Sunday paper that cost Fifteen-Sixteenths of a dollar would receive the price $0.F rather than $0.9375. Of course, there might be a few shellbacks who would object to a 16-inch foot and a 4096-foot mile, but there always seem to be diehards who will oppose anything.

THE BINARY CODED DECIMAL SYSTEM

For very small computing systems such as cash registers and pocket calculators where the data input comes from someone punching numbers on a keyboard and the data output is someone reading a display, the actual data manipulation is often performed directly in the binary-coded decimal (BCD) system.

If you cosider binary representation to be divided into nibbles of four bits each, then binary, hexadecimal and BCD are identical for the numbers zero through nine. However, here the similarity ceases. In BCD, each set of four bits describes one decimal digit. Reading from left to right, each subsequent nibble represents the next higher power of 10. Table 2-3 illustrates BCD coding.

Compared to binary, there are six unused codes in BCD. These are the same codes to which the letters A through F were applied in the hexadecimal notation system.

In pocket calculator applications and when dealing with simple money calculations as in a cash register or a gas pump, the differences are probably insignificant. On the other hand, when the machine is intended to read a digital voltmeter or program a digital power supply, the difference is striking. An eight-bit digital voltmeter can present readings from zero to 99, in other words, it has a resolution of 1 percent. Over the same eight-bit line, a binary machine can give any reading from zero to 255. It has two and one-half times the resolution of the BCD unit.

There are also differences in BCD arithmetic. For example:

Decimal Value	BCD Coding
9	I00I
+ 3	+ 00II
=12	= 000I 0I00

The BCD example on the right does not follow the binary rules of addition. Whenever the sum in a given nibble equals 10 or more, it is necessary to add six more and take the carry over to the next more significant nibble. Since the largest number which can be shown in a BCD nibble is nine, the biggest possible addition is nine plus nine plus carry.

Decimal Value	BCD Coding	
9	0000 I00I	
+ 9	+ 0000 I00I	
+ 1	+ 0000 000I	
=19	= 000I 00II	(this is not BCD)
	+ 0000 0II0	BCD Adj.
	000I I00I	
		nineteen in BCD

The BCD addition and subtraction routines are not too difficult to implement in hardware. Some machines provide an adjust-to-BCD single command instruction. In the Motorola 6800, there is an instruction for decimal adjustment which can be applied under certain very specific conditions to adjust the results of a BCD addition back to BCD. Without this feature, the programmer must provide the adjustment back to BCD in his program.

In BCD subtraction, if the minuend (the number being subtracted from) is larger than the subtrahend (the number being subtracted), the subtraction can proceed by the same process shown for binary subtraction. As demonstrated earlier, this con-

Table 2-3. BCD Coding.

Decimal Value	BCD Code	
1	0000 0001	
2	0000 0010	
3	0000 0011	
4	0000 0100	
5	0000 0101	
6	0000 0110	
7	0000 0111	
8	0000 1000	
9	0000 1001	
10	0001 0000	(note shift from binary)
11	0001 0001	
.		
99	1001 1001	

sists of complimenting the subtrahend, adding the subtrahend to the minuend, adding one more and neglecting the carry from the addition, if any. The following example shows this.

Decimal Value	BCD Coding	
$\begin{array}{r} 8 \\ -3 \\ \hline =5 \end{array}$	$\begin{array}{r} 0000\ 1000 \\ -\ 0000\ 0011 \\ \hline =\ 0000\ 0101 \end{array}$	(not a binary operation)

This is done by	$\begin{array}{r} 0000\ 1000 \\ +\ 0000\ 1100 \\ +\ 0000\ 0001 \\ \hline =\ 0001\ 0101 \end{array}$	(comp. 3)
ignoring the carry gives	0000 0101	(value 5)

If the minuend for the digit is smaller than the subtrahend, it is necessary to borrow $10 = 0000\ 1010$ from the next most significant digit. The following problem shows this.

Decimal Value	BCD Coding	
$\begin{array}{r} 12 \\ -7 \\ \hline =5 \end{array}$	$\begin{array}{r} 0001\ 0010 \\ -\ 0000\ 0111 \\ \hline =\ 0000\ 0101 \end{array}$	(not a binary operation)

36

The borrowing operation gives:

$$
\begin{array}{ll}
0000\ \text{IOIO} & \text{(binary borrow} \\
+\ 0000\ \text{00IO} & \text{(binary 2)} \\
\hline
=\ 0000\ \text{IIOO} & (\$\ OC = 12) \\
+\ \text{IIII}\ \ \ \text{I000} & (\text{comp.}\,7) \\
\hline
=\ 0000\ \text{0IOI} & \text{(answer} = \text{BCD/} \\
& \text{binary 5)}
\end{array}
$$

Note the drop of the carry in the addition,

Note that when the minuend is greater than 5, the addition in the borrow operation has a cary.

Decimal Value	BCD Coding	
18	000I I000	(not a binary
− 9	− 0000 I00I	operation)
= 9	= 0000 I00I	

The borrowing operation gives:

$$
\begin{array}{ll}
0000\ \text{IOIO} & \text{(binary borrow)} \\
+\ 0000\ \text{I000} & \text{(Binary/BCD 8)} \\
\hline
=\ 000\text{I}\ 00\text{IO} & (\$\ 12 = \text{binary 18)} \\
\end{array}
$$

$$
\begin{array}{ll}
+\ \text{IIII}\ \ \text{0IIO} & (\text{comp.}\,9) \\
+\ 0000\ \text{000I} & \\
\hline
=\ 0000\ \text{I00I} & \text{(answer is binary/} \\
& \text{BCD 9)}
\end{array}
$$

MSN   LSN

Since BCD subtractions always deal with only a single BCD digit, no single subtraction can ever yield a result greater than nine. Therefore, the operation in the most significant nibble could safely be ignored in a four-bit machine. In an eight-bit machine, it is carried out automatically.

In an eight-bit machine, when using BCD arithmetic it is possible to store two BCD digits in an eight-bit memory location with the most significant BCD digit in the MSN and the least significant BCD digit in the LSN. This requires a small routine to pack the digits upon entry and another routine to unpack them for arithmetic operations. This is sometimes necessary in single-chip microcomputers where the on-chip read/write memory might have only 64 Bytes, and memory space is at a premium. If the data arrives in ASCII or some other alphanumeric code, there might be some code bits that must be stripped off for packing two digits per register. This feature is available in a machine command in the Motorola 6809, 68000 and other advanced chips.

In the more general case, if read/write memory is available and running time is to be optimized, BCD is usually handled on a one digit per eight-bit register basis.

Even simple BCD addition and subtraction require a fair amount of manipulation which is not required of straight binary. The addition of two binary bytes will usually require only two or four machine cycles—for perhaps two to four microseconds. The BCD adjustment, which must be performed on addition, requires a test of the result and a possible binary addition. This means that BCD addition requires about three times, and perhaps as much as six times, the time to run that a binary addition would.

In subtraction, the matter is even worse with the operation including test, modify, add, increment and adjust requiring as much as four to eight times as long as a binary operation. If the matter is further compounded by having to unpack and then repack the digits, the operation can be slowed by factors as large as twenty or thirty.

If the operations to be performed consists of only a few additions or subtractions and perhaps an occasional multiplication or division of numbers with only a few digits, this slowness might be perfectly acceptable. However, it is the characteristic of calculator operations that the numbers to be handled are frequently much larger than those encountered in control applications. Since multiplication and division are generally performed by addition and subtraction, and slowdown in addition and subtraction is multiplied by the number of times that the operation must be performed. A problem such as: $24,500$ miles $\div 3.1416 = 7,798.5739$ miles radius can require several thousand subtractions. An ordinary pocket calculator will perform this calculation in something approaching one second. However, a slow routine could easily stretch the calculation out so that you might have to wait seconds or minutes for the answer.

As a general rule, if the application requires any significant amount of multiplication, division, or the addition of large multi-digit numbers or if there are going to be very many subtractions of large numbers, it is usually worthwhile to convert the BCD to binary at entry, perform all arithmetic in binary and then do a binary-to-BCD conversion on data or print output. The single conversion on each end of the process will usually run faster by a very substantial factor.

SIGNED NUMBERS

On occasion it is necessary to represent algebraically signed or negative numbers in a microcomputer application. The usual convention applied to this is to represent the negative number by setting the most significant bit to one. At first consideration, this strikes a good many people as a backward way of doing things. However, as the following examples show, it does work.

Using this convention, the counting table works out like this:

Decimal Value	Signed Binary
+ 127	OIII IIII
+ 126	OIII IIIO
•	
•	
+ 1	0000 000I
0	0000 0000
− 1	IIII IIII
− 2	IIII IIIO
•	
•	
•	
− 127	I000 000I
− 128	I000 0000

Despite the seeming backwardness of this convention, note that there is a smooth and logical transition from negative to positive at zero. Furthermore, ordinary binary arithmetic operations work without adjustment. For example:

Decimal Value	Signed Binary
(− 128)	I000 0000
+ 1	+ 0000 000I
=(− 127)	= I000 000I

Or:

(− 1)	IIII IIII
+ 1	+ 0000 000I
= 0	= 0000 0000

Note that the carry is discarded.

Subtraction also works in straightforward binary fashion.

(− 2)	IIII IIIO
−(+ 2)	+ IIII IIOI (comp +2)
=(− 4)	+ 0000 000I
	= IIII IIOO (signed −4)

In other words, signed binary numbers can be added and subtracted as straight binary numbers without error. No special attention is required in a single byte operation. On multiple byte signed numbers, the sign bit is always in the most significant bit of the most significant byte.

The principle thing the programmer must keep in mind when handling signed binary numbers is that the program must keep track of whether the contents of a given memory location is to be interpreted as a straight binary number or a signed binary number. Unless the machine is instructed otherwise, it will interpret $ FE = IIII III0 as 254 rather than as a (− 2).

Another point worthly of note is the roll-over of signed binary numbers. If you start with a cleared register (all zero's) and repeatedly add 1 (increments the register), it will eventually arrive at $7F = 0III IIII which will be read as 127 in either the signed or straight case.

With the addition of the next one, the contents of the register will move to $80 which would be interpreted as 128 in straight binary and (− 128) in signed binary. The next increment will yield either 129 or (− 127). The disparity becomes greater until the count reaches $ FF which would be interpreted as 255 in straight binary and (− 1) in signed binary.

The signed binary numbers are probably used most frequently in the operation of Digital-to-Analog (D/A) converters and Analog-to-Digital (A/D) converters which operate with bipolar voltages or currents. Use of signed binary numbers in other applications is less common.

DECODER CHIPS

A number of special purpose chips have been developed for decoding a four-line code. These can be used to drive such things as Nixie tubes or seven-segment displays. These devices come in BCD versions which decode the four input lines and manipulate the seven-segment outputs to illuminate the right segments of the display. They can also be used to select one of 10 output lines.

Other versions of the decoder are hexadecimal in nature and will decode the four input lines to manipulate the seven segments of a display to display any of the hexadecimal characters. Other versions will select one of 16 output lines. The hexadecimal chips can be used to drive a BCD display if it is arranged so that the four lines never carry any of the codes which are illegal in BCD. It should be noted that the illegal codes in BCD are sometimes used

40

to produce characters such as the minus sign, E (for error) and odd symbols for low battery, etc.

Either a BCD or a hexadecimal decoder can be used to drive an octal display simply by using only the three less significant inputs and tying the most significant input low.

The use of the decoder chips is an example of one of the trade off areas which are frequently encountered in microprocessor applications. If a latching peripheral interface adapter is available, the seven segments can be individually driven using a lookup table. In this case, the display has the flexibility that any segment or combination of segments can be individually driven to create a variety of symbols not otherwise available and printed messages such as "error" can be displayed on the seven segment device. On the other hand, the use of the decoder chip will save some running time and software programming at the cost of reduced flexibility and added hardware.

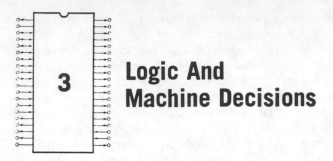

3 Logic And Machine Decisions

A great deal of what a microcomputer does in most applications amounts to the making of decisions based upon information available to the machine and the past history of the information. This has led to the use of the term *logic* which is used both as a verb and a noun. The action of the machine in providing a specific response to a given set of inputs is termed *logical operations*. The actual hardware that performs these operations is usually termed the logic. In cases where the collection of hardware pieces is specifically connected to perform one or more functions, which are defined by the way that the items are wired together, the assembly is generally referred to as *hard-wired-logic*. The hard-wired-logic term is often used to distinguish an assembly of items wired together for a specific purpose from a microcomputer type collection of hardware whose interpretation of the input data can be determined by a program in hardware, firmware or software.

In this chapter, a series of examples are used intended to expand upon and explain some of these definitions. Because it is somewhat simpler to understand. I will begin with the interpretation of some of the hard-wired-logic functions.

HISTORY

The digital computer art is directly traceable, in large measure, to the works of three people. George Boole (1815-1864) was a mathematician who set forth a technique of notation and algebraic manipulation by which certain logical processes could be formulated, solved and proved, provided that each of the statements in the problem could be defined as being either true or false (not true). Most of the written formulations in digital control work are set forth in Boolean notation and are solved by Boolean algebra. The compactness of this form of notation makes it easy to gather the various conditions to be considered in arriving at the conclusion. The technique obviously lends itself to binary manipulation since the "true" and "false" nature of all Boolean statements is a binary process.

Charles Babbage (1805-1871) comes across as a somewhat more colorful figure. Babbage, with the aid of some rather sophisticated mechanics and some substantial financial backing, managed to construct several calculating engines. He and his mistress used these engines and some of the finances in an attempt to beat the horse races. The last of these calculating engines, which was the most sophisticated, was never entirely successful. However, the principles set forth in these machines did a great deal to set the course for the mechanical adding machines, cash registers and calculators which were to follow.

A mathematician named Turing showed that, in theory, any mathematical problem could be solved by a machine that could simply print an X or an 0 in squares on a paper tape and could also erase either. The Turing machine is a theoretical concept and an actual Turing machine was never built. However, the action of a real digital computer closely resembles the action of the Turing machine since the machine writes 0's or 1's in cells or relay contacts and erases them. Given enough time, a Turing machine can solve any problem which can be solved by a computer. There are classes of problems which cannot be solved by any computer because they require so many steps that the time of solution or running time becomes impossibly long.

BOOLEAN ALGEBRA

At the time of its inception, Boolean algebra was not intended for use in digital computing apparatus. It was considered for classes of problems such as mathematical puzzles. These problems frequently involve a mathematician who journeys to a land populated only by truth-tellers and liars who answer questions only "yes" or "no" etc. The mathematician is supposed to determine whether he is speaking to a truth-teller or a liar. This type of puzzle can be written out in Boolean notation.

For control applications, the problems are actually related to the sort of deductive processes used in solving this type of puzzle. The manipulations hinge upon several basic concepts which will be covered individually.

NOT

The NOT concept used in Boolean algebra is different from the most general use of the word "not" in the English language.

Since all of the statements in Boolean algebra can be reduced to being either true of false the NOT of Boolean algebra has much more restricted meaning.

Consider that a given wire in a computer has only two possible states: the wire either has five volts on it or it has zero volts on it—the machinery will allow no other conditions. The 5-volt condition can be defined as a "true" or "I" condition and the 0-volt condition as a "false" or "0" condition. In this restricted sense, you can see that the NOT condition has a special meaning since NOT 5 volts implies that the wire has zero volts on it. Similarly, NOT zero volts implies that the wire has 5 volts on it.

From this, you can see the special meaning attached to the NOT in Boolean algebra as compared to ordinary English. If I were to say about a person "That is not Henry" I have not said anything specific about who the person really is. The person could be Mary, Otto or anyone else. In distinction, the Boolean statement tells something very specific about the condition of the wire.

To enlarge upon this concept a bit, Fig. 3-1 shows some hardware that accomplishes the direct and the NOT function. The top illustration shows an ordinary relay with "normally open" contacts. When the relay coil is not energized, the contacts are open. When a current flows through the relay coil "A" the armature is pulled down and the contacts close and the voltage "A" becomes 5 volts. When the coil is not energized, the output voltage is zero volts.

The second schematic in Fig. 3-1 shows a relay with a normally closed set of contacts. When this relay is energized, "A" is zero volts. In the Boolean sense, the output voltage of this relay is NOT "A." This is usually symbolized as $\overline{A}$ with a bar over the letter. The symbol with the bar is often read as "not A" or "A-not." The latter rendering is taught to prevent confusion with the more common English meaning of "not." Obviously, the special meaning is that the output is "true" or 5 volts only when the coil is not energized and is zero volts when the coil is energized.

Relays can and often do have more than one set of contacts. The third schematic in Fig. 3-1 shows a relay with two different sets of contacts—one of which is normally closed and the other which is normally open. This relay can accomplish both the A and the $\overline{A}$ functions.

Relays can be used to accomplish any of the control functions of "hard-wired-logic" for control or even for a whole computer. The use of relay logic in computers was very short lived because of the problems of cost, speed and reliability. Obviously, it takes some time for the armature of the relay to pull the contacts open or closed. A small, fast relay will operate in about 14 milliseconds. By contrast, even a relatively slow transistor can turn on or off in something on the order of less than a microsecond. The relay is obviously at least 14,000 times slower.

However, in control applications, the use of relay logic has persisted until fairly recently. If you examine the interior of all but

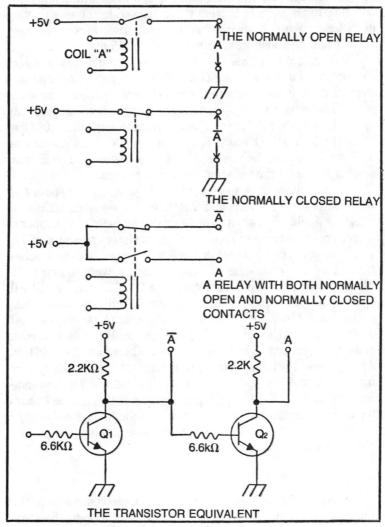

Fig. 3-1. The direct and the NOT function.

the most recent copying machines or the interior of a railway signal control apparatus, you will find banks upon banks of relay logic elements.

The bottom schematic in Fig. 3-1 shows the transistor equivalent of the double contact relay set. If the voltage at A is below about 0.8 volts, the transistor Q-1 is cutoff and the collector draws no current or very little current. The base of transistor Q-2, however, is connected through the 6.6 K Ohms and 2.2 K Ohms to the +5 volt supply. If this transistor could, it would attempt to draw 50 to 200 times as much current through its collector as is flowing in its base circuit. Allowing for the base forward drop, the base current will be about 4.8v/8800 Ohms = 0.55 milliamps.

With an unlimited supply, the transistor would draw a collector current of about 27 mA. The 220 Ohm resistor prevents this from happening and limits the actual current to about 2 milliamperes. The voltage at "A" will be lower than the 5-volt supply only by the drop due to the 0.55 mA base current through the 2200 Ohm resistor which is 1.21 volts. The voltage at "$\overline{A}$" will therefore be 3.97 volts. Each of the stages, Q-1 and Q-2 is termed an *inverter* since it performs the negating or "not" function.

If the voltage at A were taken to 3.97 volts, transistor Q-1 would saturate at 0.4 volts and transistor Q-2 would cutoff and the situation would reverse. It is obvious that an indefintie number of stages could be tacked together in this resistor-transistor (RTL) logic family. The voltages achieved are adequate to operate transistor-transistor logic (TTL) devices as well. Using some ordinary switching transistors such as a 2N2222, this circuit will operate at speeds measured in the tens of millions of switching cycles per second. The relay switching counterpart would be hard pushed to exceed 30 cycles. The relay obviously has moving parts and rubbing contacts which can wear out. Therefore, it would have a limited life. In distinction, the transistor stage has nothing moving and no well-defined wear-out mechanism and will last indefintely. The main difference in performance is that for the transistor circuit, the low is not really zero and the high is not really 5 volts. However, this is something that can be accommodated in the circuit design.

SYMBOLS

Figure 3-2 shows some common symbols which are used in the control industry to describe these devices in logic diagrams. These shorthand symbols are used in the material which follows.

Their utility stems from the fact that they describe the function being performed without resort to the basic details of how it is being specifically implemented. Note that the contacts are shown as parallel lines. This is to distinguish it from the capacitor which will always be shown with one side curved.

For the solid state inverter circuit, which is the equivalent of the Q-1 or the Q-2 circuit of Fig. 3-1, the inversion or NOT property is denoted on the amplifier triangle symbol with a small ball. The ball can be either on the input, denoting that the device is active when the input is low or on the output, denoting that the device is active when the input is high. The placement of the ball is related to the use of the device and not the device itself. Two physically identical inverters can be shown on the same drawing with the ball on the input of one and the ball on the output of the

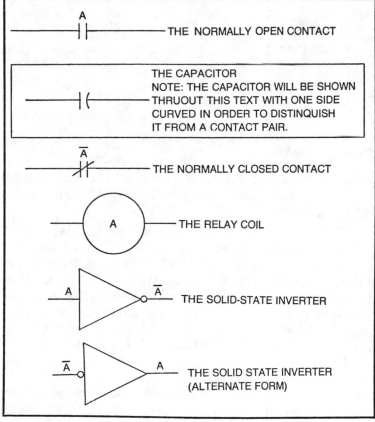

Fig. 3-2. Symbols for logic diagrams.

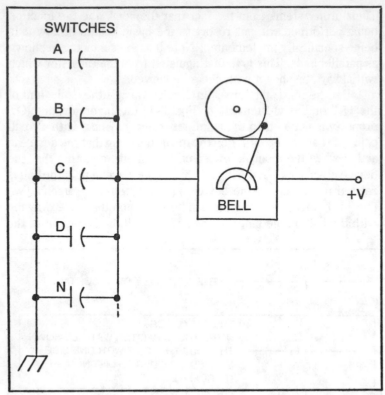

Fig. 3-3. The logical OR.

other to denote a difference in way the devices are used. This does not denote any difference in the way the device itself functions.

THE OR FUNCTION

The Boolean OR function is usually denoted by a plus sign (+) and can be combined with any number of terms. An example of an OR function is the cord that runs through a number of eyes along the side of a bus. When pulled, the cord rings the bell to signal the driver that someone would like to get off of the bus at the next stop. The passengers in row A, B, C or D .... could pull the cord and ring the bell. In Boolean notation, this could be written: Bell = A + B + C + D + ... It would be read: "Bell equals A or B or C or D .... "

Figure 3-3 shows how this function could be implemented with normally open switches. Closing any of the switches will complete the circuit through the bell to ground and cause the bell to ring. Any number of switches can be used and the result is the same no matter how many of the switches are closed.

THE NOR FUNCTION

The NOR or Not OR function is the inverse counterpart of the OR function. Suppose that you decided that it was not safe to start your automobile if any of the car doors were open or the car was in any setting other than "park." A verbal description of this situation could read: "The ignition will operate only if the right front door NOR the right rear door NOR the left front door... is open Nor the transmission is in Drive NOR the transmission is in Reverse NOR ...."

As a Boolean statement this could be written:
$$\text{Ignition} = \overline{RF} + \overline{RR} + \overline{LF} + \overline{LR} + \overline{D} + \overline{N} + \overline{R} + \overline{L1} + \overline{L2}$$

This is shown in the schematic in Fig. 3-4. Since all of the safety switches are normally closed and connected in series, the opening of any switch will interrupt the path to ground for the ignition and the ignition will not operate.

In integrated circuits, the NOR function is actually a bit easier to implement than the OR function because of the natural inverting function of the transistor amplifier. Figure 3-5 shows a pair of ways in which the multiple NOR function is realized. In the top schematic, it can be seen that if any of the transistor bases is taken high, that transistor will saturate and the output voltage will be low. Only if *all* the inputs are low will the output go high. If more than one transistor is turned on, the result remains the same.

The middle schematic of Fig. 3-5 shows the circuit configured another way. If any of the inputs is taken high, the transistor will

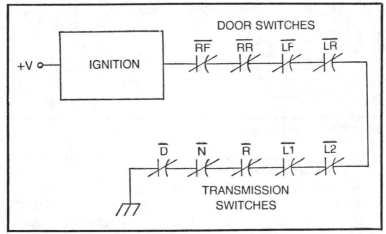

Fig. 3-4. The logical NOR.

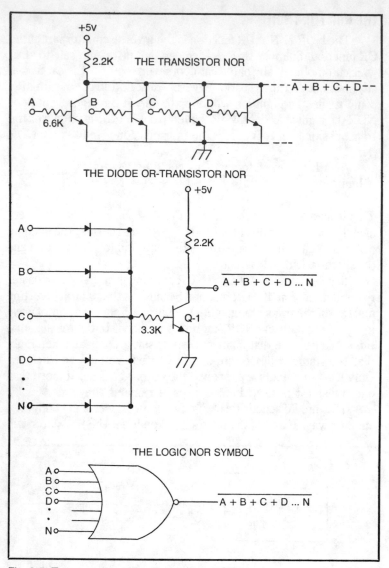

Fig. 3-5. Two ways to realize the multiple NOR function.

draw the output low. The reason for the diodes is that they isolate the inputs from one another. Suppose that B attempts to go low while all the others are high. In this case diode B will be back biased and no current will flow from any of the other inputs into B. Note that at the interface denoted by the circled ① that the connection is actually an OR connection and that the function becomes a

NOR only through the inverting action of the transistor Q-1. In this case, the base resistance has been reduced to account for the forward drop of the diode. An early logic family, the diode transistor logic (DTL) was actually fabricated in this manner.

The symbol at the bottom of the page is used in logic diagrams to illustrate the NOR function.

THE AND FUNCTION

Referring to the description of the car used in connection with Fig. 3-4 you can see that the description was sort of backhanded. For example, if the car is not in D, N, R, L1 or L2, it must be in park. Similarly, if none of the doors is open, they must all be closed. In Boolean algebra, this AND condition is designated by writing the symbols adjacent to one another as is done to signify multiplication in ordinary algebra. The condition for operating the car would be written:

$$\text{Ignition} = (RR, RF, LR, LF, P)$$

This would be read: "Ignition equals Right Rear and Right Front and Left Rear and Left Front and Park. Notice that in the case of Park, the circuit is simplified by replacing all of the switches on the gears the car was *not* supposed to be in with a single switch sensing the gear the car *was* supposed to be in. In the case of the door switches however, the actual function has not been altered. The switch is still closed when the door is closed. We have only changed the way that we look at the situation. Instead of specifying the condition of the door switches with the doors *open* we have specified the condition of the switches with the doors *closed*. Figure 3-6 shows this way of looking at things.

THE NAND FUNCTION

The logic NAND function is simply the inverse of the AND function being derived from NOT AND. As with the NOR function,

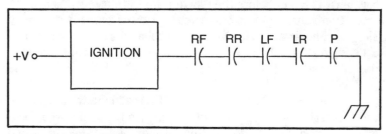

Fig. 3-6. The logic AND.

it is more easily derived from the data in solid state networks because of the natural inverting action of transistor amplifiers.

The top schematic in Fig. 3-7 shows a transistor implementation of the NAND function. Note that this has been implemented with PNP transistors rather than the NPN transistors used in the NOR function. These transistors function in the inverse way from the NPN's. If the base of the PNP transistor is taken to something close to the 5-volt emitter potential, the transistor will cut off and no current will flow. If the base of the transistor is taken to ground, the transistor will tend to saturate and draw as much current as possible. This current will be limited to about 12.5 mA by the 330 ohm resistor used as a load. In order for the output of the device to go low, it is necessary that *all* of the transistors be cutoff so that none lets any current flow through the 330 ohm load resistor. The output is therefore (A and B and C and ..... N) NOT.

A small digression is in order regarding the subject of the load resistor. Note that a 330 ohm resistor is used in the RTL NAND whereas a 220 ohm resistor is used in the RTL NOR. Since this resistor controls the current that is drawn, it means that the NAND willl draw 12.5 mA compared to only about 2mA for the NOR function. This is an obvious 6:1 disadvantage in power consumption. The reason for this change has nothing to do with the fact that PNP transistors are used in the NAND. It is there in order to make the unit compatible with ordinary TTL logic.

In standard TTL logic, each input is actually the emitter of a PNP transistor. Being an emitter, it is necessary of current, actually 1.5 mA to earth in order to turn the input to the "low" condition. The 1.5 mA flowing through the 330 ohm resistor gives a voltage drop of 0.495 volts . This is safely below the 0.8 volt level which TTL is guaranteed to accept as a "low," With the 330 ohm load resistor, the RTL NAND will "legally" drive one TTL gate and in practice it will drive several under *most* conditions. In the NOR gate, the transistor is sinking the TTL input current. The capability is larger before the 0.8 volt limit is exceeded, since the saturation voltage of a good switching transistor rises relatively slowly with current. The NOR will probably safely drive 4 or 5 TTL inputs. The ability to drive multiple devices of the family is described as the FAN OUT of the unit. The FAN OUT of the NAND is one and the FAN OUT of the NOR is four.

Since the only difference in the NAND and the NOR is due to the reversal of function, it should be fairly obvious that you could also construct a NAND by simply inverting all of the inputs and using an OR function block which itself can be made of a NOR followed by a single inverter. This approach is shown in the lower schematic in Fig. 3-7. As noted earlier, the output of the NOR will go high if and only *all* of the inputs are low. Since all of the inputs are derived from inverters, this means that *all* of the inverter inputs must be high. At the terminal labeled AND OUTPUT, the symbol would be read: "output equals A and B and C and .... N." The NAND output would be read as: "Output equals (A and B and C ...and N) NOT.

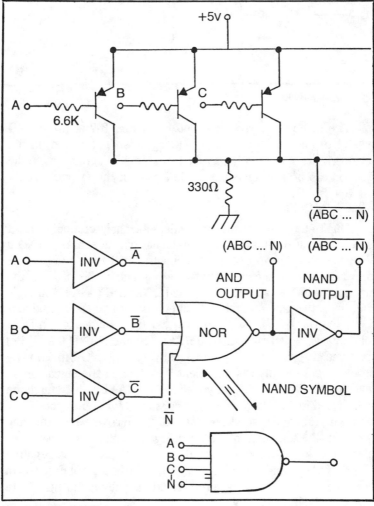

Fig. 3-7. The NAND function.

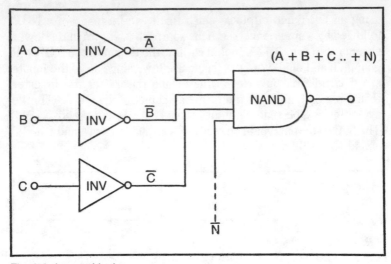

Fig. 3-8. Inverted logic.

The symbol shown at the bottom of Fig. 3-7 is the NAND symbol to be found on most logic diagrams. The labels on the schematic are not actually found on most logic diagrams since the function can be distinguished by the shape of the symbol.

INVERTED LOGIC

Due to the natural inverting action of transistor amplifiers, it is not unusual to find that a given signal will alternate between being true in the high condition to being true in the low condition. A clever designer will frequently take advantage of this. Each of the functions which have been discussed is termed a GATE in logic use. In small scale integrated circuits it is not unusual to find four TWO-INPUT NAND GATES packaged in a single 14-pin Dual Inline Package (DIP) or three THREE INPUT NAND GATES in the same size package. If the designer requires an OR function he or she might be able to implement it by finding the signals in an inverted condition and employing a NAND GATE, which might be left unused in a package which was required for some other function. This function is shown in Fig. 3-8. If you reverse our thinking regarding the schematic at the top of Fig. 3-7 you can see that if *any* of the inputs is low, the output will be high. Therefore, in negative logic an OR becomes a NAND as shown at the bottom of Fig. 3-7. In negative logic, a NAND becomes an OR as shown on Fig. 3-8. In Boolean algebra this is written:

54

also
$$\overline{(A + B + C \ldots + N)} = (ABC\ldots N)$$

$$\overline{(ABC\ldots N)} = (A + B + C \ldots + N)$$

It is not difficult to see that a clever designer can make use of this property to arrive at a design for a circuit which minimizes the package count. If on a given card one OR or NOR function and one AND or NAND function is required, it is not necessary to have a separate package for each. Inverters come six to a 14-pin package and are often required for other purposes. Spares are often available so that the functions are frequently swapped.

THE EXCLUSIVE-OR FUNCTION

In digital work, it is frequently necessary to employ the EXCLUSIVE-OR or the EXCLUSIVE-NOR function. The

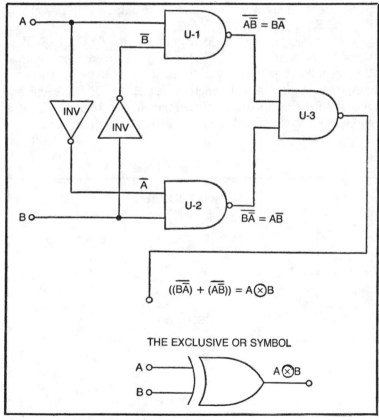

Fig. 3-9. The EXCLUSIVE-OR function.

EXCLUSIVE-OR implies $((A\overline{B}) + (\overline{A}B))$ which would be read: A and (Bnot) or B and (Anot). The EXCLUSIVE-OR is often designated by a circle with an X inside: ⊗

Figure 3-9 shows an implementation of the EXCLUSIVE-OR function using inverters and NAND gates. Remembering the action of the NAND gate, that the output will go low if and only if all of the inputs are high, you can see that if A is high and B is low then the output of U-1 will go low. This will drive the output of U-3 high. Conversely, if B is high and A is low, the output of U-2 will go low and the output of U-3 will go high. If A and B are both high, then $\overline{A}$ and $\overline{B}$ will both be low—thereby driving the outputs of U-1 and U-2 high. Since U-3 has both inputs high, the output of U-3 will be driven low. Similarly, if A and B are both low, the outputs of U-1 and U-2 will be driven high and the output of U-3 will be low. It can be seen that this fulfills the function of the EXCLUSIVE OR for all possible conditions of the two inputs. The output is high if and only if A and B are not alike.

The symbol used on logic diagrams for the EXLUSIVE-OR is shown at the bottom of the Fig. 3-9. The implementation shown at the top of the page is rarely used and is included for instructional purposes only. In actual practice, EXCLUSIVE-OR gates are available in four units to a 14-pin DIP just like two input AND gates and it is seldom justified to make use of the separate gates.

Table 3-1. Truth Table.

Two Input NAND gate Truth Table

A	B	Output
0	0	I
0	I	I
I	0	I
I	I	0

EXCLUSIVE OR gate Truth Table

A	B	Output
0	0	0
0	I	I
I	0	I
I	I	0

THE TRUTH TABLE

The output behavior of a given integrated circuit package is frequently presented in the form of a *truth table* in which all possible permutations of the input conditions are presented (Table 3-1).

For most integrated circuits, some form of truth table is generally presented in the catalog rundown on the device along with the operating voltages, currents, etc. It is obvious that for larger numbers of inputs, the number of entries in the truth table can become very large since each additional input raises the possible number of output states by a factor of two.

The various Boolean devices which have been shown give almost all of the basic parts required to build a working computer. The "almost" will be explained in the next chapter.

4 State Machines

At the close of the last chapter I noted that the Boolean functions provide almost all of the tools needed to build a true computer. To examine the shortcomings in the list, reexamine the ignition control which was shown in two forms in Figs. 3-4 and 3-6.

If you really think about that example, you will see that a control situation is set up in which it would be possible to safely protect against the possibility of starting the car engine if any of the doors were open or the car were in something other than Park. However the same system would effectively prevent us from ever driving the car! The very instant that you took the car out of Park, the ignition would be interrupted and the car would stop. Obviously, some change is required if you want to turn this arrangement into a useable system.

In reality you would like the car to be able to assume a number of different states. To be useful, the car should be able to:

—Park, during which time it is completely idle.

—Start the engine, during which time it would be desireable to interlock things so that the engine could not be started with any of the doors open or the transmission in other than Park.

—Run, during which time it should be possible for someone to exit the car without stopping the engine.

Obviously, the car should be able to assume at least three different operating regimes or *states*. The function of the control or interlock must be made to vary in accordance with the state the car currently is in. In other words, the car must remember the sequence of past events to some extent.

This is a characteristic which sets a true computer apart from the hard-wired Boolean logic devices described in Chapter 3. Each of those devices is immediate in its action. The instant that something changes on the input, the output changes. A real computer requires some latching or memory function as well. This was the missing item which was noted at the end of the Chapter 3.

In the case of the car, the simplest change possible would be to simply use the system described to control not the ignition but rather the starting motor. In this case the operation of the car engine would be the "memory" device. You could close all the doors, place the PRNDL in Park and start the engine. The engine would remember that it was running and the car would be in the RUN state.

A minor inconvenience could exist with this condition. If the engine ever stalled (as on a cold morning) it would be necessary to bring the car to a complete stop and place the PRNDL in Park again in order to restart the engine. It might be nicer if the car could be restarted when it is in the RUN condition if it were either in Park or Neutral while still reserving the condition that it would start only in the Park condition in the start state.

The revised system to do this electrically is shown in the form of the *relay ladder logic diagram* (Fig. 4-1). This form of diagram is widely used in the process control industry because of the ease with which the functions can be visualized.

In the Park state, the ignition keyswitch K is open and the rest of the system is in a "don't care" state. To go to the start state it is necessary that all the doors be closed and the PRNDL placed in park, thereby closing P. When K is closed in a command to start the engine, the relay coil A is energized, thereby closing contact A. Note that once A is closed the system goes into a "don't care" condition with regard to the door switches. Relay A is held closed with current drawn through its own contacts and the ignition keyswitch. It is *latched*.

To start the engine, the ignition keyswitch is rotated farther ON into the "start" position. This closes S and K remains closed. If the PRNDL is still in Park, the starter is energized and the engine presumably starts. Relay coil B is also energized through normally closed contacts B-2 which opens B-2 and closes contacts B-1 and B-3. The closure of contacts B-1 enables the engine to start again in either Park (P') or Neutral (N) and the car is now in the run state. When S re-opens because the driver senses that the engine has started, coil B remains energized through its own contacts B-3 and A. It is *latched*.

If the ignition keyswitch K is opened, the current through coil A is interrupted, thereby opening contact A. Thereafter, the current through coil B is interrupted. Both B and A revert to the non-energized state and the car reverts to the park state. To operate the car again it is necessary to go from the park state through the start state to the run state.

Some of the more observant will note that it would be handy to have contacts B-2 break before contacts B-3 make—otherwise S will be held closed during the switching transition.

The object of this exercise is not particularly to propose the starting interlock system but rather to illustrate the latching or memory function which causes the system to progress from one state to another and also to illustrate the use of the relay ladder diagram. Because of the relative ease with which the ladder diagram can be interpreted, it is often used in modern controllers to illustrate the operation of completely solid-state devices in which there are actually no relays at all.

As an example of this, you could write from inspection of the diagram the condition for starting:

$$Start = (((AS(P' + (N, B-1)))$$

This would be read: "starting motor equals A and S and either P' or N and B-1. The state is determined by the relays which are energized. If a non-energized coil is assigned a symbol 0 and an energized coil a symbol I, then the truth table for the system is:

COIL A	COIL B	SYSTEM STATE
0	0	PARK
I	0	START
I	I	RUN

An inspection of the table shows that there actually is one permutation of the system which is unused, namely the condition in which coil B is energized and coil A is not. The circuit actually prevents this from happening since coil B always draws its current through a set of normally open contacts on A. In general if any unused states are possible in a system, it is necessary for the designer to specifically prevent them from occurring or some very unusual performance can result.

It is possible to build a *state machine* with any finite number of states, provided you do not run out of wire, relay contacts, money or electricity. The ladder logic diagram in Fig. 4-2 shows one configuration for such a machine. Relay coil A can be energized if and only if all of the other relays are de-energized. Pushbutton 1 can then energize coil A which will stay latched through its nor-

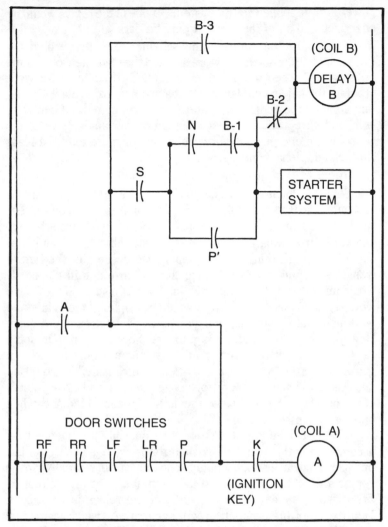

Fig. 4-1. Relay ladder logic diagram.

mally open contacts A1. With A energized pushbutton 2 can initially energize B through contacts A2, whereupon it will latch on through contacts B1. Contacts B2 enable relay C, etc. It can be seen that the system can only be operated in the sequence 1, 2, 3, . . . N. The circled symbols in parallel with the ready coils represent lamps which would "climb the ladder," lighting in succession as the buttons were pushed. The system can be reset by the reset pushbutton only when it is in the n'th state. When the power is first applied to the system,   none of the relays would be energized and all of the lamps would be dark.

Some of the variations on this scheme are relatively obvious. For example, if contacts A1 were shorted the machine would come on in state 1 when the power was applied. If contacts N2 were shorted, the ladder could be reset at any point, etc. Obviously, the only limit to the number of states lies in the number of contacts, coils and wire available. Also, instead of the lamps, each of the relays could energize or de-energize one or more external loads through additional contacts, etc.

THE TOGGLE

Suppose that it is your goal to operate the ladder from a single pushbutton so that you could advance from state to state by successively depressing the same button. If all of the pushbuttons in Fig. 4-2 were wired in parallel so that they were all closed simultaneously, a peculiar thing would happen. Depression of the button would set A and enable B. Since the button was still closed, B would immediately fire, thus enabling C, etc. In short, if the relays were relatively fast, the system would run right up the ladder and wind up in state N before you could let the pushbutton out. A quick "teasing" of the pushbutton might have the system stop in some random state, but this sort of thing is seldom desired except in games. In order to have the system controllable, it would be desireable to have the operation sense the open and closed states of the pushbutton and advance the state of the machine only when both had been accomplished.

The circuit in Fig. 4-3 shows one possible arrangement for accomplishing this end. The pushbutton is arranged so that it has one pair of normally open contacts and one pair of normally closed contacts which go to alternate ladder rungs. When the circuit is first fired up or after a reset, none of the relays is energized. Depression of the pushbutton will set relay A, which latches on through A1 and enables relay B through A2. Before relay B energizes, the pushbutton must be released. With either A or B energized, the machine is in state 1. Relay B enables relay C and the next depression of the button will set relay C and enable D, which will set on the next release of the button, etc. The machine will progress up the state ladder with alternate depressions and releases of the pushbutton. Each successive relay latches on to hold the state until the pushbutton goes to the opposite state and no amount of "teasing" of the pushbutton switch can cause a transfer of more than one state.

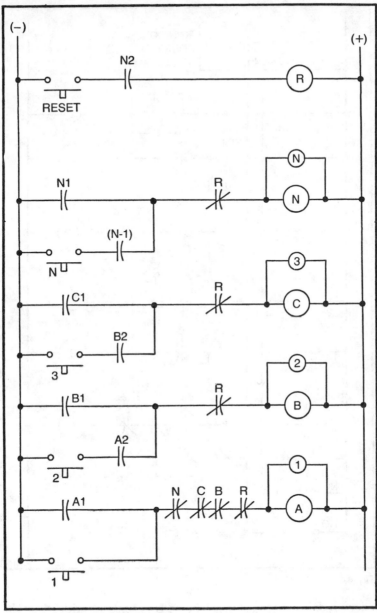

Fig. 4-2. The N state ladder.

There are several fairly obvious variations of this circuit. For example, if the dotted connection showing the Normally Open reset contacts were made, the system would reset to state 1 with D

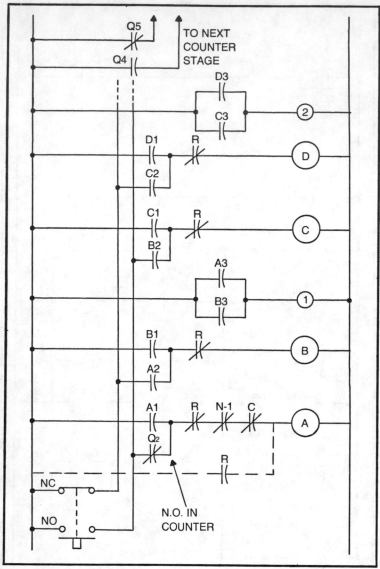

Fig. 4-3. The toggle ladder.

energized. If the contact pair labeled Q is replaced with D2 or N2 (and changed to n.o.) the ladder would climb to D or N and loop back to state 1 on the next switch depression. If contacts D2 were used the device would perform a divide-by-2 function and lamps 1 and 2 would alternately light. If contacts N2 were used the ladder would become a modulo N/2 counter and it would require N/2 depressions of the switch to make the circuit repeat.

THE COUNTER

If the highest relay in the string were fitted with two extra pairs of contacts, designated Q4 and Q5 in Fig. 4-3, it can be seen that these contacts could serve the same function that the pushbutton serves for the lowest order ladder. For example, suppose that N=D. Also assume that the dotted R connection is made (N. C. contacts C through N-1 and the N.C. R are no longer used-shorted). A reset would energize first A and then B and the machine would start in state 1. The first depression of the switch would transfer to C and the release would transfer to D. The machine would be in state 2. The next depression would transfer to A (Q2=D2) and the machine would be back in the 1 state again. In other words, every-even numbered cycle of the switch would leave the circuit in the 1 state. Every odd-numbered depression of the switch would leave the machine in the 2 state. If the state 1 lamp were labeled 0 (or simply omitted) and the state 2 lamp were labeled I the device would be a single stage binary number counter.

Contact D4 is closed and D5 is open during the time between the odd-numbered release, when the transfer from C to D takes place, and the even-numbered depression, when the transfer from D to A takes place. The action would be identical to the action of the pushbutton switch except that it would happen half as often. An identical second counter would go to state 2 and display an I on the second depression of the switch when the first counter reverted to state 1 and displayed a 0. If you presume that there are four successive identical stages with the first being actuated by the

Table 4-1. Truth Table.

Depression	Stage 4	Stage 3	Stage 2	Stage 1
Reset	0	0	0	0
1	0	0	0	I
2	0	0	I	0
3	0	0	I	I
4	0	I	0	0
5	0	I	0	I
6	0	I	I	0
7	0	I	I	I
8	I	0	0	0

pushbutton, the second being actuated by the first, and the third being actuated by the second, etc with a 0 representing state 1 and an I representing state 2 you would obtain the truth table shown in Table 4-1.

It is fairly obvious that the device is counting in a binary fashion. With four counters, the system would be hexadecimal if you chose to interpret it in that manner since 15 depressions of the button would set all four stages to I and the sixteenth would set them all to zero while outputting one "depression" on the output line from the fourth stage. This "carry" could be conducted to further counter assemblies.

If you wanted to have the system count in the decimal system you could arrange matters so that the carry came from the twentieth relay, which would represent part of the tenth state and Q=twentieth letter. Relays A and B would then represent a decimal zero, relays C and D would represent a one, relays E and F would represent a decimal nine. Nine depressions of the pushbutton would walk up the ladder to 9 and the tenth would reset the ladder to zero. The counter would have 10 stable states.

One of the advantages of the binary system is relatively obvious from this example. With the decimal counter configured this way, it would take 20 relays to count to 10—whereas the binary arrangement would permit counting to 16 using only 16 relays. It is a little less obvious, however, if you arranged some extra contacts so that a group of four binary counters would trigger the reset as follows:

$$RESET = (D_4 D_2)$$

RESET equals D of the fourth counter and D of the second counter. For this condition, the ensemble would count zero through nine in BCD and only 17 relays would be required, with the extra unit being used for reset.

THE SOLID-STATE LATCH

Except for some very special cases, the actual use of relay ladder logic for a design is seldom justifiable these days. The ladder logic is introduced only to show some of the basic concepts. One of the commonly used concepts and a sometimes used hardware arrangement is the R-S latch (Figs. 4-4A and 4-4B).

The most basic form of this latch consists of two NAND gates. With the switch in the up position, it can be seen that U1 has one of its inputs low therefore its output will be high. U2 has one input high due to the high output of U1 and a second input high due to the

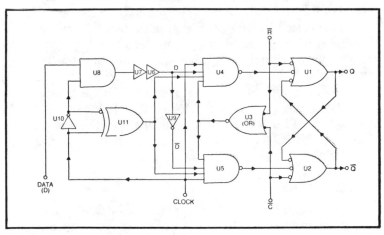

Fig. 4-4A. The RS Latch.

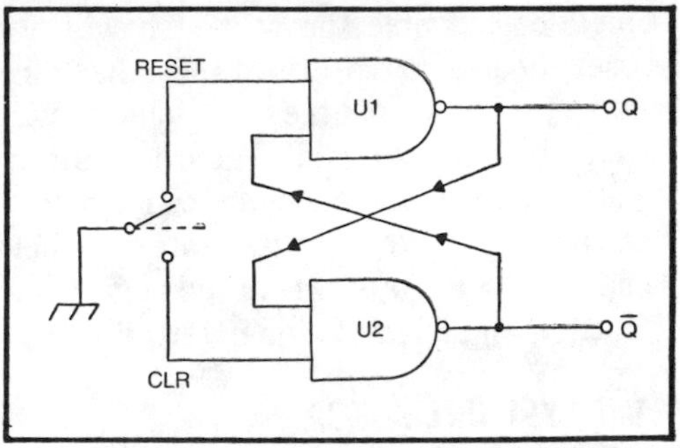

open circuit. U2 will therefore output a low or 0. Even after the switch is returned to the neutral position, U1 will have a low on one input due to the 0 on the output of U2 so U1 output will stay latched at I. Pushing the switch down will activate U2=I and U1 = 0. Whenever the device is set in one direction, it must be forcibly reset in the other direction by taking one of the inputs (but not both) to 0.

This device is very useful in a great many digital applications since it latches the last active-low input and holds that state until forcibly reset. One of the uses to which this circuit is frequently put is to de-bounce switches, relays, etc. Due to mechanical inertia and springiness, mechanical contacts tend to bounce open several items after an initial closure. The extreme speed of electronic counters and devices permits them to interpret this as multiple openings and closings of the switch. If the mechanical switch is fed through an RS latch, the latch simply goes into the set state. A

Fig. 4-4B. The type D edge triggered flip-flop.

single-pole double throw switch will not be misread because a reset requires a closure in the other direction.

The RS latch serves the same function that the latching contacts on our relays did. They hold the circuit latched in a given state. The two outputs of an RS latch are frequently labeled Q and Q̄ since they have opposite states. It should be noted that RESET and CLEAR are often *not* noted negated as R and C even when they function on active low or inverted logic.

THE TYPE D FLIP-FLOP

The circuit at the bottom of Fig. 4-5 is a type D edge triggered flip flop. The righthand portion of the figure made up of U1 and U2 is a fast RS latch. This is shown as a negative logic NOR. A low on R̄ will set Q=I and Q=0. A low on C will reverse the situation. U3 is a negative logic OR which permits the reset and set to override everything else since it disables the outputs of U4 and U5 holding both at I. At a time when the clock line is low (CK=0) the AND gate U-8 is enabled passing through DATA through U7 and U6 to U4 and negated data (D̄) to U5. However, U4 and U5 are disabled by the same low clock. On the rising edge of the clock pulse, U4 and U5 are briefly enabled during the propagation delay through U10—which is deliberately made slower. The output of U11 is arranged to be I when the inputs are alike and 0 when the inputs are different. U11 is also arranged to be a bit slower than U4 and U5 so that on the falling edge of the clock U4 and U5 are disabled by the falling clock before U11 goes briefly true. The activation of U4 and U5 transfers the data through to the RS latch which sets up and holds the data on Q and Q. If D=I then Q=I and if D=0 then Q=0. The units U7 and U6 are arranged to delay long enough for the data to clock through.

It can be seen that the data is transferred through only on the rising clock condition. At any other time, D can vary at will without transferring data. A garden variety flip-flop such as the 7474 (in TTL) will follow clock rates typically to 18 MHz. A higher speed Schottky version will typically follow the clock to 35 MHz. In general, the TTL unit will reset and clear in a few nanoseconds Figure 4-5 shows the symbol used for the type D edge triggered flip-flop along with the truth table.

THE DATA LATCH

One variation on the D type flip-flop is the data latch. For the lower schematic in Fig. 4-5 suppose that you were to discard all of the components to the left of u6 and apply the data to the junction

68

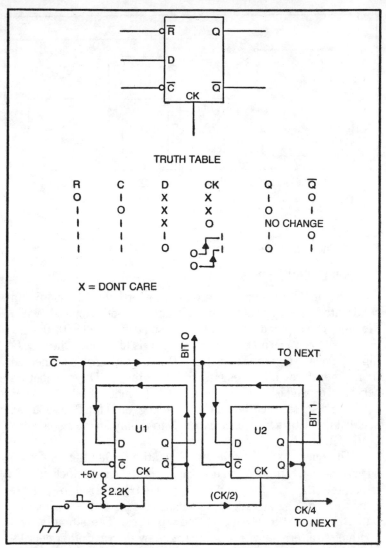

Fig. 4-5. The ripple counter (two stages) using type D edge triggered flip-flops.

marked D. For this ensemble, data would freely pass through from D to Q whenever the clock was high but would latch whenever the clock was low in the last postion held when the clock was high. This type of latch generally comes in lots of four to a 14-pin package, whereas the edge triggered variety will generally come to the 14-pin package. The data latch is frequently used to capture the status of counters, etc.

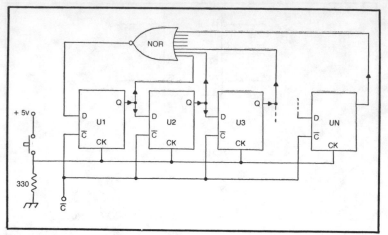

Fig. 4-6. The shift register N state machine.

THE RIPPLE COUNTER

The ripple counter shown on the lower half of Fig. 4-6 is a solid state counterpart of the ripple counter in ladder logic shown in Fig. 4-4. The negated clear lead ($\overline{C}$) is used to reset all of the binary counters to zero, as noted earlier. When $\overline{C}$ is taken low, the type D flip flop goes to Q=0 and $\overline{Q}$ = I. On U1 the $\overline{Q}$ terminal is connected to D, therefore, it represents the data input. The pushbutton serves to ground or take to 0 the Clock (CK) input of U1. From our previous discussion of the type D edge triggered flip flop, you can see that the data is transferred from D to Q only on the rising edge of the CK.

The operation is as follows. When the pushbutton is depressed it takes CK to 0. When it is released, the rising clock edge is generated, thus the I applied to D by $\overline{Q}$ is transferred to Q and $\overline{Q}$ goes to zero. The next depression and release of the pushbutton will transfer a 0 to Q since $\overline{Q}$ now is zero. The situation will continue to alternate with Q going to zero with every other depression of the pushbutton. It can be seen that the operation of stage U1 is the complete counterpart of the relay ladder of Fig. 4-4. and the device is counting in the binary system. Since the CK for U2 is supplied by the output at Q of U1, it can be seen that U2 will run at half the speed of U1 (see Table 4-2).

The counter cycles from zero through 3. On the fourth depression of the pushbutton, it reverts back to zero state and U2 outputs a rising CK to the next stage. The binary count appears at the Q terminals and the clock for succeeding stages appears at $\overline{Q}$.

With two stages, the system has four states and with N stages it has 2^N states. As described for the circuit in Fig. 4-4, the device can be made to reset at any number of stages and can be made to count in any number base. The name ripple counter comes from the fact that the count "ripples through."

THE SHIFT REGISTER

Figure 4-6 shows the solid state equivalent of the N State ladder of Fig. 4-2. The input D for U1 is derived from the NOR gate which senses the state of Q on stages 1 thru N. D can be I if and if Q=0 on all of the succeeding stages. This is the equivalent of the string of normally closed contacts in series with coil A on Fig. 4-2.

Since the circuit of Fig. 4-2 transferred on the depression of the pushbutton, the arrangement of the pushbutton is made so that the rising edge is generated when the pushbutton is depressed rather than when it was released as used on Fig. 4-5. Either arrangement would work.

Immediately after a $\overline{C} = 0$, all stages will have Q=0 and the output of the NOR will be high. At the first depression of the pushbutton, the D=I will transfer to Q1=I and the output of the NOR will fall to zero. The machine will have transferred from State Zero to State One. At the next depression of the pushbutton, D=0 and Q=I on stage one and D=I and Q=0 on stage 2. After the rising edge, Q1=0 and Q2=I. The I will shift through the stages to stage N and then "fall off the end," leaving Q=0 on all stages. The NOR senses this condition and sets D1=I and the cycle begins anew. This arrangement is useful not only in a multiple state control, but in several other very important applications.

SERIAL TO PARALLEL CONVERSION

If instead of deriving D for U1 from the NOR you were to derive the incoming data from some line coming into the system,

Table 4-2. Truth Table.

Pushbutton cycle	Q1	$\overline{Q1}$	Q2	$\overline{Q2}$
0	0	I	0	I
1	I	0	0	I
2	0	I	I	0
3	I	0	I	0
4	0	I	0	I

the current state of Q1 would be the state that the line had been on the preceding clock edge. Similarly, Q2 would be the state of the line on the second preceding clock edge and QN would be the state of the line on the nth preceding clock edge.

As you progress to more and more complex controls in practical microprocessor systems, one of the major problems becomes the large number of lines or wires which must be carried from one unit to the next. It would be very easy to get into a situation where a huge bundle of wires would be required to transfer all of the information from one location to another. If there is any significant distance to be covered, it becomes attractive to send the strings of 0's and I's in serial form over a single wire. This generally requires that the data be transformed from *parallel format* to a *serial format* and then re-converted at the other end.

Parallel to serial conversion can be accomplished by setting the Qs of each of the flip flops to the correct values using the $\overline{R}$ to set a I and the $\overline{C}$ to set a 0. The data is then taken from QN and clocked out in serial fashion using CK. At the far end of the line the data is applied to D1 and the CK shifts the data through until the serial to parallel register is full. The data can then be read out in "parallel format" by reading the Qs of the various flip-flops. In a practical situation, the number of wires can be reduced from some very large number N to only three: DATA, CK and GROUND. The only significant limitation is the time. For circuitry of the same speed, it will take N times as long to send the same data package in serial format as it would in parallel. In some cases this time limitation is not too serious.

The general process of using the same wire or device for multiple data transfer is called *multiplexing*. The technique described here is called *synchronous* or *clocked* multiplexing because the clock must be sent along with the data. *Asynchronous multiplexing* and "asynchronous data transmission" are techniques in which a small additional amount of time is traded off so that the clock need not be sent. This is advantageous in situations where the data must be sent over great distances. It can make use of rented telephone lines and the user does not have the expense of putting up poles and stringing lines. The economic advantages of the use of existing telephone or telegraph lines when the distances to be covered are measured in miles is obviously very great.

SERIAL MEMORY

The flip-flop is obviously a memory type of device since it can be used to remember or STORE the state applied to it indefinitely.

If there are only a few things to be stored, then a type D flip-flop is a reasonable way to do the job. These come two to a fourteen pin package and cost perhaps 35 cents. However, if any significant amount of data is to be stored, this process would be prohibitively expensive. A typical microcomputer routine might consist of 1000 bytes or more which would require 8000 or more bits and 4000 packages.

One of the earliest solutions to this problem was to store the data in a *dynamic flip-flop*. The data was held in a capacitor rather than in a transistor. Since the capacitor leaks the charge off and the capacitance must be kept small, these devices can store the data for only a very brief period—a few thousandths of a second at most. It was necessary, therefore, to keep transferring the data. With each

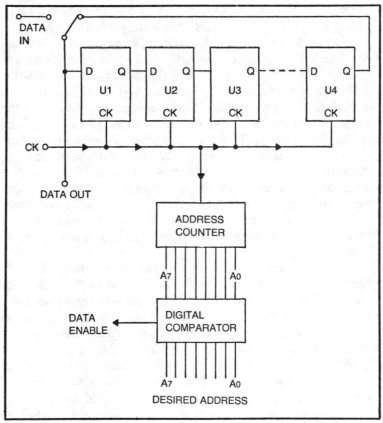

Fig. 4-7. The serial memory. The digital comparator is a summing AND device. When the desired address equals the address counter output, the data enable line is activated.

73

transfer the data is regenerated and therefore preserved. The data could be held permanently if the loop was closed and the data kept permanently moving.

If you can imagine a toy train on a closed oval track, with the train long enough to completely fill the track, I will use this analogy for the serial memory. The memory could consist of a ping pong ball placed into a car to represent a I and an empty car to represent a 0. As the cars moved by, you could place your data in the cars while they were moving. You could keep track of the location or *address* of a given bit of data by keeping count of the number of cars behind the locomotive in which the data was placed. At times when neither a *read* out of memory nor a *write* into the memory was required, the train would simply circulate. When you wanted to do either, it would only be necessary to count cars until the *data address* was reached and then read by seeing whether the car contained a ping pong ball or write by removing or inserting a ball.

Figure 4-7 shows the solid state implementation of this analogy. The address counter has exactly the same number of states as the shift register has flip-flops. With the data switch in the position shown, data from the nth stage is fed into the first stage. A read can be performed at any item by simply examining the data line at the instant when the address counter has the correct address showing on the pins A_0 thru A_7 To write data in, the system waits until the correct address is present and then flips the switch, *writes* and flips the switch back. The circuit shown is a *one-wide memory*. Only a single bit is written or read at each address. However, the clock can drive—and the address counter can just as easily keep track of—a large number of loops. Therefore, with four tracks you could have a *four-wide memory* and with eight tracks you would have an eight-wide memory.

The advantage of this format for the memory lies in the "pin count", which is a significant part of the cost of any solid state package. If all of the circuitry for the *N-wide memory* is placed on a single chip, you would need only to have pins coming to the outside to carry the *N* data bits, the number of *decoded address bits* from the address counter, the *CK*, and a *READ/$\overline{WRITE}$* signal as well as power and ground. You could access any location in memory by merely waiting for it to come by. Chips with N=1024 and a width of eight bits with an onboard address counter are sold commercially.

The principle problem with the serial memory is the latency time. On a 1024 long memory running at 1 MHz CK you would have to wait as much as a millisecond to get data in or out if the data address had just passed. On the average, you would have to wait a half millisecond. This tends to considerably slow the processor in most cases. An exception is in the data for a CRT display or TV display where the data is cycled through in order and the read and write commands are relatively infrequent. Because of the slowness, serial memorys had largely fallen into disuse except for displays as noted. More recently, the serial memory has begun to come back into use in *charge coupled devices* (CCD) and *magnetic bubble memorys* which can be very densly packed. These memorys are now being offered in capacities up to a million bytes with still larger devices in the offing. These devices are generally used for *archival storage* where very large amounts of data are to be stored and access to the memory is relatively infrequent. Faster working *random access memory* (RAM) is used for program and frequently accessed data.

THE ADDRESS DECODER

The primary difference between the serial memory and the RAM is that in the serial memory the data can only be accessed in sequence. To obtain data from a new address, it is necessary for the machine to wait until the desired address cycles by. In the random access memory it is possible to jump to any address in the same short period of time. The machine does not have to wait for a number of unwanted addresses to cycle by. In order to do this, it is necessary that the RAM be equipped with an *address decoder* which will instantaneously decode the address being asserted and enable the correct storage element.

If there are very many bits to be decoded, address decoders tend to get a bit complicated to follow. The example shown in Fig. 4-8 is selected to be simple. It will decode the four possible conditions of lines A and B. The BUS running down the left hand side of the illustration carries both the positive and negated values of A and B. The binary value of zero corresponds to having both A and B low. Therefore, the inputs of U1 are connected to A and B. With both A and B low, the negated values of both are high. Thus the output of the AND gate U1 goes high. A little study of the circuit reveals that the successive outputs of the various ANDs will respond to the Boolean conditions listed on the output which in turn correspond to the decimal numbers in the column on the right.

This decoder is very straightforward since it follows the Boolean expression directly in hardware. For example, for a decoder to decode four lines on the binary value of nine you would use

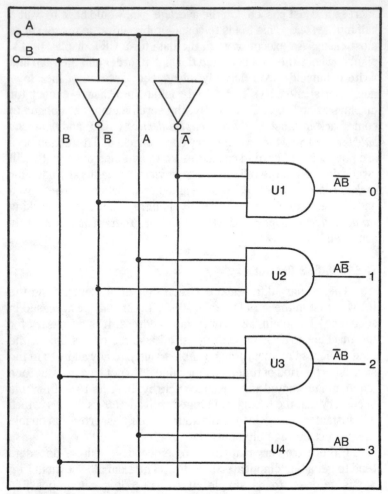

Fig. 4-8. The address decoder.

four input AND gates and the Boolean expression would be: $9 =$ I00I $9 = D\overline{C}BA$ where D is the most significant bit and A is the least.

Decoders to decode four lines are available in a single chip in the 74154 and others. On many of these chips, the 16-line output is configured in the active-low condition where all of the lines except the active one are high and the selected line goes low. In addition to the four input address lines, there are usually one or more chip select lines which will take all of the outputs high. On the 74154, the two chip select lines are active low and the selected line will not go low unless both of the chip selects are low.

Figure 4-9 shows a typical RAM organization. The eight address bits are interpreted in terms of 16 rows and 16 columns and each memory address corresponds to a row and column intersection. Since the decoder can drive a number of these row and column

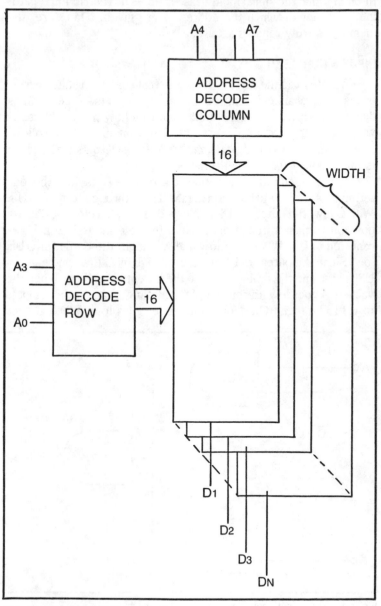

Fig. 4-9. A typical RAM organization.

matrices, the memory can be given any width. A fairly common size would be a 256 × 8 wide RAM. From the circuit of the decoder in Fig. 4-8 the speed of selecting any address is limited only by the speed of operation of the gates involved and the number of gates through which the signal must pass. There is no restriction regarding the order in which the addresses are given. Therefore, the memory is truly random access.

INPUT MULTIPLEXING

A state machine will often require that change in state corresponds to a change in source of data or signals. Like address decoders, which get a bit complicated to follow if the address is very wide, input multiplexers are also a bit difficult to follow. Figure 4-10 shows the *digital double pole double throw switch*, which is the simplest form of multiplexer to follow.

For this circuit, when the control line C is low the odd terminal of U1 is held high and data will pass through from A to U3. With C low, the output of U2 is blocked high. Therefore, U3 is in a position to pass through data. Note that the inversion in U1 is canceled in U3. When C is low and A is high, the output of U1 is low. Since the output of U2 is blocked high by C low, one input of U3 is high and the other is low so the U3 output is high. When the value of A goes low, the output of U1 goes high, causing both inputs to U3 to be high. Therefore, the output goes low. When C goes

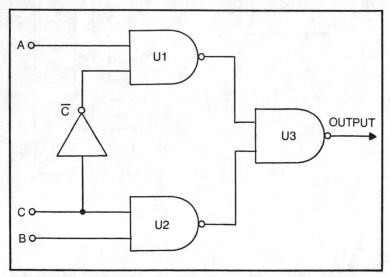

Fig. 4-10. The digital double pole double throw switch.

high, the opposite situation prevails. One input of U1 is blocked low, therefore the output of U1 is blocked high and the data passes through U2. A multiple line data selector of width N would use an N-input NAND for U3 and would require N two-input NANDs for the switching function. It would also require an address decoder to select which of the two input gates to enable to let the data through. Eight to one and 16 to one selectors are available in single chip packages.

SUMMARY

All true stored program computers are state machines. Their response to a given set of inputs can change from state to state and is a function of the architecture of the machine as well as the history of the operation. The machine might proceed from one state to the next in either fixed or variable sequences. For example, in the car control discussed earlier, the control could pass from park only to start. However, from start it could go back to park of forward to run but from run it can only go back to park and not to start. The state machine is characterized by the existance of multiple input/output relationships depending upon its memory of past actions.

5 Flow Charting and Documentation

Some of the basic techniques of flow charting were developed a number of years ago to bring some order out of the chaos of computer programming. The computer is an extremely literal-minded device which (when all the hardware is functioning properly) will do precisely what you told it to do. The problem is that what it does might not always prove to be what you had intended it to do. The flow chart was conceived as an orderly mechanism to graphically illustrate what you are asking the machine to do.

The basic technique of flow charting proved to be so serviceable that the use was extended beyond the original range to include PERT and CRITICAL PATH diagrams in management situations. The technique has a wide basic usefulness when directed toward any task in which multiple goals must be accomplished more or less simultaneously and the results must come together to achieve the desired end result. The chart sets forward in an easily visualized manner the various tasks and nodes so that pacing items can be singled out and properly attended. For example, if the task is to produce a new automobile, there is no point in scheduling road tests before the engine construction is complete.

In working with microcomputers, I have somewhat extended and embellished the use of the flow chart as the main time of documentation in programming. When properly used and annotated, this technique will permit the original programmer or any other qualified programmer to find any particular step or constant in even large and very complex machine-language programs. This particular point is very important since the principal objections to machine language programming (with the attendant efficiency in equipment requirements, memory requirements and running speed) stem from the difficulty in following the program. The technique which follows can make a machine language program as easy to follow as a high-level language program.

SYMBOLS

The symbols to be used in this flow charting technique are illustrated in Fig. 5-1 with a brief definition beside each. The symbol set has been somewhat embellished over the American Standards Association (ASA) X3.5 standard for this usage.

Rather than try to define the symbols by themselves, refer to Fig. 5-2 which represents a Saturday flow chart.

In Fig. 5-2, you can see that the system under consideration starts with the end point symbol in the upper left hand corner and proceeds along one of several pathways to arrive at one of several goals or to launch into other parts of the program. The numbered nodes show that a given end point or continuation can be arrived at by means of several possible paths. For example the system can

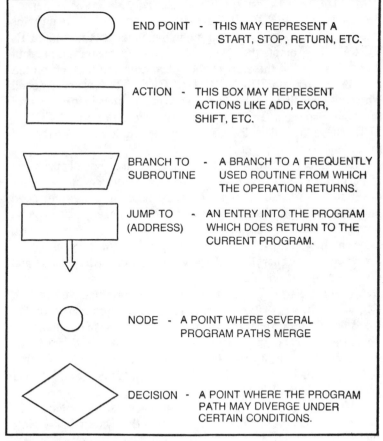

END POINT - THIS MAY REPRESENT A START, STOP, RETURN, ETC.

ACTION - THIS BOX MAY REPRESENT ACTIONS LIKE ADD, EXOR, SHIFT, ETC.

BRANCH TO SUBROUTINE - A BRANCH TO A FREQUENTLY USED ROUTINE FROM WHICH THE OPERATION RETURNS.

JUMP TO (ADDRESS) - AN ENTRY INTO THE PROGRAM WHICH DOES RETURN TO THE CURRENT PROGRAM.

NODE - A POINT WHERE SEVERAL PROGRAM PATHS MERGE

DECISION - A POINT WHERE THE PROGRAM PATH MAY DIVERGE UNDER CERTAIN CONDITIONS.

Fig. 5-1. Flow chart symbols.

arrive at node 1 and subsequently the continuation or JUMP TO (Go Play Golf) by either the route of having WIFE approve or by mowing the lawn and still having time left. The box is called a continuation or a JUMP TO because it implies that further action will result. Go Play Golf would represent a considerable program in itself.

The BRANCH TO SUBROUTINE box is a little less evident. Most microprocessors have a BRANCH TO SUBROUTINE or JUMP TO SUBROUTINE command available. With this command, the machine will store the status of all registers required to remember what it was doing, drop that task and perform the subroutine function or program and then pick up where the main program left off. This differs from a JUMP TO since the JUMP TO does not automatically come back and pick up where it left off. JUMP TO departs for something entirely different, whereas BRANCH TO SUBROUTINE always comes back to the main path. The last command in a subroutine is usually something like RE-TURN. This prompts the system to retrieve from storage the data that was stored at the start of the subroutine and take off on the main program again. BRANCH TO SUBROUTINE is usually used when the same little routine is required many times in the course of the main program. The whys and wherefores of BRANCH TO SUBROUTINE will be discussed at some length under the topic of microprocessor architecture.

Not all of the paths on the flow chart need be equally probable of occurrence. For example, the jump from the second weather observation to node 2 is not highly probable since weather good enough to prompt a discussion of golf would generally also be good enough for mowing the lawn.

The flow chart itself is fairly self-evident. Merely follow the arrows about the chart through the various paths as they merge and diverge at nodes and decision points.

A somewhat more practical flow chart is illustrated in Fig. 5-3, which reverts to the car interlock of the ladder diagram of Fig. 4-1. Looking at the diagram, you can see that if any of the doors are open, the flow chart stays locked in the tight little loop between the first decision block and node 1. If the answer is no on any of the first three decision blocks, the flow circles through node 1 and the car remains in the PARK state.

Upon satisfaction of all of the first three decision blocks, the flow chart shows A enabled or latched and the system passes into the START state. Opening of the key will take the system back to

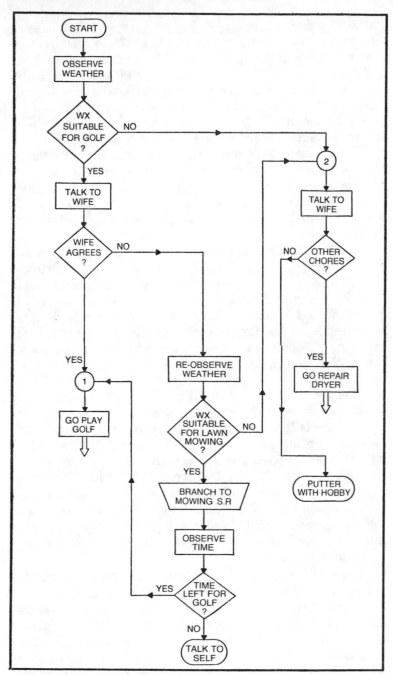

Fig. 5-2. A Saturday flow chart.

PARK. However, a failure to satisfy the next two blocks simply leaves the system locked in the START loop. When all three of the tests are satisfied, the system proceeds to the RUN loop. The RUN loop contains a DO action. If all three of the tests in the RUN loop are satisfied, the starter is energized. However, the system stays locked in the RUN loop. The only escape from the RUN loop is the condition KEY = Open. In this case, relay A is cleared which in turn clears relay B and the system returns to PARK.

In relay ladder logic diagram in Fig. 4-1, the use of the three loops is somewhat arbitrary since all of the tests are performed simultaneously. For example, the door switch contacts and the PRNDL switch are all tested simultaneously since they are wired into a series AND. To all intents and purposes, the speed around the loop is infinite.

In a microcomputer system, on the other hand, this is not so. The microcomputer would probably actually perform these tests one at a time and the steps would be spaced out in time. It might take only ten microseconds for each test, however, the speed around the loop would be finite and the steps would be done in sequence. Depending upon the input/output arrangement used and the nature of the program, it might be possible to double up in a few places. Nonetheless, the tests would tend to be done on a step-at-a-time basis.

Make no mistake about it, the microcomputer system would do the overall job much faster than the relay logic circuit. For example, the task of setting or clearing relay A would require not less than 14 milliseconds, whereas the electronic latching of the equivalent of relay A could be done in microseconds. However, it is well to keep in mind that in the microcomputer each of the tests would represent a small block of instructions which would have to be read from memory. The microprocessor would then have to get the data, gauge it against a standard and then either jump back to the node or go forward to the next instruction if the test was satisfied.

Each of the nodes and blocks represented in the flow chart will actually have a discrete address in the memory of the computer. The four-digit numbers placed above each of the blocks represents the address in memory where the specific step or small train of steps is to be found. This procedure is a definite departure from the more usual flow charting, which serves as only a general guide to what is going on in the computer. With the address of each specific step identified on the flow chart, the flow chart becomes a "master wiring diagram" for the system.

There is another basic difference in the type of flow charting shown in Fig. 5-3 compared to the more usual flow charts. The

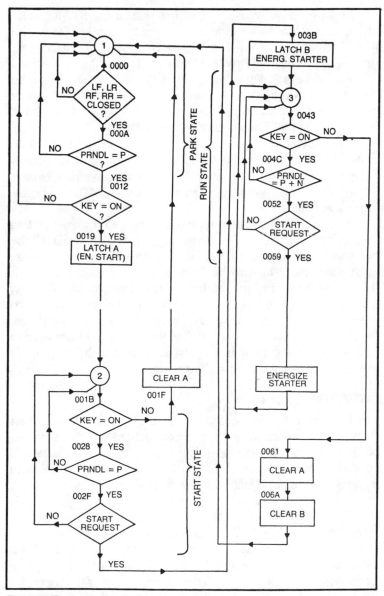

Fig. 5-3. The car interlock flow chart of Fig. 4-1.

difference is essentially a matter of degree. However the type of flow charting shown goes into much greater detail of the basic programming. It is wise to show a block for every step or small group of 2 or 3 steps when using this technique so that you can keep track of the various things that are going on.

As an example, consider the first test in the START state where the machine looks to determine whether the key is on. The actual language, spelled out in English (not machine instructions) for this sequence would resemble Fig. 5-4.

The address $0000 is the location of node 1 as shown on the diagram. If the condition is satisfied, the program simply skips over the next sequence of instructions which tell it to clear relay A equivalent and then jump back into the PARK loop at the start. If the keyswitch is no longer ON (it had to be on one to get into START) the machine does not skip the next instructions. It clears Relay A and jumps to the start of PARK. If the keyswitch is on it simply skips the instructions from $001F through 0017 and commences at 0028.

This is a fairly common type of procedure for implementing decisions in a computer. You write a test of some kind and tell the machine that if the test is satisfied it should jump over some instructions and go on with the main program. On the other hand, if the test is not satisfied the machine does not jump or skip the next instructions and those instructions tell the machine to go elsewhere in the program. The reverse logic is also used at times. In this case, if the test is not satisfied the machine is instructed to jump to a new location. If the test is satisfied, the machine is instructed to just go on with the program.

INSTRUCTIONS AND DATA

In most microcomputers, the same set of lines, the DATA BUS, is used for diseminating both instructions and data throughout the machine. On an eight-bit machine, this DATA BUS will consist of eight wires numbered D_0 through D_7. The data bus will sometimes contain an instruction such as shift, add, complement, exclusive-or, etc. On one cycle and might contain data such as operands, addresses, etc. for the next one or two cycles (and in some cases no cycles). The eight-bit instructions range in value from $00 to $FF just as the numbers in data do. When viewed independently, it is impossible to distinguish whether a given entry is an instruction or data. The second portion of the documentation method makes use of a data sheet in which the specific

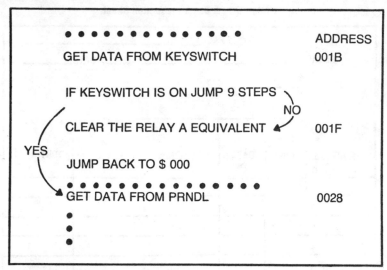

Fig. 5-4. Sequence for the START state.

program entries are recorded step-by-step and segregated into instructions and data. The blank instruction sheet is filled out only after the flow chart is complete. The instruction sheet keeps track of the address of each instruction and that address is then transferred to the flow chart. A provision is made for recording notations regarding the meaning of each instruction. A blank instruction sheet is shown in Table 5-1.

To illustrate the way this works, consider a simple but useful program loop: the DELAY LOOP. The first step in laying out this program is to work up the flow chart diagram. This is shown on Fig. 5-5. There are a great many times when you might like to have a microcomputer pause and essentially do nothing or wait for some specified period of time before doing something. For example, when sensing a keyswitch or a mechanical switch of some sort, the machine can be set to sense the switch closure, dally for a specified period of time and then go back and sense the closure again to make sure that the first reading was not just a noise pulse or glitch on the line. Before the reading is accepted as a valid switch closure, two successive yes answers are required. Another reason for a SOFTWARE TIMING LOOP is if the machine is sending code such as Morse over the radio or Baudot or ASCII on a teletype. Since each code character is sent at a specific speed, the machine is instructed to output an 0 or I and then hold the character for a specific period of time. In a control for a machine such as a

Table 5-1. A Blank Instruction Sheet.

| PAGE_____ _____ |
| PROGRAM_____ DATE_____ |
| _____ |
| _____ |

ADDRESS	COM	DATA	OPERATION	ROUTINE
0				
1				
2				
3				
4				
5				
6				
7				
8				
9				
0				
1				
2				
3				
4				
5				
6				
7				
8				
9				
0				
1				

dishwasher or a copier you will want to turn on a motor and have it run for a specific period of time. There are unlimited uses for a software timing loop.

Some of the one-chip microcomputers incorporate one or more programmable timers so that the software timing loop will not be required. However, timing loop can be incorporated in nearly any microcomputer and there are few if any control applications which are not required to have timing control. There are always tradeoffs to consider regarding the use of extra hardware versus extra software. In units like the 6800 or 6802 in which the timer is not offered as a standard feature, the use of a software timing loop is often the most economical approach.

THE 6800 SOFTWARE TIMING LOOP

The 6800 microprocessors are NMOS devices and they are at least partially dynamic. Some of the flip-flops are built using

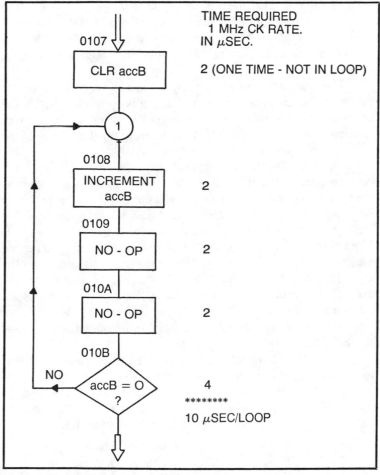

Fig. 5-5. The 6800 software timing loop.

capacitor storage. The processor cannot be stopped without losing information. Even when you want the device to do nothing—it has to work at doing nothing. The standard devices will run at a clock rate up to 1 MHz—which is usually generated with a 4 MHz crystal and divided down to get the 2 phase clock—which is actually used by the device. For the program in Fig. 5-5, assume that the software timing loop is a portion of another larger program and that the timing loop begins at address $0107.

As the first step in the program, clear accumulator B. The 6800 actually has two accumulators, A and B—which are each 8 bits wide. These accumulators are the place where most of the arithmetic is done. Although either accumulator could be used for this timing loop, B is used in this example.

The clearing operation sets accumulator B (accB) to the value $ 00. It is now empty. The next step after the node 1 is to add one to the contents of accB. The first time through the loop the contents of accB = $01.

The next two steps in the program are NO-OP. They simply take up time and program space. Internally to the computer, the only thing that happens is that the program counter is incremented. The machine simply moves to the next program step. None of the registers is changed.

The 6800 (6802, etc) contains a register called the condition code register or the HINZVC. This register is set with a code as the result of operations like add, increment, load, etc. Here we are interested only in the Z in HINZVC. The Z stands for Zero. If the last operation resulted in a zero, the third significant bit is set to I. Most of the branch instructions in the 6800 are based upon testing individual bits in the HINZVC. There is one instruction with the code $26 which tells the machine to branch if the zero bit (Z) is not set. This instruction has a mnemonic BNE, which stands for Branch if Not Equal. If the last instruction does not set Z=I, the machine will branch according to the byte immediately following the $26 instruction.

The byte which follows a branch instruction is always treated as a binary signed number. If the first bit is set, it is considered to be negative. A negative branch instruction has its complement subtracted from the program counter. This makes the machine jump backward in the program. This works out as follows:

$$\begin{array}{lll} & \text{if used as a branch} \\ \$ \text{ FF} = \text{IIII IIII} = -128 & \text{no steps backward} \\ \$ \text{ 80} = \text{I000 0000} = -0 & \text{128 steps backward} \end{array}$$

$$\$ \ 7F = 0III \ IIII = + 127 \qquad \text{127 steps forward}$$
$$\$ \ 00 = 0000 \ 0000 = + 0 \qquad \text{no steps forward}$$

The positive branch instruction simply has its value added to the program counter, which makes the machine jump forward. Since in the case of the timing loop you want the machine to jump backward to node 1, you immediately know that the DESTINATION BYTE must lie in the range between $FF and $80. Since the backward branch is a short one you know that it will be close to $FF rather than $80.

On the first tour through the loop, the contents of the accB = $01. On the second time, it will be $02, etc. Obviously, neither of these instructions would set the Z bit in the HINZVC, so the machine will branch back to node 1. On the 255 pass through the loop, the contents of the accB = $FF = IIII IIII. Obviously, the 256 pass will set the contents of the accB = 0000 0000. This will set the Z bit and, incidentally, it will set the carry bit (C) of the HINZVC as well. With the Z bit set, the test is no longer true and the machine will not branch but will proceed on to the next step in the program. The loop is complete and the delay is over. The programming sheet is now ready for preparation.

THE PROGRAMMING SHEET

Figure 5-6 shows the programming sheet. For this example, assume that the program which precedes the timing loop runs up through address $0106. Therefore, the first step in the loop is $0107.

The M6800 Programming Reference Manual or other source of programming information lists instructions for clearing accumulator B as $5F. This instruction is written on line $0107 to start the loop. The address of the instruction is also written on the flow chart above the box for the instruction. Clear accB is a single byte instruction and has no data to follow it. Therefore, there is an entry in the COM(mand) column but no subsequent entry(s) in the data column. The OPERATION column shows the mnemonic in parentheses and description of the operation. For hand programming, the mnemonic is not particularly useful. It is included here only for identification. The programming manual lists the machine commands in the alphabetical order of the menmonics. The increment command and the loop command are both also single byte commands which require no data. They are listed and the address transferred to the flow chart.

The final command in the loop is the branch-if-not-equal $26. This is a two byte command which must have a data byte following so that the machine knows where to branch to. Note that the sheet extends beyond F. It is good practice to keep multiple byte commands together on the same sheet. For example, the command:

COM	DATA	OPERATION
7E		
	00	jump to $0000
	00	

The programming might be such that the $7E could fall on line XXIF. Therefore, the destination data would be on lines XX20 and XX21. It is better practice to write lines XX20 and XX21 on program sheet XX10 so that the bracket can be used to tie the command together. Be sure when doing this to cross out lines 0 and 1 on page XX20. If the extra lines are used on one programming they *must* be crossed out on the following sheet or an address error will be propagated through the subsequent programming.

When entering the data into a machine via a hex keyboard, it is only the data in the COM and DATA columns which is punched in. On most machines with a hex keyboard, there will also be a six digit LED display. The first four digits show the address into which the data is being inserted. The next two will show the data which you enter. The distinction between the COM and DATA is entirely for the benefit of the operator. The machine itself recognizes $7E as a 3-byte command and it will intepret the next two bytes it encounters in the program as the higher order and lower order bytes of the address it is to jump to. In the address of the timing loop in Table 5-2 the higher order byte of the address of node 1 is $ 01 and the lower order byte is $08. For data entry from the hex keyboard, the codes are simply punched in order, regardless of whether they are commands or data.

THE BACKWARD BRANCH

A technique for calculating the value of the backward branch is shown in the right-hand margin. The destination of the branch is $0108 and the source of the branch is $010C. If you start at the destination with a value of $ FF and count backward in hexadecimal until you are on the source, the count at the source will be equal to the DISPLACEMENT data required for the backward branch, as shown by the column. An alternative method is to cut the address

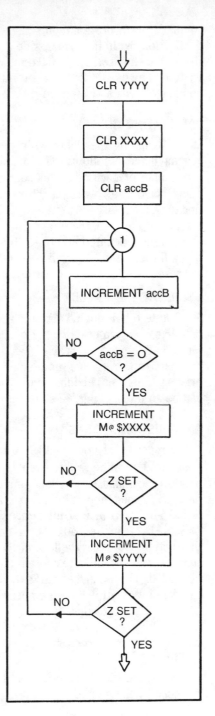

Fig. 5-6. The multiple timing loop.

column from a programming sheet and line up the F with the destination, with the strip upside down. The last hex character of the displacement will then fall opposite the source where it is to be written. The most significant bit must be calculated by noting the number of cycles of 16 from the destination to the source.

CALCULATING THE DELAY

Calculating the delay which is shown on the flow chart is accomplished as follows. The manual for the processor will give the number of machine cycles required to process the entire command including its own data. These command times can be added to find the execution time for the loop. In this case, assuming a 1MHz machine cycle time, the total comes to 10 microseconds. Since the loop will be executed 256 times before the machine falls out, the delay through the loop will be 0.002562 seconds including the 2 microseconds for the original clear of accB.

USING THE TIMING LOOP

Quite often in control applications, there is some repetitive task like the scan of a display or a keyboard which must be performed at regular intervals. The time for such a routine can be calculated and used as a time base for a software timing loop. The processor need not be idle during the timing loop. The timing loop can be an integral part of some other necessary program.

AN ADJUSTABLE TIMING LOOP

Suppose that you would like to have a timing loop that was some predetermined value such as 1 millisecond. It is possible to preload accumulator B with a numeric value such as $ 64 which is equal to 100 and then count down to zero. This program is shown in Table 5-3. The principal differences between this program and that of Table 5-2 is in the load accB instruction and the decrement accB instruction. Note that the load accB instruction is a 2-byte instruction with the second byte containing the data with which accB is to be loaded. This is termed a LOAD IMMEDIATE instruction since the data byte with which the accumulator is to be loaded follows immediately. Note that the use of a two byte instruction pushes node 1 by one step to $0109. Other than the two instruction changes and the address changes, the flow chart would be identical to Fig. 5-5.

It is notable that accB could also have been loaded from memory by the sequence:

Address	COM	DATA	OPERATION
0107	F6		
8		00	Load from memory address
9		25	$ 0025 into accB
A	5A		Decrement accB

Table 5-2. Timing Loop 0107-010C.

PAGE _____ _____

PROGRAM_____ DATE _____

_____

_____

ADDRESS	COM	DATA	OPERATION	ROUTINE
0100				
1				
2				
3				
4			EARLIER PROGRAM	
5				
6				
7	5F		(CLR) clear accB	
8	5C		(INC) increment accB	$ FF
9	01		(NOP) no op	FE
A	01		(NOP) no op	FD
B	26		(BNE) branch ifnot equal	FC
C		FB	to destination of branch (0108)	FB
D			SUBSEQUENT PROGRAM AFTER	
E			DELAY IS COMPLETE	
F				
0110				
1				
2				
3				
4				
5				

With the three byte instruction node 1 is pushed one more step to $010A.

One of the advantages of loading from memory is that the 6800 also has instructions for incrementing memory and decrementing memory. Therefore, the delay can be made to grow longer or shorter with each execution. If the time base is simply written into memory before each execution, it can be made to vary in any manner. If different delays are required in different parts of the program, the timing loop can be made as a subroutine and the appropriate constant inserted just before the command to JUMP TO SUBROUTINE or BRANCH TO SUBROUTINE is written. If this loop were written as a subroutine, the 3-byte load instruction would have pushed the destination instruction to $010E and instruction $010F would be $ 39, which means RETURN. The JUMP TO SUBROUTINE instruction is:

COM	DATA	OPERATION
BD		Jump to subroutine at
	01	$ 0107
	07	
NEXT		

Upon encountering this instruction in a program, the processor would carefully store the contents of its program counter register in what is called the STACK in memory. It would also move the stack pointer so that another branch to subroutine or interrupt could be accomodated. It would then set the program counter to $0107 and commence doing the delay loop. When the delay loop was finished and the processor dropped out to encounter the $39 instruction, it would reload the processor program counter register from the stack, then move the stack pointer back and commence with the program instruction labeled NEXT in the example above. A subroutine can be placed right up against other programming. However, the instruction immediately before it must be such that the machine does not "walk" into the subroutine since the $ 39 = RETURN instruction would have no defined meaning. A subroutine must always be entered only by a JUMP TO SUBROUTINE or a BRANCH TO SUBROUTINE command.

JUMP ERRORS

Referring to Table 5-3, suppose that you made an error in counting the jump destination inserted into $ 010D and had made the value $ F9. In this case, the machine would run once through

96

the loop and decrement the accB once. It would then note that the contents were not zero but $ 63. It would therefore jump back to $ 0107 due to the error in the displacement calculation. At $ 0107 it would reload with $64 and try again. Obviously, it would never succeed and the machine would be stuck in an endless loop.

Table 5-3. Timing Loop 0107-010D.

PAGE				
PROGRAM			DATE	
ADDRESS	COM	DATA	OPERATION	ROUTINE
0				
1				
2				
3				
4				
5				
6				
7	C6		Load Immediate accB	
8		64	with $ 64= 100	
9	5A		Decrement accB	
A	01		noop	
B	01		noop	
C	26		branch if not equal to	
D		FB	0109	
E				
F				
0				
1				
2				
3				
4				
5				

An even more drastic result would be obtained if the displacement were miscalculated as $ FA. In this case, after the first pass, the machine would jump to $ 0108 and it would misread the instruction as:

ADDRESS	COM	DATA	OPERATION
0108	64		Logic shift right the contents
		5A	of the memory at the IX addr + $ 54

It would still be in an endless loop since it would not be decrementing accB after the first pass and there would be a mistake in a location in memory.

A still worse result would obtain if the time constant at $ 0108 were a jump command such as $ 7E or a branch like $ 20. In this case, the machine would read the data as:

ADDRESS	COM	DATA	OPERATION
0108	7E		Jump to address $ 5A01
		5A	
		01	

Depending upon what is found at address $ 5A01, the machine could do just about anything—including scribbling over sections of the data in the read/write memory, etc. Whenever the machine jumps, it reads the first instruction at the jump address as a command and acts accordingly. Probably the largest source of problems in programs written by beginners is due to faulty offset calculations. These jump the machine to a false address, whereupon the whole thing runs wild.

CALCULATING FORWARD JUMPS

The forward jump is calculated in a somewhat different manner than the backward jump. Consider the program fragment in Table 5-4. When the machine walks up to $ 0107 it reads the command to compare the contents of accB with $ 86. If accB = $ 86 it jumps 3 steps to $ 010E and if not it reads $010B and jumps to $ 0185. The forward jump is calculated by counting the steps *between* the source and the destination as shown in the right-hand margin of the sheet.

MACHINE CALCULATION OF OFFSETS.

The Motorola MEK DII kit has a procedure for calculating offsets. However, I find it to be awkward and cumbersome. The

Table 5-4. Forward Branch Calculation.

| | | | PAGE _____ _____ |
| PROGRAM _____ DATE _____ |

_____

_____

ADDRESS	COM	DATA	OPERATION	ROUTINE
0100				
1				
2				
3				
4				
5				
6				
7	C1		Compare Immediate the	
8		86	contents of accB with $86	
9	27		Branch if equal to	
A		03	offset destination $ 010E	
B	7E		jump to $ 0185	$ 01
C		01		02
D		85		03
E			remainder of program	
F				
0110				
1				
2				
3				
4				
5				

program in Table 5-5 serves well and it is easily written into the
machine. The source address least significant byte is written into
$ 0000 and the destination address is wrtten into $ 0001. After
running, the answer will befound in $ 0002.

To use this program, it must first be entered into the machine.
To do this on the MEK DII follow the steps below:

- ■ Key E to clear the machine and obtain the prompt (−) sign.
- ■ Key in 0000 then key M. This tells the machine that you want to write in memory starting at $ 0000.
- ■ Key in the source address and hit G. The memory address will now read $0001.
- ■ Key in the destination address and hit G.
- ■ Key in 00 and hit G. The memory address will now read $0003.
- ■ Key in program bytes from $ 0003 through $ 000D.

B6	
00	
01	
B0	
00	
00	Hit G between each byte and
4A	note memory address advance.
B7	
00	
02	
3F	

To run the program:

- ■ Key E and get prompt.
- ■ Key in 0003 and hit G. The display will blink and then read $ 000D 3F.
- ■ Key in E and get prompt.
- ■ Key in $ 0002 and hit M. The display will read $ 0002 ZZ where ZZ is the proper displacement.

To calculate a different offset, simply enter the new source in $0000 and the new destination in $ 0001. Hit E and repeat steps seven through 10. It is possible to write a longer program which will show the source byte, the destination byte and the offset byte in the display. However, this takes a bit more programming. The above program is easily loaded and not too awkward to use. It is handy for calculating larger offsets.

MULTIPLE LOOPS

There is no reason that timing loops cannot be nested within one another to obtain longer timing delays. For example, Fig. 5-6 shows three nested loops. The inside one, which runs in register

100

Table 5-5. Machine Offset Calculations.

				PAGE_____ _____

PROGRAM_____ DATE_____

_____

_____

ADDRESS	COM	DATA	OPERATION	ROUTINE
000 0	XX		enter source address here	
1	YY		enter destination addr. here	
2	ZZ		find calculated offset here	
3	B6		Load accA with the contents	
4		00	of memory address $ 0000	
5		01		
6	B0		Subtract from accA the	
7		00	contents of memory	
8		00	address oooo	
9	4A		decrement accA	
A	B7		Store accA in memory	
B		00	address $ 0002	
C		02		
D	3F		Software Interrupt	
E				
F				
0				
1				
2				
3				
4				
5				

accB, takes about 6 microseconds for one turn and 1.536 milliseconds for the 256 turns required to drop out. When this happens it increments the loop running in memory location XXXX once, branches back to node 1 and starts the inner loop again. After 256 of these cycles, 0.39326 seconds have elapsed. A decrement or increment of a memory location will also set the Z bit for the test. The third loop runs at 1/256 of the speed of the second loop so it will time out in 100.663 seconds. A fourth loop would time out in 7.15828 hours and a fifth loop would require 76.355 days and a sixth loop would require 53.516 years.

This shows one of the great advantages of the microprocessor in control applications: the extreme flexability of the unit. With only a slight change in software, you can change the operation of the machine from time bases measured in a few microseconds to years. Within the same program, the machine could test for a switch closure every 50 microseconds, turn a lamp on at sunset and off at sunrise, disable the lamp on Saturdays and Sundays, keep the lamp disabled from July 6 through July 22 for a planned vacation shutdown and restart the electric hot water heater on the night of July 22 so that there will be hot water when the plant reopens on July 23.

The interior of the timing loop does not have to be made of no-ops, it can contain any form of programming of constant length. If the programmer is clever, allowance can be made for programs of non-constant length by keeping track of the disparity and resetting the clock. For example, if the sensing of the switch closure caused a branch to a subroutine which was longer than the basic loop, the subroutine might subtract an appropriate number of counts from the register being used to keep tally of the time. In general, the only limitations on the control tasks which can be performed by the processor are the imagination of the programmer, the speed of the processor and the size of the memory available.

SUMMARY

In this chapter, I have shown a technique by which a program can be designed using a flow chart and can be accurately documented using programming sheets. The annotation of the program step address onto the flow chart turns the flow chart into a master wiring diagram by which any state and any individual program step can be quickly located. This documentation is very important and should not be neglected in any step. Otherwise, the program will be completely incomprehensible to even its originator a week later.

Boolean Functions And Input/Output Functions

6

The operation of a microcomputer can generally be divided into the following categories:
- —Input sensing.
- —Data manipulation.
- —State changing.
- —Output generation.

Particularly in control applications, the data manipulation is very likely to consist principally of the various Boolean functions. The use and implementation of the Boolean functions are examined in this chapter.

INPUT SENSING

Before discussing data manipulation, it is appropriate to devote a brief treatment to the acquisition of data from the outside world. There are some microprocessors which actually have input and output lines on the processor chip itself. The RCA 1802 has one. Among the general purpose processors, the number of input/output lines is very limited for reasons of PIN COUNT. Most of the 8-bit machines have an 8-bit DATA BUS, 16-bit ADDRESS BUS and a variety of clock, timing and control lines. Since the bonding of the chip lands to the pin frame is largely a manually controlled operation, every additional pin tends to significantly increase the cost of the finished chip. Competetive pricing generally limits the number of pins to 40 on 8-bit machines so there are few pins left for input/output operations.

Some machines, such as the 1802 alleviate this problem by alternately using the lower 8 bits of the address bus in a memory address/data multiplexed operation. This does free 8 pins but it does so at an increased cost of memory since all devices on the memory bus are required to latch the address and then hold it while data is being sent. It also about halves the operating speed of the machine since address and data cannot be asserted simultaneously.

A fundamentally faster and cleaner way to do this is to address all input/output devices in the same way that memory is addressed and to use an input/output chip which accepts and outputs or inputs data to the data bus just as if it were an ordinary read/write memory. This is the approach used on the Motorola 6800 family. The single-chip microcomputers in this family do have input and output on the chip, but from the standpoint of the programmer, they operate in exactly the same way that the external device does.

THE 6821 PERIPHERAL INTERFACE ADAPTER

The chip designed for parallel input/output operations in the Motorola 6800 family is the 6821 Peripheral Input Output chip (PIA). This chip is designed to hang across a few of the address lines and across the entire data bus. Some of its ADDRESS DECODING is done by external hardwired logic. This affords some flexability in assigning the address of the chip. It has two, 8-bit wide input/output registers which connect the microcomputer to the outside world. These registers are latching devices on output and will hold the last data sent them on a TTL compatible (but limited drive capability) line until they are reset. Any single bit on either of these registers can be made an input or an output under program software control. This lends great flexability to the system since any single bit or any combination of these bits can be used as an input and a few commands later the same line or lines can be used as outputs.

With external hardware, the PIA can be given nearly any memory address. However, in the interest of being specific and clear the next few examples use addresses for the two PIA chips found in the MEK DII kit. In the kit, the PIA wired to the input/output edgeboard connector has the following addresses:

$ 8004	Input/output register A
$ 8005	Control Register A
$ 8006	Input/output register B
$ 8007	Control register B

The other PIA uses addresses $ 8020 through $ 8025 in the same sequence. This is the PIA which drives the display and senses the hex keyboard operation. With two exceptions, it is not available for other outside use with out some wiring changes.

Once the PIA has been initialized, it can be treated as any other memory location. For example, the following instructions will read the data on the A and B registers.

COM	DATA	OPERATION
F6		Load accB from memory
	80	address $ 8004.
	04	
B6		Load accA from memory address
	80	$ 8006.
	06	

This would read the data from I/O register A into accB and the data from I/O register B into accA. The following instructions would output data.

B7		Write accA into output register
	80	(memory location) $ 8004.
	04	
F7		Write accB into output register
	80	(memory location) $ 8006
	06	

These same instructions could be used to write the contents of accA or accB into any other memory location. An important fact is that a read instruction of these registers when they are in the write condition will get back the data last written into that register without disturbing the contents of the register. The registers actually behave like a true memory address. This is quite an asset in certain control applications. Because of the multiple paths due to different states, the machine might not know how the outputs were last latched. The fact that the PIA is readable makes it unnecessary to take steps to store the information elsewhere.

INITIALIZING THE PIA

With all of the flexability of the PIA, it is relatively obvious that you must somehow tell it how to behave with respect to commands. For example, consider that you would like to set bits 2,3,4 and 5 to *write* or output data and have the remaining bits set to read. You would like to use output register B. You have also elected to use accA as the data source. Table 6-1 illustrates the procedure.

Referring to the illustration, you can see that you first clear accA or set all bits to zero and write it to the control register for the B bank of 8 bits of the PIA. The fact that bit 2 is zero tells the PIA that you want to access the DATA DIRECTION REGISTER. Any other command in which bit 2 was low would have acocmplished this end. For example, $ FB could have been used. The other bits in

Table 6-1. PIA Conditioning.

PAGE_____ _____

PROGRAM_____ DATE_____

_____

_____

ADDRESS	COM	DATA	OPERATION	ROUTINE
FCO 0	4F		Clear accA	
1	B7		Write to $ 8007	
2		80	this selects the data direction	
3		07	register of the PIA	
4	86		load accA imm. with $3C	
5		3C		
6	B7		Write accA to $ 8006	
7		80	This sets bits 2, 3, 4 & 5	
8		06	to write or output and rest to read	
9	86		Load imm. accA with $ FF	
A		FF		
B	B7		Write to $ 8007	
C		80	this de-selects the data	
D		07	direction register	
E	4F			
F	B7			
FCI 0		80		
1		06		
2				
3				
4				
5				

the control register have other uses and are essentially ignored here.

The next group of steps is $ FC04 through $ FC08. Use an immediate load accA with the data $ 3C and write this into the data direction register. Every bit which is high will be programmed to be an output and every bit which is low will be programmed to be an input. The data direction register uses the same address as the output register. If you had wanted to set all bits to read you would have written $ 00 and for all bits set to write you would have written $ FF.

To complete the operation, de-select the data direction register so that you can use bank B of the PIA to input and output data. This is done by loading accA with a character in which bit 2 is set. In this case $ FF is used but it could have been $ 04. This is written into the control register and the B bank is now ready for use. If you write $ 00 into the output register bits 2,3,4 & 5 will be set low. Conversely, if you write $ 3C into $ 8006, the same bits will be set high. After the initialization, it is adviseable to set all of the write bits into the condition you want to have them in.

The initialization of the A bank could have proceeded on the same program and the writing could have been done just as easily from accB. Either accumulator can read from or write to any location in memory.

There are a number of other things which can be done with the control register. These will be treated later since they are a little ahead of the sequence here. For the time being simply read and write the A and B output/input banks.

THE BOOLEAN AND FUNCTION

For an example of the Boolean AND function, consider the arrangement in Fig. 6-1 showing the PIA hooked to some external devices. The unit has been preconditioned or initialized as in the preceding program. There are four normally open switches on PBO, 1, 6 & 7 and there are lamps on the outputs. Do not take the lamps too literally. The PIA would require a booster amplifier or electronic switch to drive them. They are merely shown here to symbolize some physical output to the outside world.

Suppose that you wanted to test the four switches to see whether they were all open and if so to light lamp PB2. The Boolean expression for this is: Lamp PB2 = (PB1, 2, 6,7). You can see that this is an AND expression. The flow chart and abbreviated program sheet to the right show the procedure. AccB first reads the PIA data. It must be remembered that PB2, 3, 4 & 5 are in the write mode. Therefore, a read operation will simply tell you what you last wrote into them. If you are going to do a comparison on the contents of accB, you must do something to MASK out these bits so that they do not effect the results of the comparison. This can be done by ORing the contents of accB with $3C as shown below.

all sw. open   IIXX XXII   contents of accB
                         00II II00   OR mask ($3C)
                         IIII IIII   = $ FF result

The OR is applied on a bit-by-bit basis. Any bit in the OR mask which is I will always turn out to be I in the accumulator after the OR operation. You can see that if, and only if, all four switches are open will the results of the OR be $ FF. If PB7 had been closed the result would have been 0III IIII = $ 7F. The AND has been implemented. The series of instructions following the comparison and decision simply light the lamp.

THE BOOLEAN OR FUNCTION

Suppose that instead of the above situation, you would like to have lamp PB2 light if any of the switches were open. This would correspond to the Boolean OR of the switches and would be described by the expression: lamp PB2 = (PB1 + 2 + 6 + 7). This function could be simply accomplished by changing the comparison data to be equal to the mask ($ 3C) and changing the branch comparison to branch if equal ($ 27 , 05). Opening of any switch would cause the contents of the accB to differ from $ 3C after the OR mask. The machine would therefore not branch and lamp PB2 would be lighted.

THE EXCLUSIVE OR FUNCTION

Suppose that you wanted lamp PB2 to light if PB1 were open and PB2 closed or if PB2 were open and PB1 were closed. This is the Boolean EXCLUSIVE-OR function and would be written: lamp PB2 = PB1⊗PB2. To accomplish this, change the mask to $ FC. This would mask all bits except PB1 & 2 to I. The two desired conditions after the OR mask would then be: IIII III0 = $ FE and IIII II0I = $ FD.

Two comparison tests would be required one to $ FE and the second to $ FD. What happens next is a little tricky so refer to the flow chart in Fig. 6-2. If either of the tests is satisfied, the program jumps to node 1 and lights the lamp. On the other hand, if neither test is satisfied the program runs into a branch always ($ 20) instruction with a displacement to jump over the lamp lighting routine. The exclusive or is accomplished.

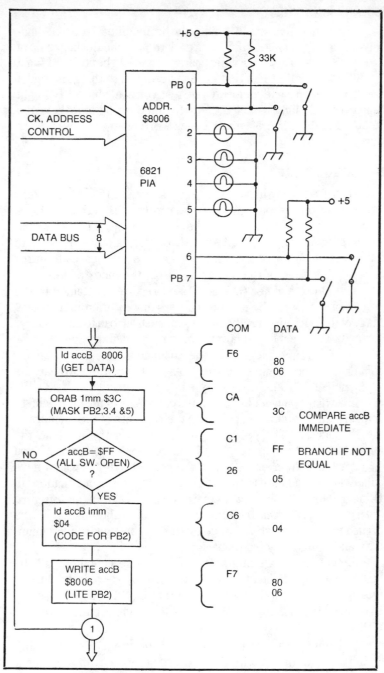

Fig. 6-1. The Boolean AND function.

109

ONE AND ONLY ONE

The above test could obviously be modified to a one-and-only-one with a change in the mask back to $ 3C and the inclusion of two more tests. The other valid characters would be: 0III IIII = 7F and I0II IIII = $ BF. The tests need not branch to the same node. For example, on a one-and-only-one test you could have PBQ light lamp PB2, PB1 light lamp PB3, etc. In this way you could have the output identify which of the switches were open and which were closed.

THE LOOKUP TABLE

With the four switches, there are obviously 16 separate combinations of on and off which can be represented. This could be solved and each condition could be uniquely traced by expanding the program in Fig. 6-2 to 16 tests. However, another approach is the use of the *lookup table*. The lookup table also serves to introduce another facet of the 6800 processor: the index address.

The index register (IX) is a 16-bit register contained in the processor which can be used to address any location in memory. Many of the operations of the processor such as load from memory, compare with memory contents, increment memory, etc. can be addressed through the IX. These commands are always 2-byte commands. For example, in the lookup table routine we use the command $ E1, $ 00. The first byte is the command which tells the machine what you want done. In this case, $E1 is the command to compare the contents of accB with the contents of the memory at the IX address. The second byte ($ 00) tells the machine the numerical offset to apply to the IX address: in this case zero. If you had written a different offset in the second byte, it would have added the second byte to the value in the IX for the destination. In IX addressing, the second byte is considered to be an *unsigned* binary number. It can only go forward unlike the offsets for the branch instructions which are considered to be signed binary numbers and can go forward or backward.

Before the program starts, write a table containing all the values of interest. The table can be written anywhere in memory. If it is to be permanent, it can be written in ROM. Here I will assume that the table is a permanent feature of the machine and it is written in ROM at $ FC30 through $ FC3F.

The flow chart in Fig. 6-3 shows the program. The first thing to do is to load the IX with the address of the start of the lookup table. AccB then gets the data and masks it as before. AccB then is

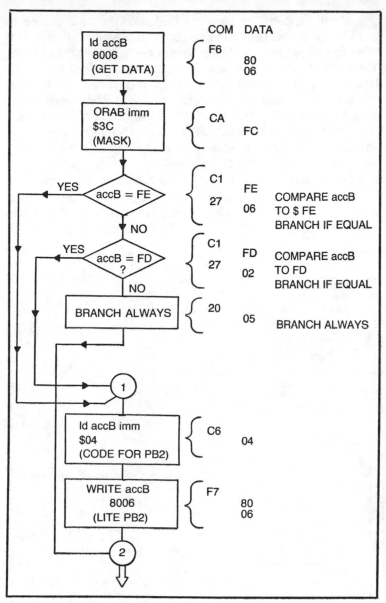

Fig. 6-2. The EXCLUSIVE-OR function.

compared with the contents of the memory at the IX address. If it does not match, the IX is then incremented. The test determines whether the test is finished. If it is not, the program jumps to node 1 and makes the comparison with the next table entry. This continues until the data is matched or all values of the table have been tried. Since in this case there are only 16 possible answers and there are 16 entrys in the table, the answer will always be found. The last instruction could have been a branch always ($ 20 , $F6). However, in many cases there are unused codes and the table is shorter than the memory. The end of table test is therefore included for generality. The entrys can be in any order on the table.

Lookup tables have advantages and disadvantages. One of the advantages is in *translation*. Suppose that you wanted the N possible input codes to respond with N possible outputs with both the input codes and the output codes being arbitrary. You could then create two tables with a one-for-one correspondence between the input codes and output codes. When you find the entry which corresponded to the contents of accB you could simply load accB

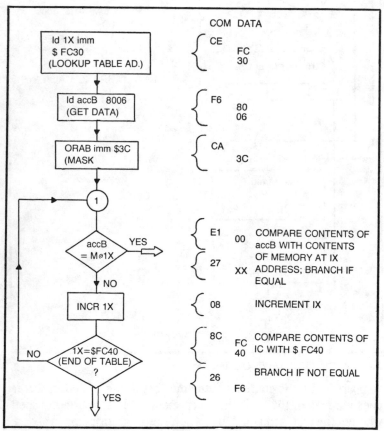

Fig. 6-3. A flow chart of a lookup table program.

with the contents of the memory at IX plus the offset between the tables and write accB to output. This form of translation is frequently used for encoding seven-segment displays and other devices which require an arbitrary relationship between input and output. The principle disadvantage of the lookup table routine comes in the matter of running time. If you look up the running time, it turns out that the IX operations require more running time than most of the same operations done with direct or extended addressing. For the routine of making a direct comparison as in Fig. 6-3, find that the running time for each comparison is 6 microseconds. For an N entry lookup, you would therefore, at most require 6N+6 microseconds.

For the lookup table routine, the time around the loop is 20 microseconds and the preamble 9 microseconds. Therefore, an N entry lookup would require 20N+9 microseconds to accomplish in the worst case.

Both methods could be made to perform the same functions—including the arbitrary input/output scrambling. No relative advantage for one over the other could be obtained in running time by placing the most probable inputs low on the table. The straight line N-fold comparison would require $4N + 7$ lines of memory. The lookup table requires only $18 + N$ lines for the single table in each case. In the translation case, the relationships would be raised by N. Obviously, if N is large, the tradeoff becomes one of running time against program memory space. The choice can be made upon the basis of which parameter is to be optimized.

OTHER BIT MANIPULATIONS

For the next example consider that the machine is being used as a controller and that the four lamps are being used as prompt lamps with legends such as:

lamp PB2 = Insert Coins

      3 = select sandwich content (meat, cheese, etc.)

      4 = select mustard, catsup, etc.

      5 = select roll or bread

We would like to have only one lamp lit at a time indicating to the customer what was expected of him next. We would also probably like to have a "clear" button which would permit him to erase the last choice and back up one step. This could be accomplished by reading the register into either accumulator and going through a fourfold comparison and encoding the output to the appropriate previous state.

This would be the most flexible way of doing the job since there are no constraints upon the way in which the thing is handled. Note, however, that if there were no button marked "deliver" on the machine, a bad choice on the bread could not be corrected since the machine would have to deliver the sandwich as soon as the bread had been selected. You would probably like to have the ability to rescind choices restricted as well. For example, the choice of mustard, catsup or horseradish could be made and the seasoning not applied until the bread was selected. However, once the filler had been applied with seasoning, you would prefer the choice to be irrevocable. Otherwise, the vending machine operator could wind up with a lot of peanut butter, jelly and horseradish sandwiches due to either chance or malice.

SETTING A SINGLE BIT

Under some circumstances, it is necessary to take the contents of an output register and toggle a single bit to make it a zero if it is a one or vice versa. For example, suppose that you desired to toggle bit PB3. This could be done by reading the register into accB (or accA) and EXCLUSIVE-ORing it with a word in which only the desired bit was I. For example:

	xxII 0Ixx	contents of register & accB
	0000 I000	EXOR mask
	xxII II00	result - write to output
or		
	xxII IIxx	contents of register & accB
	0000 I000	EXOR mask
	xxII 0Ixx	result - write to output.

You can see that this simple program would toggle a single bit in the output. Of course, more that one bit could be handled in this manner on a single pass by simply adjusting the mask. The EXCLUSIVE-OR immediate is a two-bye command $ C8 for the accB.

Using the above routine, it is possible—with the use of a timing loop—to create a square wave signal generator at one or several of the output ports. If the timing loop draws the time constant from memory, the memory location can be incremented on each pass through the loop or perhaps on every tenth pass to cause the generator to sweep in frequency. This is a very useful feature in certain types of electronic test instruments. A signal generator with a frequency that can be programmed to walk through a range of frequencies and then back up, stop, read out the

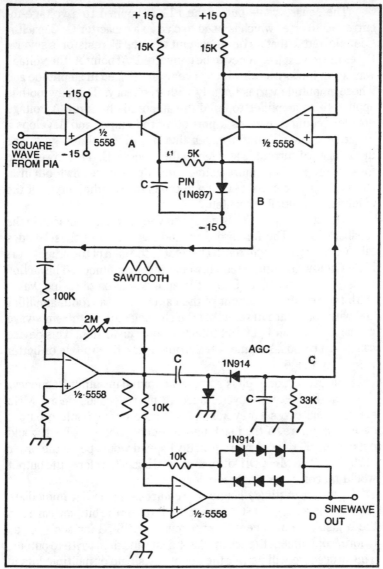

Fig. 6-4. An analog squarewave to sinewave converter.

frequency on its own display, etc. can greatly simplify the testing of frequency sensitive devices.

One of the principle problems with the use of square waves in testing is the very high harmonic content. Some form of square wave to sine wave converter is usually desireable. The circuit shown in Fig. 6-4 will do a reasonable job of this conversion.

The square wave out of the PIA is applied to a voltage-to-current converter which is used to charge a capacitor C. Capacitor C is selected so that its time constant with the 5k resistor is several times the lowest frequency to be converted. At point A, the voltage waveform is a sawtooth which is very diminished in amplitude and whose amplitude varies linearly with frequency. This sawtooth is applied to an amplifier to build the amplitude back up. A voltage doubler rectifier rectifies a portion of the output and develops a negative voltage. The stronger this negative voltage gets, the more forward current is applied to the diode at B. This lowers the forward drop and therefore voltage amplitude of the sawtooth in an automatic gain control (AGC) and tends to hold the output of the amplifier essentiallly constant.

The output amplifier is equipped with a series of diodes in the feedback loop. The forward drop and resistance of these diodes falls with increasing current. Therefore, the gain of the amplifier is higher at low amplitudes and lower at high amplitudes. This action massages the sawtooth into a fair approximation of a sine wave. With the proper adjustment of the gain on the sawtooth amplifier and with some care in selecting the shaping diodes, the sine wave can have less than 1 percent total harmonic distortion. This device can hold a reasonable sine wave shape over a five-to-one or better frequency range.

The processor itself is somewhat limited in output frequency. The read-EXOR-write cycle takes 10 microseconds on a 1 MHz machine and two such cycles are required on a complete output cycle. Therefore, if the machine were doing nothing else it could not exceed 50 KHz. A more practical speed would be on the order of 30 KHz. The MEK DII kit runs at 680 Khz. Therefore, the output would be correspondingly slower.

A way of setting a single bit requires only an OR immediate with the bit set at one ($CA for accB). To clear the bit, you can read the register, compliment the accumulator ($ 53 for accB) or as before, compliment the accumulator again and then write to output. This procedure will permit the set of any single or multiple bits in the output while leaving the remainder of the register unchanged.

AUDIO OUTPUT

The toggling of a single bit on the PIA output is sometimes used as a technique for the generation of electronic tones for warnings, alarms, games and even electronic musical instruments. The available range of frequencies is more than adequate to cover the entire audio range. The generation of high quality musical tones requires the use of a filter set and some amplitude control mechanism. For warnings and annunciators, however, it is adequate to simply attach an audio amplifier to the PIA output port selected for the purpose.

On the MEK DII kit, the PIA at location $ 8020 through $ 8023 was used for the servicing of the keyboard and the display and was therefore not available. This is not entirely true. In the control register, lines CA2 and CB2 can also be used as outputs. This can be accomplished by the routines below.

To set CA2 high:

COM	DATA	OPERATION
86		Load imm. accA with $ 3C
	3C	
B7		Write to control register A
	80	
	21	

To set CA2 low:

COM	DATA	OPERATION
86		Load imm. accA
	34	
B7		write to control register A
	80	
	21	

On the MEK DII kit control register A is unused and can be employed for an audio output or other output purposes.

Most high quality musical instruments incorporating a microprocessor do not generate the tones in software but instead use a top octave generator chip. These chips take care of generating the top octave on the piano keyboard and provide certain other features. Some of these chips are intended for game use. Some even feature sound effects such as sirens, whistles, zooming airplanes or explosions. These features are available upon transmission of coded data to the chip.

CODE TRANSMISSION OF SERIAL DATA

Various PIA output ports can be toggled fast enough to send serial output code and to receive serial input code in the form of Morse, ASCII, etc. At the slower code speeds, the processor is quite capable of keeping up with the code and the entire code transmission can be accomodated in the software. Alternatively, there are a number of serial to parallel code converters which can take a large burden of software off the shoulders of the processor. Devices such as the Motorola 6850 ACIA (Assynchronous Communications Interface Adapter) will accept data in parallel format as a single byte. They will then add such things as parity, start and stop bits under program control and output the byte in serial format with the coding protocols included. On reception, they will perform the reverse function: accepting serial data, checking for parity and alerting the processor that data is ready. One of the chief advantages of these units is their ability to speed up the process. Using the ACIA, data transmission rates up to about 500 KHz can be accomodated.

SUMMARY

In the chapters up to this point I have attempted to introduce the concepts of programming, addressing, machine operations, Boolean functions and input/output operations without attempting to introduce a wholesale description of the machine internal construction. With this background, some of the basic details of the processor internal functioning should be a little easier to understand. Since the intention of this book is not to teach people to design microprocessor chips, but rather how to use them, the approach in the next series of chapters will deal mainly with the functional aspects of the devices.

Microprocessor Architecture

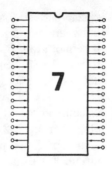

7

The general structure of the FUNCTIONAL BLOCK DIAGRAM of a microprocessor is generally referred to as the *architecture* of the processor. The term is applied to the functional actions of the device rather than to the individual gates and transistors. The user will seldom if ever get a look at the actual gates and transistors since they are hermetically sealed from the outside world in the package and can be accessed only by destroying the device. They are visible only under a powerful microscope and only with the aid of a set of drawings and diagrams could the user identify and locate them.

The architecture of the processor actually describes the way the machine performs and responds to commands by the user. It is this concept that will be examined in this chapter.

ADDRESSING

In the preceding chapters, some of the addressing techniques used in the 6800 processor are given. Here I will go into a bit more detail on the subject of addresses and addressing. To begin with, consider an analogy for the address situation. The 6800 and most 8-bit processors have an address bus which is 16 bits wide. There are 16 pins on the chip which are dedicated to propagating the address throughout the system. Counting all of the possible states on the ADDRESS BUS, the processor can assert and address for $0000 = 0 to $ FFFF = 65,535. If you consider the continuum of these addresses as a circular street or drive lined with special mailboxes where each mailbox has eight slots, you will have a picture of the special closed world in which the processor lives. The processor itself can be considered to be a bicycle with only one fixed speed forward which always covers the distance betweeen two adjacent mailboxes in exactly one clock period. However there are certain things which can cause the bike to take a zigzag path so that it will take an extra clock period or two to go between two adjacent mailboxes. The bike cannot go backward and it cannot stop. It normally proceeds along the street from $ 0000 toward $ FFFF. Since the street is in the form of a closed circle, the address after $ FFFF is $ 0000 and the bicycle starts another trip around. The bicycle has one very special property. Under special circumstances, it can disappear into a space warp and reappear elsewhere in 1, 2 or 3 clock cycles—anywhere on the circle. It can also sometimes manage to do something to any mailbox on the circle. For example, it can place something in or take something out or just read the contents of the box without disturbing anything in one or two or three clock cycles.

There are some neighborhoods along the street which have some special properties. For example, whenever anyone or anything presses the RESET button, the bike obtains the contents of $ FFFE and $ FFFF and stuffs these into the high and low order bytes of the 16-bit *program counter*. This causes the bike to reappear from the space warp at the mailbox specified by the program counter. This is the normal way in which the machine starts up. On controllers, the reset often consists of an RC circuit designed so that the reset line is held low until all units have power. As long as reset is held low, the address lines are held at $ FFFE.

The address to be found in $ FFFE and $ FFFF is frequently $ FC00 (which is just 1024 addresses below $ FFFF) or $ F800 (which is 2048 addresses before $ FFFF). The reason for this is that ROM's commonly come in these lengths and the jump takes the 6800 to the first address on the particular ROM. In general, addresses $ FFFX must be relatively permanent and non-volatile since the machine goes to these first—before you have anything written in the memory. When first powered, the read/write memory is full of garbage and the machine has no instructions to tell it to sense a keyboard, etc. For this reason, it must have some ROM which does not change its contents when the power is turned off. Since $ FFFF must be included in the ROM, it is customary to start a 1024 byte ROM at $ FC00 and a 2048 byte ROM at $ F800. The ROM could be placed elsewhere, but it would considerably complicate the chip-select lines which tell the ROM that the bike wants data from one of its mailboxes.

Consider for a moment the addresses themselves:

$ FFFF = IIII IIII IIII IIII A_{15} A_{10} A_0
$ FC00 = IIII II00 0000 0000

You can see that over the entire range the highest order

address lines, A15, through A10 are all I. A simple 6-wide NAND hung across these lines would produce the $\overline{CE}$ (Chip Enable not) required so that the ROM will know that it is being addressed and will enable it to respond. Bits A15 through A11 suffice for the range $ F800 through $ FFFF. On the 1024, byte ROM address lines A9 through A0 are connected to the address lines on the ROM itself to tell the ROM which particular address in the ROM is being addressed.

Presume that the bike has made the jump to $FC00. It interprets the contents of the mailbox there as a command. The bike has an internal mechanism which interprets the contents of the box into microinstructions which tell the individual gates what to do. It also tells the bike whether the instruction, is one, two or three bytes long. Some instructions such as noop ($ 0I), clear accA)$ 4F) and complement accB ($ 53) are only one byte long since the machine has no requirement for further information. The place where the thing is to be done is implicit in the instruction. For these instructions, the machine will interpret the next thing it encounters as another instruction.

After reading the first byte and interpreting it, the machine increments the program counter and goes to $ FC01 (in the example). If the instruction at $ FC00 was interpreted as a 2-byte instruction or a 3-byte instruction it considers that the contents of $ FC01 is data to be handled as commanded by the preceding instruction. For example, if the contents of $FC00 had been $ 86, the machine interprets this as a load immediate instruction for accA. This means that the byte at $FC01 is the data with which accA is to be loaded. If the contents of $ FC01 were also $ 86, the machine would load accA with $ 86.

If the contents of $ FC00 had been $ B6, the machine would have recognized this as a command to load accA from the memory address described in the bytes in $ FC01 and $ FC02: the two following bytes. If these two bytes had contained $ B6 and $ B6, the machine would have gone to address $ B6B6 and loaded accA with *contents* of that mailbox.

The point is that except for sequence, the machine cannot distinguish between command bytes, data bytes or address bytes. The machine always functions in one of three cycles; Command, Command or Command, Data or Command, Data, Data. Depending upon the starting command, the machine decodes whether the following bytes are another command, one data byte or two data bytes.

ADDRESSING MEMORY

The addressing schemes in different processors are different. However, many have features similar to the 6800 family. For the two accumulators, the modes of addressing available are INHERENT, IMMEDIATE, DIRECT, EXTENDED and INDEXED.

Inherent Addressing

In inherent addressing, which is always a single byte command, the address is actually inherent in the command itself. For example, the command $ 1B tells the machine to add the contents of accB to the contents of accA and deposit the result in accA. The single instruction is complete by itself. Other instructions such as $ 5F, clear accB, require no further information. The machine is told what to do and where to place the result.

Immediate Addressing

In immediate addressing of the accumulators, the byte immediately following the command is the data which the command byte operates upon. In some of the examples used previously, the command $ CA, which means OR the contents of accB ($ 8A for accA) with the data byte in the next memory address, is used. For the accumulators, the immediate address is always a 2-byte command. The accumulators are only eight bits wide and can therefore accept only a single byte. The immediate address commands for the 16-bit registers will be discussed shortly.

Direct Addressing

The direct address is another 2-byte instruction. The second byte tells the bike how many houses up the street to go to deposit data or extrate data. For example, the command $ 97, $ 03 tells the machine that the contents of the accumulator accA are to be deposited in the mailbox of the third house. The direct address is *not* interpreted as a signed binary number. It only goes forward. In essence, the direct address is the same as an extended address with the most significant byte assumed to be $ 00. Obviously, since the direct address is a single byte, it can cover only the first 255 steps from the start of memory.

Extended Addressing

The extended address is intended to cover the complete range of address from $ 0000 to $ FFFF. An extended address can cover any location in memory. Obviously, in order to do this it requires two bytes of address data. Extended addressing is also sometimes referred to as *absolute addressing* since it specifies the complete address. In our analogy, the extended address would correspond to:

2 Round Trail Drive
Pittsford, NY 14534

Compared to this direct addressing would be:

The second house on the street.

This is similar to the *relative* addresses discussed earlier except that a relative address can be either five doors up or five doors back from the present location.

Indexed Addressing

One of the registers aboard our bike is the index register (IX). This register, like the program counter, is a 16-bit register. It is wide enough to accommodate any address in the machine memory. Unlike the program counter which increments with each instruction, the IX will increment or decrement only when told to. Its contents will be what was last written into it. As shown earlier, the index register is very handy when you want to read from contiguous blocks of memory or write into contiguous blocks of memory as shown in the lookup table example. All index addressed commands are 2-byte commands, with the second byte representing an offset. For example, the command $ E7, $ 02 would write the contents of accB into the address two bytes from the IX contents. Suppose the IX = $ 0010. The contents of accB would be written into $ 0012. As with direct addressing, the offset can be up to 255 steps forward.

The index register can be loaded via immediate, direct extended or indexed commands from two contiguous memory locations. The lower address gets the most significant or high order byte and the higher address gets the low order byte. For example, the command $ CE, $ 00, $12 will load the IX with the contents of memorq locations $ 0012 which will contain the high order byte and $ 0013 which will contain the high order byte and $ 0013 which will contain the low order byte. If $ 0012 = $ FC and $ 0013 = $ 00; after the operation, IX = $ FC00.

The contents of the IX can also be stored via direct, extended or indexed addressing. For example the command $ EF, $ 02 following the previous example would be:

$ FC02 = FC   High order byte
$ FC03 = $ 00   Low order byte

The ability to load the IX from memory and store the IX in memory can be very handy for transferring from one table to another. In addition, there are certain tricks which can be done using the IX.

A register can be used for counting events by the expedient of incrementing the count whenever the event occurs. However, the accumulators and the memory are only eight bits wide. Therefore, the count can go only to 255 before the memory overflows. There are a number of ways around this, however, and one of the simplest is to keep the count by incrementing the IX. In this way, counts up to 65,535 can be kept and tested using the compare IX immediate ($ 8C, $ XX, $ XX), a 3-byte instruction. If the IX is required in other parts of the program, it can be stored and loaded with 2- or 3-byte instructions.

THE STACK POINTER

One of the very convenient features of the 6800 family stems from the use of the stack pointer (SP). Whenever the processor is required to BRANCH TO SUBROUTINE ($ 8D, $ XX), JUMP TO SUBROUTINE ($ BD, $ XX, $ XX for extended address or $ AD, $ XX for indexed address), answer an INTERRUPT from external hardware or a SOFTWARE INTERRUPT from program ($ 3F) or a WAIT FOR INTERRUPT ($ 3E) it is necessary for the various processor register contents to be somehow saved so that at some later time the processor can return to its location at the time of the command resume the operation.

In some processors, this is implemented with internal storage registers and in others it is done by transferring control to an entirely different set of registers. For example, an entirely different register is used for the program counter, etc. This can have certain advantages in terms of speed of operation. In the 6800 family, this operation is implemented in the *stack*.

The stack is just about what the name implies. A physical analogy would equate the stack to the gadget you see in a cafeteria which doles out the plates. As a plate is placed on the pile the pile sinks so that one plate is always level with the surface of the counter. If you consider the plates each to have one byte of memory written on it, then it will take seven plates to save the contents of the processor. The 16-bit registers require two bytes each and the 8-bit registers require a single byte each. The information goes on in the order:

ADDRESS IN MEMORY   **CONTENTS**

STACK POINTER $ XXXX   Program Counter low byte (PCL)
                       XXXX-1 Program Counter high byte (PCH)

XXXX -2	IX low
XXXX -3	IX High
XXXX -4	accA
XXXX -5	accB
XXXX -6	HINZVC (condition code)

Before it is placed on the stack, the program counter is incremented so that when the stack is recovered the operation will commence with the program step following the one being performed at the time of the interruption. The step in progress will always be completed before the transfer to the stack and the jump is made. The stack pointer is also automatically decremented to $ XXXX - 7 so that a new location is available for more stack operations. In the analogy, the stack pointer always represents the surface of the coutertop. It is always necessary to load the stack pointer once at the start of a program with a 2-byte address if these features are to be used.

The loading of the stack pointer can be done with a load immediate ($ 8E, $ XX, $ XX), a load direct ($ 9E, $ XX) load extended) $ BE, $ XX, XX) in which case the stack pointer is loaded with the *contents* of $ XXXX, or by a load IX'ed ($ AE, $XX) in which case the SP is loaded with the *contents* of the memory addressed by the IX + XX. In the direct, extended and indexed modes, the high order byte of the SP is taken from the location addressed in memory and the low order byte is taken from the next higher byte in memory (M + 1). This order is used in all transactions where a 16-bit register is loaded from memory. It applies equally to the program counter (PC) and the IX.

The stack pointer can also be stored by direct, extended or indexed commands. The contents of the stack pointer can be transferred into the IX and the IX can be transferred into the SP.

The large number of operations required of the processor will obviously give this technique a net disadvantage in running speed compared to the techniques where the functions of registers are simply swapped. A typical interruption will occupy nine or 10 clock cycles by the time the PC is incremented and all the registers are stored in memory. A typical return from an interruption will require 5 clock cycles. There is, however, one very major advantage in the matter of nested subroutines.

Suppose that you are using a subroutine and you want to branch to a second subroutine before returning from the first. This is termed a *nested subroutine* and consists of a subroutine within a subroutine. With the register transfer schemes, there is obviously a fairly stiff restriction on the number of full function registers that can be made available. Therefore, there is a restriction upon the number of subroutines that can be nested. With the stack scheme, the number of subroutines that can be nested is limited only by the extent of the read/write memory which is available for the stack. Some of the available processors will allow only the nesting of two subroutines.

At first glance, it might seem that a restriction nesting two subroutines might not be too onerous since a subroutine branch can always be replaced by simply writing out the subroutine steps. However, some subroutines—such as a division subroutine—can be fairly long. Within each of these longer subroutines there can be repetetive shorter routines which are repeated many times. If each of these could be written just once and used as a subroutine, it can save a considerable amount of program memory.

Added to this is that the branch to subroutine might be conditional: it happens only under certain conditions of data. The number of nestings is, therefore, often a function of the data which has been received. Sometimes the only way to find out how many subroutines will be nested is to consider all of the possible combinations and sequences of data that can be received. This can prove to be computationally impractical with even the largest computer.

Another factor which must be considered is the possibility that an external device interrupt might occur just when the processor is in the deepest nesting.

In general, a branch to subroutine which cannot be accomodated will cause the machine to run wild. A usual result is that, somewhere along the line, data will be read as a command. Once the machine gets out of sequence, the probability that it will ever get back in sequence is very small since the sequence is the distinction and the *only* distinction between data and commands. It is also highly likely that the read/write memory will be scribled over and most or all data lost.

In a TV game, this might not be too serious. However, in a controller this type of crash can cause the oven temperature to be set to maximum, the throttle to be set wide open, the brakes to be locked or a million other horrendous possibilities. There are also certain illegal commands which can alter the operation of the machine in such a way that the processor will not even repond to a reset. In this case, the only way that control can be restored is to shut off the electricity and start over. Usually this an unattractive requirement.

This discussion emphasizes the point made earlier that a subroutine should be entered only with a subroutine instruction. If the processor simply walks in during program execution, the stack will not be loaded and the return instruction at the end of the subroutine will cause the processor to be loaded with the garbage behind the stack pointer. This will almost invariably cause a crash.

Another less obvious pitfall awaits the unwary. The subroutine must always be exited via a RETURN FROM INTERRUPT ($ 3B) or a RETURN FROM SUBROUTINE ($ 39) as appropriate and never via a simple jump or branch.

Every time a jump out of a subroutine occurrs, the data in the stack is not taken back out and the SP is not incremented. This can lead to a very pernicious form of software crash. The failure to push the SP back up means that it will slowly walk down through memory. If the jump is a relatively infrequent occurrance, it can take a long time for it to work its way out to the point where it starts overwriting memory reserved for other tasks. The machine might have to be in continuous operation for weeks in order for the crash to occur. The nasty part of this is that you can design and test a product over some significant period of time and never have the crash occur since enough of the illegal jumps did not happen during the testing program. Then the customer installs the product and it crashes at the end of the first week. You restore the power and test it and it is perfectly okay. But three days or nine weeks later it crashes again, etc, etc.

The BRANCH TO SUBROUTINE and JUMP TO SUBROUTINE instructions are a little different from the various interrupts in that only the contents of the program counter, properly incremented, are saved. The SP is also properly incremented by these instructions. However, if the subroutine alters the contents of other registers and if you want them restored on RETURN, it is necessary to explicitly write them into memory at the start of the subroutine and to read them back into the registers prior to RETURN.

In this regard, there are two other instructions which are very useful: PUSH and PULL. These instructions will push the contents of the accumulator onto the stack—thereby saving it and pull the contents from the stack—thereby retrieving it. The commands are:

accA	accB	
$36	$37	Push acc. to stack
$32	$33	Pull data from stack to acc.

Note that these operations (push and pull) can be separated only by complete stack operations. After a push any operation that writes to stack must be followed by another operation that reads from stack or else the data will be scrambed and a crash will result.

Another caution is that between a push and a pull there should never be a test which causes one to be used without the other or you will have the built-in software bug of creeping SP with the attendant possibility of long delayed crashes noted for jumping out of a subroutine. PUSH and PULL should be treated like Siamese twins.

With the cautions noted, the use of the SP in the 6800 family is a marvelously flexible mechanism allowing nearly unlimited nesting of subroutines, interrupts, etc. The processor does not have a direct mechanism in the form of an instruction to compare. However, SP can be written to memory and the two memory bytes can then be compared. A simpler test would store IX, transfer SP to IX and compare IX which is a single instruction. The SP can be adjusted if necessary be incrementing SP ($31) or decrementing SP ($34) or completely rewriting SP with one of the write SP instructions previously noted. The IX could then be restored from memory. This is one gambit for protection of a program against "creeping SP" which might otherwise be very difficult to locate and diagnose.

THE ACCUMULATORS

The 6800 family has two accumulators which are nearly, but not quite, identical. The accumulators are the place where most of the arithmetic will be done with the processor and where the input and output data is normally handled. Most of the 72 instructions that the 6800 and the 6802 will handle are addressed to the accumulators. The similarity between the two registers is so great that it is perpaps easier to first dispose of the differences.

The asymmetry of the accumulators is found in 6 instructions which are listed below in numerical order:

INSTRUCTION **OPERATION**

$06   Transfer HINZVC to accA
$07   Transfer accA to HINZVC
$10   Subtract accB from accA cont. result to accA
$11   Compare accA - accB)cont. of neither changes)
$19   Decimal adjust accA. This instruction is used only after an add into accA and presumes that both

128

addends were BCD numbers. It readjusts the contents of accA to BCD.

$ 1B   Add accB into accA: result in accA.

From the above instructions it can be seen that there is a net advantage in doing most decimal arithmetic in accA. In some cases, there is also a slight advantage in doing binary arithmetic in accA since the results of additions and subtractions wind up in accA. The only outside access to HINZVC directly is also through accA. The remaining asymmetry stems from the fact that a comparison of the registers behaves like a subtraction of accB from accA, although the contents of neither register is altered. The result of the comparison sets N, Z, V, and C in HINZVC. Actually, there would be no net advantage to inclusion of a symmetric comparison test.

The symmetrical commands for the two accumulators form a much larger list. Both can be written into memory, loaded from memory, added-to from memory and have the contents of memory subtracted from them—including a carry or with the carry eliminated. Since the 6800 addresses everything including input/output devices as memory, the above statements apply to I/0 as well.

The addressing of the commands can be direct, IX extended or immediate, following the discussion for these modes of addressing previously given. The direct and IX modes have only forward offsets.

The accumulators also have certain bit and byte manipulation modes. They can be inclusive OR'd and exclusive OR'd in each of the address modes. They can be rotated left and right in one of two modes. In both modes the bit at the end of the accumulator in the direction of the rotation winds up in CARRY in the HINZVC. In the one mode, the space evacuated by the rotation is filled from the contents of CARRY before the move. In the second mode, the evacuated space is filled with a zero.

The rotate command is useful for masking since in the second mode all of the unwanted bits can be set to zero. The rotate commands are also useful for examining the contents of the register on a bit-by-bit basis. The contents of the register are rotated one bit and CARRY tested for set or clear. Then the next rotation is called, etc. This form of test is frequently used in input and output subroutines to test the condition of individual switches and devices. If the devices have an order of priority or urgency, they can be connected to the PIA in order of descending or ascending priority and the rotation arranged so that the highest priority device is tested first and the lowest priority device tested last.

The presence of two accumulators is extremely handy in a juggling routine. Suppose that you were creating a list in which you wanted all of the entries to go in numerical order into a table of some fixed length and it then became necessary to insert an entry somewhere in the middle of the list. Figure 7-1 shows one compact way of accomplishing this end. The data to be inserted is placed in accA and the address for insertion of the data is loaded in IX. Next, accB obtains the data from the memory at IX to save it and accA deposits the insertion. The saved contents from accB are then transferred to accA. The IX is then incremented and tested to see whether the space allocated for the table has been exhausted. If not, the cycle repeats. You can see that this routine would walk right up the table until the table was exhausted. The last table entry is, of course, lost.

Suppose that the table actually contains a message for a sign which you would like to scroll across the display like the news sign at Times Square. If you initially loaded accA with the last table entry and began at the first table entry, the entire message would scroll around the list in an endless loop with no data being lost.

Another use for this routine would be in the creation of a numerically ordered list of every configuration of the input data from some PIA bank. Since the largest number of possible 8-bit entries is 256, you need only make the table 256 memory addresses long to ensure that no data will be lost.

THE HINZVC

Any true microcomputer will have certain bits or registers which are automatically set by certain operations. These registers or bits are used as the basis for CONDITIONAL COMMANDS such as "branch if zero," "branch if carry is clear," etc. Obviously, these conditional commands must have some source on which to base the judgement of whether the test is true or false. The variety of such commands differs from machine to machine. However, all have some such commands which must seek the state of the bits or registers set by the preceding operations. In the Motorola 6800 series, the registers are referred to as the CONDITION CODES REGISTER or the HINZVC. The contents of this register are tested for all conditional operations. Each of the bits in the HINZVC has a distinct meaning and each is set, cleared or left undisturbed by each operation of the machine. The nature of the operation or the result of the operation is the determining factor in what is done with each individual bit.

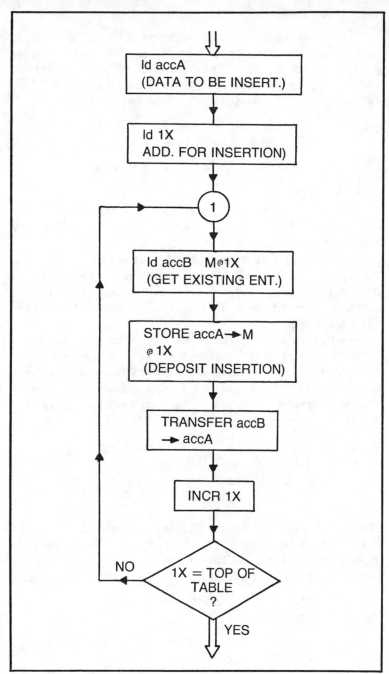

Fig. 7-1. The insertion algorithm.

C = Carry

The lowest order bit or the carry bit of the HINZVC is set when a carry is required. For example, suppose that the current contents of accA = $ 80 and the contents of accB = $ C0 and you give the next command to the machine to add accB into accA ($ 1B). The arithmetic of the operation would be:

$$
\begin{array}{rclcl}
\$\,80 & = & 1000\ 0000 & = & 128 \\
+\ \underline{\$\,C0} & = & \underline{1100\ 0000} & = & \underline{192} \\
\$\,1\ 40 & & 1\ 0100\ \ 000 & = & 320
\end{array}
$$

Carry: *1* and *I*.

The result $ 40 would wind up in accA and the carry bit of the HINZVC would be set. The carry bit sets whenever there is a carry from the most significant bit in the result.

Carry is also set if an arithmetic borrow is required, as when the subtrahend is larger than the minuend, for example 7- 8. In this case, you would have a borrow required to correctly perform the operation. In doing arithmetic within the processor, the carry is frequently required.

The instructions to increment or decrement a given ac-cumulator or a memory location *do not* set carry. However, the rotate instructions for either accumulators or memory can set carry. For example, suppose the contents of either an accumulator or a memory address were $ 81 and you gave the machine the command for either an arithmetic shift left or a rotate left. The result would be:

Carry	register	
X	1000 0001	before
I	0000 0010	after

The rotate instructions differ in what is done to the vacated space. For the arithmetic shift left, the vacated space is filled with a zero as in the above example. This is equivalent to multiplying the contents of the register by two. In the example, the decimal value

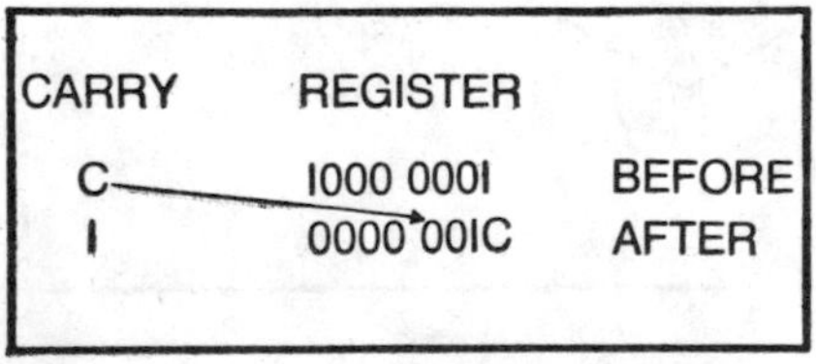

CARRY	REGISTER	
C⎯⎯⎯	1000 0001	BEFORE
I	0000 0001C	AFTER

Fig. 7-2. The rotate left instruction.

132

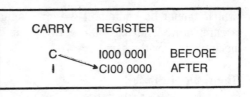

Fig. 7-3. The rotate right instruction.

```
        CARRY    REGISTER
    C           I000 0001    BEFORE
    I          CI00 0000    AFTER
```

before the operation is 129 and after the operation if you consider that the value of the carry bit is 256, the sum of CARRY + REGISTER = 256 + 2 = 258.

The rotate left instruction, on the other hand, will fill the unused bit with the contents of the carry bit before the operation (see Fig. 7-2). The logical shift right routine reverses the above proceedure. The least significant bit is pushed into carry and the most significant bit is filled with a zero.

The rotate right operation fills the most significant bit with the contents of carry before the operation (see Fig. 7-3). It can be seen that the logical shift right is equivalent to division by two:

Carry	Register	Decimal
x	I000 000I	129
I	0I00 0000	64 + ½

The value of the carry is the first place to the right of the binary point or ½ in this case.

The machine is equipped with commands to set carry ($0D) or clear carry ($ 0C). It is also equipped with commands to BRANCH IF CARRY SET ($25 $ XX) and BRANCH IF CARRY CLEAR ($ 24, $XX). The $ XX is the offset which determines the destination of the branch.

Carry enters into other operations as well. For instance, at some times it is necessary to add into one of the accumulators from memory and ignore the carry which might have been set by some previous operation. The command for this operation for accA is $ BB, $ XX $ XX in the extended address form. On the other hand, the previous operation might have been a previous addition from which the carry must be included. For accA, the command for this is $ 89, $DD in immediate address form (where $ DD represents the data to be added). There are also separate command sets for subtracting memory from accumulators with and without carry. Commands exist for immediate, direct, extended and indexed addressing for each of these operations.

Later chapters will be treating the properties of the processor in performing arithmetic, particularly on larger strings of numbers which cannot be contained within a single memory register or accumulator. The use of the carry bit is required in order to perform this arithmetic.

The H Bit of HINZVC

The H bit of HINZVC operates on additions but not subtractions or rotation in the same manner as the carry—except that H refers to carry out of the fourth bit: B3. The presence of the H bit is handy in cases where BCD arithmetic is being done. There is only a single BCD digit being stored in a register since it signals a decimal carry after a decimal adjust operation. There is no direct test to branch if H is set. However, the HINZVC can be loaded to accA as previously noted and then accA can be masked and tested for H set or clear.

The Z Bit of HINZVC

The Z bit is set whenever an operation results in the contents of an accumulator or a memory register being set to zero. This can be as a result of an addition, subtraction, increment, decrement or clear instruction. The use of the Z bit tests was demonstrated in the timing loop example.

The N Bit of HINZVC

The N or negative bit of the HINZVC simply senses and repeats the most significant bit of the last addressed register. If the number in the register is considered to be a signed binary number, then the most significant bit is the sign bit. Whenever an operation results in $B7 = I$, the N bit is set. The processor will test the N bit on the instruction: BRANCH IF MINUS (\$ 2B) or BRANCH IF PLUS (\$ 2A).

The V Bit of HINZVC

The V bit of the HINZVC is the two's compliment overflow bit. It is set if there was a two's compliment overflow as a result of the operation. In Boolean notation, after an addition from register to accumulator, or accumulator to accumulator, with or without carry, the condition is: $V = A7, B7, \overline{R7} + \overline{A7}, \overline{B7}, R7$. Consider this statement briefly. The terms represent the seventh bit of accA and accB before the operation and the Rs represent the results. Considering only the seventh or most significant bits in an addition you would have:

$$\begin{array}{c} I \\ +\underline{\;I\;} \\ = I\;0 \end{array} \quad \text{or} \quad \begin{array}{c} 0 \\ +\underline{\;0\;} \\ = I \end{array}$$

In the left-hand example there was obviously a carry out of the register and C would also be set. In the right-hand example, there obviously had to be a carry out of B6 to obtain the result.

V also is set on a rotate instruction if after the completion of the instruction either N is set and C is clear or C is set and N is clear. Therefore: $V = N\overline{(x)}C$. There are two branch instructions using N alone: BRANCH IF OVERFLOW IS CLEAR ($ 28) and BRANCH IF OVERFLOW IS SET ($ 29).

The I Bit of HINZVC

The I bit of the HINZVC is the interrupt mask bit. The 6800 will respond to two types of interrupts, maskable and non-maskable interrupts. The processor must respond to the interrupt on the non-maskable interrupt line. In this case, it jumps to the address listed in addresseses $ FFFC and $FFFD (high order and low order bytes respectively) after it has completed the instructionit is currently processing. It then proceeds to store the contents of all registers on the stack and begins the interrupt subroutine listed in the contents of the program which begins at the address listed in the contents of $ FFFC and $FFFD.

With the MASKABLE INTERRUPT, the machine might or might not respond depending upon whether CLEAR INTERRUPT MASK ($ 0E) has been issued or SET INTERRUPT MASK ($OF) has been set. The maskable interrupt responds to a low transition on the interrupt request line (LRQ). The action is similar to the non-maskable interrupt except that the processor jumps to the address specified in the contents of memory addresses $ FFF8 and $ FFF9.

The maskable interrupt is a valuable addition to the 6800 since it makes it possible to disable the interrupts in portions of a program where the processor is involved in a critical task and to enable interrupts when the processor is involved in something less critical. The interrupt mask can be read by loading HINZVC to accA and then testing the contents of accA. Conversely, the mask can also be set by transfer from accA to HINZVC.

THE SOFTWARE INTERRUPT

The software interrupt is a command, $3F, which can be written into program. It goes through the same routines as the other interrupts except that it takes its "jump to" address from the contents of $ FFFA and $ FFFB. Since the software interrupt is in itself a command which would only be accessed at the close of another preceding command, the machine does not have to wait until the completion of the preceding command. The software interrupt can be employed at any point or points in the program or programs where it is desirable to return the machine to a special housekeeping routine. For example, in the MEK D II kit the software interrupt contains the address $ F in the J-Bug ROM which places the prompt mark or dash in the display lefthand digit, clears the remainder of the display and places the machine back under the control of the Hex keyboard and control buttons. The non-maskable interrupt contains address $ F which represents the recovery routine. It is electrically connected to the EXIT button (second, colored E on the keyboard of the MEK). Since this interrupt is non-maskable it will interrupt nearly any routine of the processor and bring the unit back to keyboard control.

These interrupts are generally used on a small general purpose routine to throw the machine back into housekeeping routines. On any of the routines listed thus far in the book, there are no instructions to scan and interpret the keyboard. Therefore, you would find that the keyboard will not accomplish anything during the operation of the programs. The only control the operator would have would be through EXIT or RESET. Under certain circumstances, after the issuance of certain illegal codes such as command $ 9D, the machine can go into a mode in which it will even refuse to respond to these. The only way to regain control is to shut off the electricity.

WAIT

The wait instruction $ 3E will cause the machine to store the contents of the registers on the stack and then idle until an interrupt is received—provided that the interrupt bit is not set.

HALT LINE

One of the inputs to the 6800 processor is the $\overline{\text{HALT}}$ line. When this line is high, the processor functions normally. When the line is taken low, the processor will halt in its tracks with the address frozen on the 16 address lines. Because of the dynamic nature of the machine, if the line is held low for more than a few clock cycles, the contents of the processor registers will be lost.

The two unused bits in the condition code register are set to I.

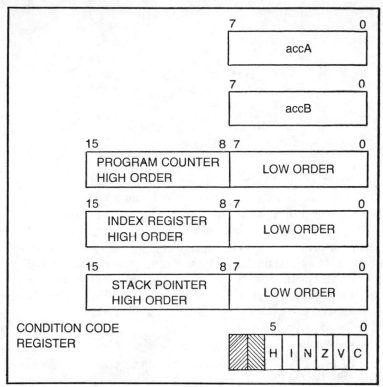

Fig. 7-4. 6800 register architecture.

REGISTER ILLUSTRATION

Figure 7-4 illustrates the registers I have been discussing. These can be thought of as being some of the principle devices on the bike. They are the items which provide most of the functions of the bike.

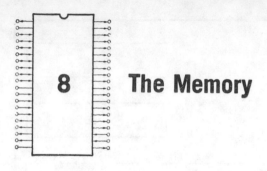

8   The Memory

At the start of the discussion on architecture I launched an analogy in which I discussed the processor as being a bike which could traverse in only one direction around a long circular boulevard: the memory. Although the bike could only go forward it also had certain abilities to dissappear and reappear at other locations nearly instantaneously. It could also examine any mailbox along the boulevard of memory with the same speed and alter the contents of any mailbox regardless of its current position. This chapter will examine the properties of the memory boulevard.

THE DATA BUS

As noted in the earlier discussion, the 6800 family makes use of a dedicated data bus. The bus is 8 bits wide—numbered from D0 through D7. The bus is always used for data and only used for data. Furthermore, since the 6800 family addresses everything as memory, all communication to and from the processor must pass over the data bus. This reveals several things about the nature of the data bus. First of all, the bus itself must be *bi-directional* since data must sometimes pass from the processor to memory, PIA's, ACIA's, etc. and sometimes from memory, etc. to the processor. Secondly it reveals that *every* device connected across the data bus must be *tri-state*.

The tri-state organization is used in order to prevent bus connection. Unlike a cocktail party where everyone seems to talk simultaneously, a microcomputer can have only one voice on the data bus at any time. It must function like a well-run and formal meeting in which a chairman designates each speaker and only one person is allowed to speak at a time. The reasoning behind this is fairly obvious. Suppose that two devices were trying to simultaneously output something on D7 and the first device was set at 1 and the second was set at 0. The D7 line would probably assume an *illegal level* halfway between I and 0. This could be interpreted in any way by the devices on the bus or else one of the devices would burn out. Neither alternative is desirable.

DATA SOURCE SELECTION

Under most circumstances, the designation of who is going to speak on the data bus is made by the processor. This is done by controlling the status of two distinct lines, READ/$\overline{\text{WRITE}}$ and CE or $\overline{\text{CE}}$ (sometimes both are used). Their operation and derivation is a little different, therefore they are explained separately.

The line READ/$\overline{\text{WRITE}}$ (R/$\overline{\text{W}}$) comes from a dedicated pin on the processor itself and is used to signal to all memory devices whether the processor (acting as chairman) intends to talk or to listen. When this line is in the I state the processor is in the listening condition. It then is designating that it will yield the floor to some memory device. Conversely, when R/$\overline{\text{W}}$ = 0 it indicates to all memory devices that the processor intends to speak and that all memory devices must be silent. This line must obviously be carried to all devices on the data bus which are capable of speaking.

CHIP ENABLE

Although the R/$\overline{\text{W}}$ line tells all of the devices on the data bus whether the processor intends to speak or to listen, it cannot designate which device(s) it intends to speak or listen to. This function is performed by the CE (or $\overline{\text{CE}}$).

The CE function is implemented indirectly by the processor through a series of ADDRESS DECODE functions which might or might not utilize additional external hardware. Some devices feature multiple chip selects which can be either active in the high state or negated and active in the low state. The address on the address bus, which is usually asserted by the processor, is the thing which is used to designate the source or the destination of the data which appears on the data bus. The use of multiple chip enables on the peripheral device make it possible to minimize the number of chips which are required to implement a controller.

To illustrate this point, refer to Fig. 8-1. This illustration shows one of the simplest possible configurations for a controller device. With only a total of four chips (excluding power supply) it is possible to implement a full controller having input and output functions, a program in ROM and an internal scratchpad in the 6802 processor. A number of lines have been left off of the figure for simplicity.

To begin with, look at the ROM. The ROM has most, but not all, of the address lines brought into it. You can see that the Boolean conditions for the ROM are: ROM = A15, $\overline{A11}$, (VMA, 02). In other words, the ROM will be activated (and out of the tri-state condition) whenever A15 is high and A11 is low. The binary state of the address bus is:

IXXX 0XAA AAAA AAAA

where: X = don't care

A = address bit is decoded in the ROM itself

With the range allowed by the don't cares, the ROM would be active when the most significant byte was:

$ F8 = IIII I000	$ FC = IIII II00
$ F9 = IIII I00I	$ FD = IIII II0I
$ FA = IIII I0I0	$ FE = IIII III0
$ FB = IIII I0II	$ FF = IIII IIII

From this it can be seen that the arrangement suffices to decode the addresses for the ROM for 2K bytes.

There is a point of interest, however, in the fact that the omission of the address lines does not make the address *fully decoded*. For example, the first nibble of the address could just as well have been: $8, $9, $A, $B, $C, $D, or $E. In the operation of the machine, $ F8XX would be indistinquishable from $ 88XX and the two addresses could be used interchangeably.

For the PIA the boolean condition is: PIA = $\overline{A15}$, A11, (VMA, 02). The binary state of the address bus is: 0XXX IXXX XXXX XXAA. Because of the large number of don't cares, it can be seen that the PIA has a much larger number of valid addresses beside the fundamental $ $ 08. However, none of these lie within the range of the ROM addresses.

The internal scratchpad memory in the 6802 processor lies in the address range $ 0000 and $007F. Therefore, this address decoding scheme is adequate to keep from having address contention, since an address to either of the peripheral chips will have either bit 11 or bit 15 set.

VALID MEMORY ADDRESS

At the bottom Fig. 8-1 note the valid memory address (VMA) line. The reason for the use of this line is to signal when the memory address on the address bus is valid. On a 16-bit bus like the address bus, it takes a finite amount of time for each line to switch from 0 to I and vice versa.

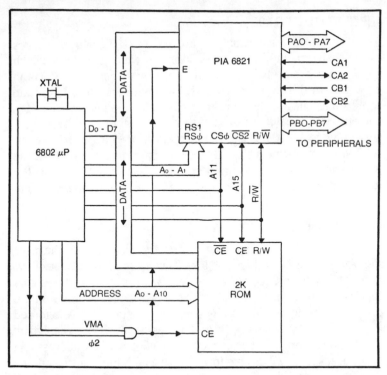

Fig. 8-1. A simple controller.

Since the drivers for each individual address line cannot be made precisely identical, and since the loads on each bit cannot be made precisely identical, there is a slight variation in the switching time from bit to bit. In order to avoid errors or glitches in decoding, the VMA is made slightly slower than any of the address drivers so that the address will have settled out on the address bus by the time that VMA goes high. VMA is commonly AND'd with the address decode to avoid glitches.

A similar line of reasoning applies to the data bus. The 6800 family employs a two phase clock and the data is normally shifted into registers on the falling edge of the Ø2 clock. This clock is normally derived by dividing the XTAL frequency by four to provide Ø1 and Ø2 which are out of phase. One of the distinctions between the 6800 and the 6802 is that the 6802 has an on-board clock oscillator, whereas the 6800 requires an external oscillator. The 6802, however, does have an output on Ø2 provided for the express purpose of providing the precise time to read memory.

THREE STATE CONTROL

It was noted earlier that the processor itself generally serves as the chairman and issues the addresses which designate which speaker is addressed or is to speak. Three state control (TSC) is an exception to this, however, and it is sometimes used. In certain applications such as the refresh cycle of a video display, etc. it is sometimes advantageous to have something other than the processor be able to directly access the memory. For example, to read out of or write into memory directly without passing through a PIA, the processor, etc. Obviously, this saves a great deal of time for the interchange which can be important if interchange occurrs regularly.

DIRECT MEMORY ACCESS

To accomplish a *direct memory access*, (DMA) take the *three state control* (TSC) line high and lock Ø1 clock high and Ø2 clock low. When this happens, the *bus available* (BA) line goes low to signal that the bus is available and all of the address and data lines on the processor are forced into a high impedance state. VMA is forced low to prevent erronious reads and writes on any device enabled by VMA. The external device can now take control of the address and data busses and R/W is also forced into a high impedance state so that the external device can either read or write into memory.

One of the main cautions in this matter is that the 6800 is a dynamic device. If the Ø1 clock remains locked up for more than about 4.5 microseconds, data will be destroyed within the processor and a crash is almost inevitable unless all registers are carefully stored before DMA and contents are returned at the termination of DMA. This is a tricky operation requiring external logic. Since a load accumulator or a store accumulator from memory requires 4 clock cycles at 1 microsecond each, another processor has barely enough time to read or write to a single memory address. This is, however, one of the things which will permit multiprocessor operation in which two or more processors can share a single memory.

If fast memory is available, some relatively sophisticated hardware can accomplish a half dozen read/write operations during the 4.5 microseconds PWØH time that the clock can remain locked without data loss. One technique which has been used on a computer with a TV-type display is to toggle TSC back and forth so that the display gets a crack at memory and the processor gets a crack alternately. If this is timed properly, the display and the processor can share the same memory without contention. However, it

142

should be noted that the speed of the processor is effectively reduced by the duty cycle. The processor will effectively run only a one-half or a one-fourth as fast.

FULL ADDRESS DECODING

As the term implies, full address decoding requires that all of the address bits are decoded in the determination of CE and that there are no address ambiguities. In an earlier example of the

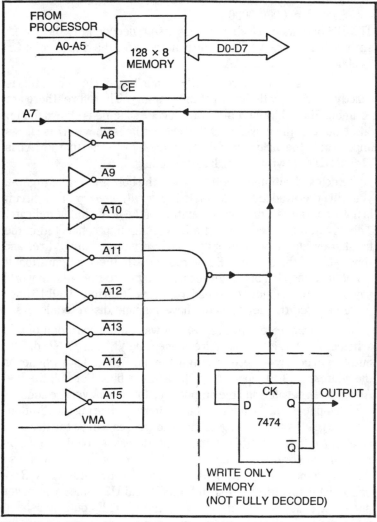

Fig. 8-2. A full decoding scheme.

placement of ROM I noted that a 6-wide AND gate would fire on any of the 1024 addresses lying between $ FC00 and $ FFFF if placed across A10 through A15.

Suppose that you would like to add an external 128 byte memory to a 6802 and that for reasons of programming simplicity you would like to make it contiguous with the internal scratchpad so that it ran from addresses $ 0080 to $ 00FF. The binary relationship would be:

$ 0080 = 0000 0000 1000 0000
$ 00FF = 0000 0000 1111 1111

The 128 byte memory chip will, by itself, decode fully the lowest six bits. Therefore, you have the conditions for the chip enable: $\overline{CE}$ = 0000 0000 IXAA AAAA.

You can see that there is still one don't care. However, this is exactly covered by the width of the memory. Therefore, there are no ambiguities. The circuit for this decode scheme is shown in Fig. 8-2. Note that the negation of the address lines above A7 is just as important as the inclusion of the true lines. Note also that VMA has been AND'd in with the address decoding.

Enclosed within the dotted box at the bottom right of Fig. 8-2 you will note an added block labeled *write only memory*. This circuit is not as trivial as a first interpretation of the name might indicate. The circuit simply consists of a D type flip flop connected in the familiar divide by two configuration. Every time that $\overline{CE}$ fires and then relaxes, the output will reverse state. In this configuration, it is *not* fully decoded but it serves as a contact to the outside world saying that the memory was read from or written into. If all 16 lines were decoded the device could have a single discrete address.

The arrangement in Fig. 8-3 shows another variation of this scheme. For U1, all of the address lines and VMA are AND'd. The output will go low—thereby setting the flip-flop for Q=1 whenever the address $ FFFF appears on the address bus. For U2, the line A8 has been negated and the output goes low whenever the address $ FF7F appears on the address bus—thereby clearing the flip-flop. Either a read from or a write to these addresses will do the trick. Of course, a different set of set and clear addresses could be used by negating one or more of the address lines to change the address.

Since the addresses listed are in ROM you could negate $R/\overline{W}$ and AND it in with the rest in both U1 and U2. Since you never should be required to write to ROM, the WRITE could be used to uniquely distinguish the output command.

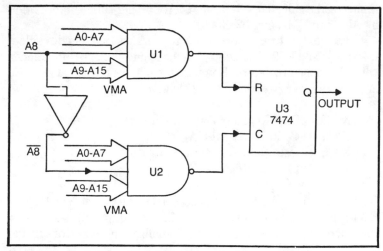

Fig. 8-3. A reset/clear write only memory output arrangement.

One of the advantages to an arrangement of this type is that the output stays latched. The programmer can set it and forget it until a change is required. This is a feature which inherently comes with the PIA which is more flexible than the scheme presented here. Furthermore, the full decoding requires quite a few chips. You can see that if you wanted to AND the 16 address lines along with VMA and negated R/$\overline{W}$ you would require an 18-wide AND gate. There really is no such arrangement and you would have to synthesize the action from three or four packages of standard logic for the U1 and U2 functions.

INCOMPLETE DECODING

Because of the hardware requirements for complete decoding, it is often worthwhile in small systems to deliberately select an incomplete decoding scheme because of the hardware savings which can result. In the discussion of input/output actions in Chapter 6, I noted that the Motorola MEK DII kit employed addresses $ 8004 through $ 8007 for one of the PIA's and $ 8020 through $ 8023 for the second unit (which is dedicated to keyboard and display purposes). It is instructive to examine the rationale behind this selection.

First of all, suppose that you would like to reserve addresses in the range $ FC00 through $ FFFF for ROM. Next examine the architecture of the PIA itself. First of all, you find that the chip is fitted with an ENABLE (E) terminal which determines all of the timing on the chip. This chip can receive proper timing information by AND'ing VMA and Ø2 clock.

The next feature of note is that the PIA has two register select lines: RS1 and RS2. The coding on these lines selects the A and B control and data registers. If you tie these lines to the data bus A0 and A1, the last two bits make selection:

XX00 = Data Register A/Data Direction Reg. A
XX0I = Control Register A
XXI0 = Data Register B/Data Direction Reg. B
XXII = Control Register B

The question of whether you access a data direction register or a data register is determined by the last write into the associated control register as described in the initialization section of Chapter 6.

The next feature to note about the PIA is that it is equipped with three chip select lines; CS0, CS1 and CS2. The last of these lines is negated. Can these three chip selects be used to do the necessary decoding without the use of any additional hardware? Figure. 8-4 shows one such scheme. The binary representation of the coding to select the upper PIA is: Upper PIA = IX0X XXXX XXXX XIAA. The primary address range for this is:

$ 8004 = I000 0000 0000 0I00 = DATA REG. A
$ 8005 = I000 0000 0000 0I0I = CONT REG. A
$ 8006 = I000 0000 0000 0II0 = DATA REG. B
$ 8007 = I000 0000 0000 0III = CONT. REG. B

For the Lower PIA the binary coding is: Lower PIA = IX0X XXXX XXIX XXAA. The Primary address range for this is:

$ 8020 = I000 0000 00I0 0000 = DATA REG. A
$ 8021 = I000 0000 00I0 000I = CONT. REG. A
$ 8022 = I000 0000 00I0 00I0 = DATA REG. B
$ 8023 = I000 0000 00I0 00II = CONT. REG. B

From this, it can be seen that it is indeed possible to partially decode the necessary address arrangement with only the chip lines available and without the use of additional hardware. The question remains, however, to determine whether the address select scheme is sufficient to uniquely select only PIA's without contention from other devices.

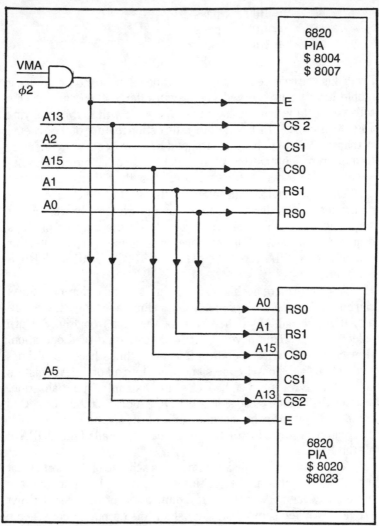

Fig. 8-4. An incomplete decoding scheme.

For the first cut at this, note that A15 must be asserted true. This means that only addresses $8XXX through $$FXXX need be considered. Considering only the most significant nibble you can see:

$8	= I000	pass	
$9	= I00I	pass	pass for A13=0
$A	= I0I0	fail	fail for A13=I
$B	= I0II	fail	

$C	= II00	pass
$D	= II0I	pass
$E	= III0	fail
$F	= IIII	fail

From this you can see that $A, $B, $E and $F in the most significant nibble have been reserved. They will offer no contention. This tells you that the scheme as shown will work with ROM occupying $FC00 through $FFFF. Another interesting feature of the scheme is that the MEK DII has a scratchpad RAM or read/write memory located from $A000 to $A07F which is used for internal housekeeping. The scheme offers no conflict with this either.

The most obvious advantage of this sort of scheme is that it minimizes the hardware required for the system. By the use of some ingenuity, the designer has reduced the number of chips required on the board. Furthermore, the scheme is expansible. For example, other PIA's could be placed at $8008, $8010, $8040, $8080, etc.

A slightly more sophisticated point is that a different address can be used to select all of the outputs simultaneously. For example, if A2=I and A5=I then *both* of the chips on Fig. 8-4 are selected. You would never want to do this on a read operation. However, on a write operation it is sometimes handy and time-saving to be able to write the same word into all of the A registers or all of the B registers of the PIA's. For example, at initialization, a single instruction could select the DDRA of all of the PIAs. This could be followed by the data direction words on a one by one basis. Thereafter, a single instruction could de-select all of the DDRA of all the PIAs.

The most obvious disadvantage of a scheme of this sort is that it is limited in the number of times that it can be done and it is wasteful of memory range. An examination of the pass/fail list previously given shows that the use of this output select scheme means that the output addresses occupy half of the upper half of the memory address range of 16K of the total 64K bytes while providing only about ten possible primary output addresses and about forty secondary addresses. In a great many small microcomputer applications, this loss of memory is of no serious consequence. If written in compact machine language, 1K or 2K of ROM will provide a pretty sophisticated control algorythm. For example, high speed algorithms to initialize memory at startup, do 15 digit add, subtract, multiply and divide and a limited precision sine, cosine and tangent routine can be squeezed into 1K of ROM. From the address scheme, it can be seen that there is actually room for 16K of ROM. However, the ROM is not contiguously addressed and an essentially full decoding scheme would be required to use it unambiguously. This might defeat the advantage of incomplete addressing for the output and a more advantageous balance of hardware might result from the use of a little more decoding for output.

QUASI MEMORY OPERATIONS

One of the features of the 6800 family which is not to be found on a number of processors is the ability to perform a number of operations with single commands as though they were actually taking place in memory and to have the HINZVC respond as if the operation were monitored in memory.

For example, the left and right shifts and rolls can be addressed to memory by either extended or indexed addressing. The contents of memory can be incremented or decremented or negated. In each case, the HINZVC responds exactly as if the operation had been performed in one of the accumulators and the various conditional operations will perform exactly as if the operation had taken place in an accumulator.

Actually the operation does take place in an accumulator. The machine stores the contents of the accumulator, retrieves the memory, performs the specified operation, sets the HINZVC flags, returns the result to memory and retrieves the contents of the accumulator. Without this feature, the programmer would have had to program this routine on a step-by-step basis as above. Therefore, the savings in program space are very significant and the savings in running time are also substantial—although the quasi memory operations are among the slower operations that the machine performs. For example, the logical shift right of an accumulator takes two machine cycles, whereas the logical shift right of a memory contents requires six if extended addressing is used to specify the memory and seven cycles if IX addressing is used. This is still a great deal shorter than the extended routine noted above. An example of the use of quasi memory operation was given in the nested timing loop example where the increment memory instruction was employed.

ROM AND RAM USAGE

At the outset of this discussion it is perhaps worthwhile to clarify a few definitions. It was shown earlier that memory could consist of long circulating shift registers which featured serial access to the data. *Serial access* is a natural feature of shift register memorys, bubble memorys, disc memorys and tape memorys. The sequence above is listed in increasing order of latency time or the time in which a given memory location can be accessed in the average case.

It was also shown that other types of memories could be constructed (in solid state or core) in which any address in memory can be accessed in the same period of time. This type of memory is described as *random access memory* (RAM). A single clock cycle usually suffices for a read-from or a write-to a RAM register.

Before a computer can do anything sensible, it must have some kind of a *housekeeping algorythm* loaded into it. If the computer is equipped only with volatile read/write memory, every time that the power is turned off the contents of the memory disappear and restoration of the power finds the memory filled with garbage. In order to get the machine to do anything useful, it is necessary to write a minimal *bootstrap* program into read/write memory to give the machine enough "smarts" so that it will follow a tape, teletype or disc which then loads the OPERATING PROGRAM. This initial loading is sometimes done by *direct memory access* using a row of switches and lights to set every binary bit for each memory entry on a one-bit-at-a-time basis. It does not take much imagination to figure out how tedious this task is even for very short bootstrap programs. For industrial controllers, the operating program is frequently contained in a punched paper tape which is mechanically read into the machine.

It is not difficult to imagine that the microcomputer would not have achieved very widespread acceptance if every power interruption had to be accompanied by a several hour session setting switches or a reading of several minutes or a half hour from a $700 punched paper tape recorder.

The development that made the difference came along about 1970 in the form of the *read only memory*. In the earliest form of this device it consisted simply of a 3×5 inch printed circuit card which was made double sided with a row and column matrix printed on the two sides. An address decoder similar to the 74154 was used to pull one of the 16 output columns low or pull none low if $\overline{CS} = I$. For the data output, every row that wanted to be 0 had a diode soldered in place and every row that wanted to be I did not receive a diode. The code was permanently written in by soldering in diodes and was therefore non-volatile. It did not dissappear when the power was removed. The device used *negative logic* in that a low represented an I and a high represented an 0.

The advantage of this negative logic lay in the fact that the diodes turned the data lines into a DIODE OR. The data lines from multiple sets of the cards could be wired together. The particular card was disabled by setting $\overline{CE} = I$ and the correct card enabled by setting $\overline{CE} = 0$. It can be seen that 16 of the cards could be used if one extra 74154 was tied across A4 through A7 with its outputs 0 through 15 used to derive $\overline{CE}$ for cards 0 through 15. The entire ROM could be disabled by setting $\overline{CE} = I$ on this card selector chip.

This arrangement did not work badly. It is nearly as fast as the TTL driver and the negative true logic really did not present any major problem except for an adjustment of thinking on the part of the designer. The wired OR arrangement meant that the cards could be simply daisy chained together at the socket. The principle problem was the size and power consumption. A 16-card ROM of this design would measure about $4 \times 6 \times 10$ inches and would consume about 950 mA from the + 5 volt supply for 4.76 watts. If there was not too much capacitance on the line, switching times on the order of 75 nanoseconds could be achieved. That is more than

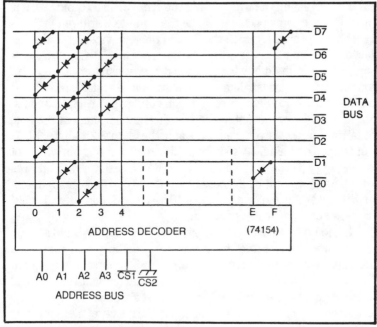

Fig. 8-5. An early form of diode ROM.

fast enough for most of the contemporary devices and is indeed faster than a good many of the single chip ROMs in use today. The main point was that the assembly offered 256 eight- (or more) bit bytes of non volatile memory which was ready to go at any time that the power was turned on. Furthermore, it had the advantage of being field programmable if a bag of 1N914 diodes and a soldering iron was handy. The information content was such that the computer could simply be turned on and the housekeeping chores were taken care of so that the machine was ready to run and answer the keyboard and inputs after a few milliseconds.

This type of ROM found a certain amount of popularity in dedicated control applications, particularly those operated with the central processor constructed from small scale or medium scale TTL chips.

Obviously, a kluge of this nature was destined for only a very limited popularity in an industry as dynamic as the solid state electronics industry. One of the first and most obvious improvements consisted of placing the line select logic and the diodes on the same chip. Among other things, this had the advantage of reducing the pin count. After all, the card had only four address inputs, two chip select inputs and eight outputs plus—of course, power and ground. The whole thing could be run in a 16-pin DIP if it were all in the same package, since the outside world required no access to the line selects. In the first of these devices, a diode was placed at every intersection of the matrix and a fusible link was incorporated in the diode lead. If the drive transistors were made somewhat more robust than the fusible link, an address could be selected and a carefully controlled high voltage pulse applied to the data line for every unwanted diode—thereby burning out the link. Voila! the chip was programmed and the entire 256-byte ROM could be run on a single 3×5 inch card with no daisy chain wiring of sockets, etc. Through the use of the MOS transistors, the power consumption was cut by a factor of eight or 10. The access time of the ROM was slowed by a factor of 10 as well, but as later proved, this was not a particular problem.

It should be noted that the problem of volatility could also be solved through the use of magnetic core memory, but there is a hitch involved in this when the system to be contructed is small. Core memory tends to require a fairly large amount of overhead hardware and even in the late 1960s it cost about $1,000 to get any core memory running at all. A fairly large core memory was cheaper on a per-bit basis than a solid state memory at that time.

However, the $1,000 price tag on openers very definitely restricted the possibility of using computer techniques in most control applications.

By the early 1970s, the price of read/write MOS memory was falling sharply on the "learning curve." However, it was still too great on a per-bit basis to make much of a dent in the computer mainframe business except for small fast cachet memory where the big mainframe did scratchpad type things. It seemed that it would be a long time before the volume on MOS memory would get up to the level where the price per bit would be attractive for mainframe or even minicomputer makers.

Intel Corp. was heavily involved in MOS memory and they had an axe to grind in this matter. In what would seem to have been a brilliant act of confidence, they set about to solve the problem in a unique manner. In 1972, Intel introduced the MCS-4 which, for the first time, combined all of the *central processor unit* (CPU) functions on a single chip, and the microprocessor was born.

While this 4-bit chip could be used to make a rather slow and very clumsy general purpose computer, the Intel goal was not this market, but rather the more mundane applications such as "smart" cash registers, controls, instruments, etc. The price was low enough to consider inclusion of such a machine into gasoline pumps for multi-grade fuels, etc. More important, however, was the fact that such devices would use small solid-state memories. The $100 price of a 1K byte memory was much more attractive than the $1,000 needed for openers for core. At the outset, the MCS-4 was offered at a money losing price in order to gain the profit on the solid-state memories required in order to use it. This proposition gets even better today when you consider devices such as the Motorola 68000. It will take 2048 of the new 64KBit memory chips to fill the 16MByte addressable memory.

At about the same time that Intel was developing the MCS-4 microprocessor, they were also developing a new type of ROM which could be electrically programmed. In this device, a MOS field effect transistor (FET) replaced the diode at each of the row and column crossovers. This FET could be permanently biased on by appropriately pulsing the gate and source lines with high voltage. This would cause a charge to become trapped under the gate and the cell would be permanently set in the ROM. The ability to electrically program the ROM is of course a very great advantage. The program which was eventually to reside in the ROM could be developed in read/write memory and then transferred under program control to the ROM. This process could, however, be duplicated with the blown-diode type ROM also. The real advantage lay in the fact that the biased transistor ROM could be erased by exposing the device to ultraviolet light for a few minutes. This caused the charge to leak off of the various set gates and returned the ROM to the original condition—ready to receive a new program.

For a while, there was a great distinction made regarding the difference between the *programmable read only memory* (PROM) and the *erasable programmable read only memory* (EPROM). Physically, the package showed a difference in that the EPROM is fitted with a quartz window to let the ultraviolet light through to the chip while retaining the hermetic seal. However, in operation the differences between the two was negligable and in more recent literature a ROM is referred to only as ROM regardless of the mechanism involved.

An even more recent development is the *electrically alterable read only memory* (EAROM) which can be erased as well as written electrically. Sometimes these devices are referred to as *read mostly memorys*. They are actually capable of read/write operations but not on the same scale as normal read/write memorys.

Most of the memory manufacturers offer to produce ROMs into which the program is written by masking the connections at the time that the chip is manufactured. In large production runs, the masked ROM is by far the cheapest with 1K chips running on the order of a dollar. However, there is a one-time masking charge of $ 1,500 to $2,000 which must be paid to the manufacturer. Changing even a single bit will mean a repeat of the masking charge. Therfore, most people will want to be certain of the program before committing themselves to the mask charge.

The PROM is used in many low-volume situations because of the mask charge and because it is cheaper than the EPROM which tends currently to run about $32 for a 1K × 8 NMOS chip which will operate on a single-supply voltage. The EAROM is even more expensive and is generally used only where the ability to alter the program in-circuit is an advantage. It should be noted that most of these EAROM devices require that voltages and pulse shaping circuits be made available which are not used elsewhere in the computer. Therefore, the costs for these must be added to the product as well.

Most microprocessor systems to be made in only single units or a few tens of units are constructed using ultraviolet erasable

PROMs which are generally programmed in an external machine. This has the advantage during development that the program can be written, altered and rewritten as the product begins to take shape. In between steps, the PROMs can be erased and reused. If the operating program is developed in small modules, the use of the EPROM will result in a savings over the use of a non-erasable PROM which would have to be used up in some considerable quantity. There are gradual steps being made by some of the chip manufacturers to offer a line of plug-compatible chips in EPROM, PROM and ROM (masked). If these are offered, it becomes possible to do the inital development, prototyping and field acceptance testing with the relatively expensive but reusable EPROM chips for the first dozen or so units.

When the quantity demand reaches 100 or more units, the switch can be made to the less expensive PROM units without requiring any hardware changes. When the demand for the product rises to multiple hundreds, the economics of the situation will favor a switch to the use of masked-program ROM provided that no hardware changes are required in the equipment. For example, a parts cost saving of $ 20 per chip would be realized by the switch from PROM to ROM. The $ 2,000 mask charge could be amortized over 100 units. This would, of course, be accompanied by a loss in flexability since the operating characteristics of the product are not "cast in bronze" and are not available for alteration.

There is a fundamental difference in philosophy which appears at this point between large volume manufacturers and small volume manufacturers. Unless a very large mass market is anticipated for the product from the outset, the use of masked ROM is relatively unattractive because it negates one of the very attractive features of the microprocessor—namely the flexability. For the small volume manufacturer, the ability to alter or tailor the operation of the product to the needs of a specific customer often makes the difference between a slae and no sale. On a per-function basis these tailor-made products are very expensive compared to the mass-market products.

For the mass-market producer, on the other hand, the product price is a very potent influence and the prospect of tailoring a product to a specific customer requirement is not attractive since it will occupy a high-overhead engineering group in tasks not directed toward increasing factory yield. If you do not like the TV game or microwave oven, there might be 100,000 others who do and who would not pay the extra dollars that an option would add.

ROM VERSUS RAM

It should be noted that the actual operation of nearly all ROM is actually on a random access basis and not on a serial access basis. In current usage, the term RAM is used to describe random access read/write memory to distinguish it from ROM even though the ROM is itself a random access memory.

THE STARTUP PROGRAM

At the startup of the operation, all microprocessors must have some initialize program which sets up the processor in a specific configuration and operation sequence There is a little more going on than meets the eye. Figure 8-6 is essentially a flow chart of the invisible action internal to the processor. This loop is completed with every one- two- or three-byte command of the processor. The flow chart is termed invisible because it is built into the processor and proceeds without any action on the part of the programmer. This loop represents a flow chart reiteration of the processor operation to this point.

Figure 8-7 represents a typical inital ROM program for a processor which has a hexadecimal display and a hex keyboard with some command keys such as memory, run, clear, advance, enter, etc. It is presumed that the computer is intended to run on programs entered into memory from the keyboard and that the ROM is used only for housekeeping. In this case, the program is shown for clarity with a great many of the instructions lumped together. This is a high level flow chart which does not treat the details of the contents of most of the blocks.

As shown at the top left-hand corner of the chart, the depression of the reset button sends the processor to addresses $ FFFE and $ FFFF where it reads the contents $ FC00. This is the bottom address on the same ROM. It reads the first instruction which tells it to lead the SP with $ 00EF. That is the place where you would like to have the stack start. In this example, I have assumed that the microcomputer has only 256 bytes of read/write memory or RAM. Note that the last 16 bytes have been reserved for flags, display data, etc.

The next step is to initialize the appropriate PIA(s) for driving the display. Next, the machine initializes the display register with something which will tell the operator that the machine is ready to operate. For example, the message HELLO or a - can be used. Up to node 1, the program is linear and is performed only once after reset. The remainder of the program is multiply looped and con-

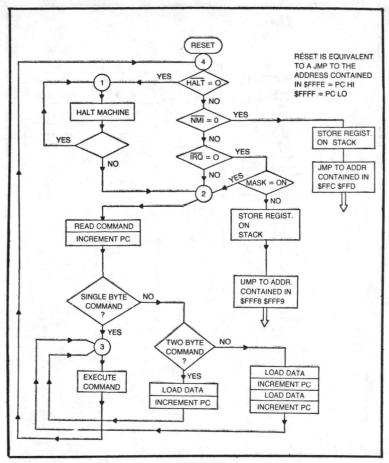

Fig. 8-6. The invisible flow chart (6800).

tains information and programming for the servicing of the display
and the keyboard.

Below node 1, set up IX with the data for the register in
memory which contains the data of the first display character. The
machine then writes the character to the display and tests the first
keyboard row. If no key is closed, it increments the IX and tests to
see whether the display is finished. If the display is not finished the
processor loops to 2 and displays the next character. If the display
is finished, the processor loops back to 1 and re-sets IX.

If a key is closed, the processor jumps out of the display loop
and identifies the key. If it is a data key, the processor enters the
data and tests for an open key. This delay and test for an open key

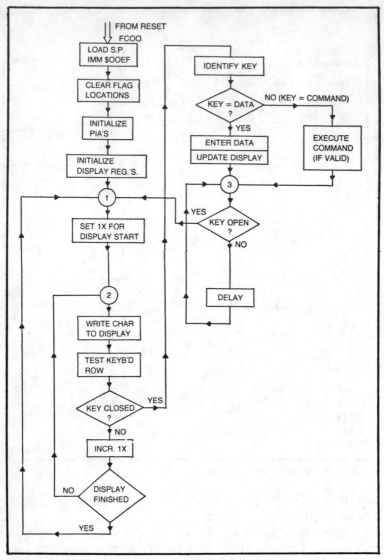

Fig. 8-7. A typical initial ROM program for a processor.

routine assures that a single key depression will enter only one character or one command for each key closure. If the key is identified as a command key, the processor tests for the validity of the command.

For example, if the command is RUN, the machine tests to determine whether a valid four hex digit address ($ AAAA) has

158

been entered. If not, the machine simply aborts the process and jumps to node 3. If a valid address has been entered, the machine simply jumps to $ AAAA and commences operation. This operation might or might not return the operation to node 3. It depends upon what has been written in the program beginning at $ AAAA.

For memory operations, the unit could accept four digits from the keyboard. The depression of the memory key following this would then fetch the contents of that memory location and add them to the display for a manual reading of that memory location. If the operator wants to write to memory, he could then enter the correct digits and press ENTER. If he only wants to read the contents of that memory address, he would press ADVANCE and the memory address would increment and be displayed. The contents of that memory address would be fetched and displayed as well. Rough speaking, this ROM routine would grant the programmer the ability to write into any location in memory, examine the data in any memory and start execution of a program at any point in memory. For any general purpose computer, this is the least capability that will give control of the machine operation.

If you simply buy a microprocessor chip, a ROM and a PIA and intend to use these to create a four-chip computer such as shown in Fig. 8-1, a program akin to this must be created and written into ROM. I have touched only lightly upon this housekeeping routine. In later chapters I will explain the concept further. However, it is presented here to illustrate the usage of ROM to perform housekeeping and to bring the processor into a condition where the operator can control the machine. It should be obvious that the housekeeping is dependent upon not only the specific processor (the 6800, 1802, 8080, etc.) but also upon the total hardware which is used (PIAs ACIAs memory, etc.) and the intended operation of the general machine (general purpose, motor control, etc).

9 Other Architectures

As it was noted in the introduction, this book will attempt to reduce the various fundamental principles of microprocessor usage to practical levels through the use of some rather specific examples intended to demonstrate the mechanisms and proceedures by which the hardware and software engineer manipulate these devices. Up to this point, the examples have been almost entirely concerned with the Motorola 6800 family machines; most particularly the 6800 and the 6802. This chapter covers another type of processor having a rather different architecture.

For an example, I have selected the RCA 1800 family. The reason for this choice is the significant contrast between the machines in the way in which some of the fundamental operations of the machine are handled on both the hardware and the software levels. The differences are sufficient so that most other processors lie somewhere between the two.

Viewed objectively, microprocessors of any type have a great deal in common. They all generally have some form of data bus, some form of address bus and they all tend to proceed down the memory boulevard in much the same way. Also, they all make use of the same binary arithmetic and the same Boolean algebra and most will have equivalent sets of commands. However, there are a number of nuances involved in the handling of each individual type.

It is very difficult to clearly demonstrate the superiority of one machine over the other. One of the principal techniques for evaluating the relative merits of one processor against another is the *benchmark* test in which the machines are individually programmed to perform some task and then compared for running time, program bytes required, hardware required, etc. The trouble with this form of testing is that a great deal of the outcome depends upon the skill of the operator. In any but the most trivial tasks, the ingenious programmer can generally out perform the less skilled programmer even though the less skilled person might be using a machine with certain intrinsic advantages. Referring to the lookup table example in Chapter 6, note that on the *same* machine, the IX and lookup method required fewer lines of code but more running time—after the number of table entries exceeded a certain level. With such differences in a relatively simple routine on an intra-machine comparison, it is easy to see that inter-machine comparisons are very difficult to evaluate independent of the operator skill.

A PHYSICAL COMPARISON

The first and most obvious difference between the 6800 family and the 1800 family is in the basic transistor scheme employed. The 6800 family is NMOS and operates on a single +5V ± 5 percent supply. It will typically consume 0.6W and might reach 1.2W from the supply. The registers on the 6800 are dynamic and the standard unit (not the 68A00 or 68 B00 selected for high-speed operation) will operate with a clock speed no slower than 100KHz and no faster than 1 MHz.

The RCA CDP1802 is a CMOS device employing complimentary p- and n-channel transistors for each ladder. For the operation of this mechanism refer to Fig. 9-1. The illustration shows a pair of field effect transistors of which Q1 is a p-channel and Q2 is an n-channel device. When the switch S is in the grounded position, transistor Q1 turns on to saturation and Q2 is completely cutoff. Since the saturated ON resistance of a FET is on the order of an ohm and the cutoff resistance is on the order of megohms, the output terminal rises to within a few millivolts of V+. Furthermore, if a second such stage is connected to the output, the input resistance of that stage is also measured in megohms or higher. Therefore, the current drawn by the stage is measured in microamperes or less. With the switch up, the reverse condition occurs. This has a profound effect upon the power consumption and the voltage tolerance of the device. First of all, the output swings nearly to the + and − rails. Therefore, the device is much less voltage-sensitive than an NMOS + resistor scheme. Secondly, the power consumption is orders of magnitude lower. Only during the transitions from high to low and low to high does the device draw any significant current from the supply in order to change the gates and the miscellaneous stray capacitances on the chip. The power drawn by a CMOS circuit tends to be frequency-sensitive—rising linearly with switching frequency. For the 1802, the allowable supply voltage range is 4V to 10.5 V and the power consumption is 10 to 100 mW nominal at 4 MHz. The vastly reduced power consumption and the elimination of the requirement for strict regulation is an obvious advantage in battery powered equipment.

Another advantage for the inherent power efficiency of the CMOS structure is that it is not necessary to skimp on devices to keep down power consumption. For this reason, the CMOS processor can be made fully static. The 1802 can use any clock frequency between 0 and 6 MHz and the clock can be stopped indefinitely without loss of data. A clock frequency on the order of 4 MHz is common with the use 3.58 MHz color burst TV crystals being popular because of the economic advantage of large scale production.

CYCLE TIME

The clock frequency deserves a certain amount of attention at this point. There are rather wide differences between the frequencies used in the clocks of different processors. They range from over 18 MHz for the 8080 to a few hundred KHz for some of the older PMOS units. However, in inter-machine comparisons the presence of a faster clock does not necessarily imply that the machine will run through a given cycle faster or that it will run a given program faster. A discussion on clock and cycle timing is therefore in order here.

Figure 9-2 shows a mechanism similar to the one employed in the 6802 to derive a two phase clock. It should be noted that this circuit might not exactly satisfy the requirements of the 6800 for which 02 should rise a little after 01 falls and fall a little before 01 rises. Most processors are relatively fussy about the details of rise and fall of the different phases, etc. These details are specific to the device itself and should be taken from the device literature. Most manufacturers provide a special clock chip for their devices. For the 6800, this is the MC6870 series. The circuit in Fig. 9-1 is intended for instructional purposes.

The easiest way to obtain a two-phase clock is to operate the clock oscillator at four times the desired processor cycle time and to divide the frequency by four. This is the mechanism used in the example. Inverters U1A and U1B perform a double inversion. Therefore, the feedback through the crystal is in-phase at the resonant frequency of the crystal. Capacitor Ct is used to tweak the crystal frequency to a standard value over a range of plus or minus a few KHz or tens of KHz. The RC net on the input of U1B might be

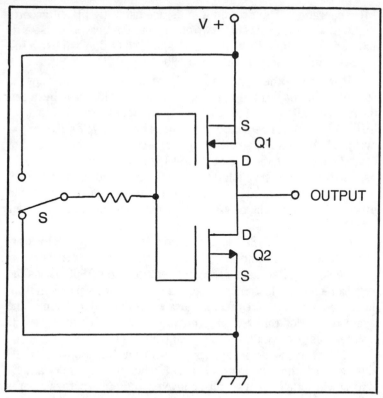

Fig. 9-1. The CMOS totem pole.

required for reliable starting. The two D type flip-flops, U2A and U2B, are arranged in a divide by four configuration ripple counter. Since the Q and Q output are out-of-phase, the basic requirements of the two-phase clock are met. However, attaining the correct delays between the various rises and falls might require some doing.

On the 6800, a clock frequency of 4 MHz is used. Therefore the machine cycle frequency is 1 MHz. As noted earlier, the shortest instructions on the 6800 require two clock cycles or two microseconds. Some of the longest, such as branching to interrupt and indexed mode addressing, can require up to 7 clock cycles or microseconds. When the 6800 chips are tested, they are run at 1.2 MHz first. Those that fail are rejected. They are then tested at 1.7 MHz and those that pass are tested at 2.5 MHz. The units which pass at 2.5 are labeled 68B00 and guaranteed for 2 MHz operation. Those that pass at 1.7 are labeled 68A00 and guaranteed for 1.5

MHz operation. The premium units are naturally priced accordingly. Also, it is obvious that two otherwise identical processors do have execution time related to clock speed. A 68B00 will execute a given program twice as fast as a 6800.

However, other processors have substantial differences. Suppose that you wanted to ensure a precise relationship between the rise and fall times of the phases. If the clock crystal is run at 20 MHz and 01 is arranged to be high for the first 10 cycles and low on cycles 11 through 20, and 02 were arranged to rise on the end of cycle 11 and fall on the rise of cycle 19, you would have a precisely established timing in which 02 rose 50 nanoseconds behind the fall of 01 and fell 50 nanoseconds before the rise of 01. On some processors, the timing requirements are such that three and four clocks are required.

The RCA CDP1802 is equipped with an on-board clock arrangement which requires only the addition of an external crystal (like the 6802). Because of the architecture of the 1802, it has the requirement for a large number divisor to provide various multiplexing signals which are of short duration compared to the machine cycle time. For this reason, the rate of the machine cycles is arranged as one-eighth of the clock frequency.

The machine normally operates in one of two states: SO during which time the instruction is fetched from memory and S1 during which time the instruction is executed. Each of these states occupy eight clock cycles. For a 4 MHz clock, this would require 2 microseconds for each state.

Because of the architecture of the 1802, it is possible to make most of the instructions operate in the sequence S0, S1: therefore requiring 4 microseconds. The long branch and long skip instructions, however, require three cycles and operate S0, S1, S1: thereby requiring 6 microseconds. Some of the 6800 instructions will operate faster and some of the instructions will operate slower than the 1802. However, this does not yet explain which machine will run a given program faster since the various commands have different *power* in which a given instruction can accomplish more than another. Furthermore, the question is raised whether, in a given program, the fast 6800 commands or the slow ones predominate. In the 1802, the fast instructions nearly always predominate.

MEMORY ADDRESSING

The 1802 employs an eight-bit address bus to address a 65,536-byte memory. The addresses must obviously be multip-

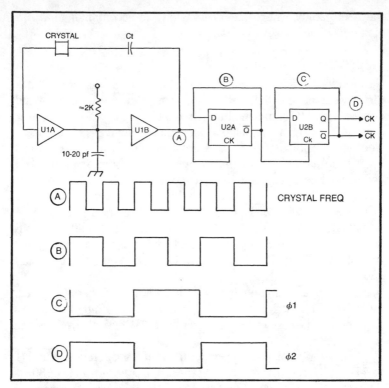

Fig. 9-2. A two phase clock circuit.

lexed onto the address bus. This is accomplished through the use of output lines TPA and TPB. If you assume that S0 begins on the fall of the clock, the data bus is turned off during the 0 cycle of the clock. At the same clock fall, the high order address byte for memory is asserted on the address bus. At the fall of the 0 clock cycle, TPA rises and latches this address into the high order address latch. At the fall of clock cycle 1, the low order memory address is asserted and TPB is high during the fall of clock cycle 7. Therefore, TPA and TPB serve to identify which byte of memory address is being presented. The high order bus must be somehow latched into the memory. The RCA CDP 1822 CMOS memories (256 × 4) are equipped to latch the memory address byte.

The 1802 is also equipped with two read/write flags called $\overline{MRD}$ and $\overline{MWR}$. These are active low for read and write respectively.

The latching, multiplexed address bus and the use of two read/write lines represents a significant hardware difference from the 6800 family where the de-glitching is accomplished with a single R/$\overline{\text{W}}$ and VMA plus 02.

INPUT/OUTPUT STRUCTURE

Another significant difference in hardware is that the 1802 is directly equipped with four I/O flags labeled $\overline{\text{EF1}}$ through $\overline{\text{EF4}}$ and a three-wide I/O command line labeled N0, N1 and N2. The latter are used to designate which of the seven I/O devices is addressed. The actual data comes to the processor via the bi-directional eight-wide data bus with the designation decoded from the I/O command lines. The single byte command 6N (where N = 1 through 7) will set these lines with the designated binary number. When decoded with $\overline{\text{MRD}}$, this can be used to latch output data in an output latch device. When the instruction 6N with N = 9 through F is used, the unit will accept inputs and write them into memory and the data register. This action will be discussed in more detail shortly.

The 1802 is also equipped with a one line data output latch labeled Q. This latch can be used for serial data output or to drive a flag, etc. It is set by the instruction $ 7B and cleared by the instruction $ 7A.

The 1802 is also equipped with two lines labeled $\overline{\text{DMA OUT}}$ and $\overline{\text{DMA IN}}$. It is in this area that the static operation of the 1802 is used to full advantage. When $\overline{\text{DMA IN}}$ is taken low, the machine stops and deposits the data asserted on the address line in the memory location listed in R(0). It also advances the contents of R(0) by 1. After a reset operation R(0) = 0. Therefore the combination of a reset followed by a series of $\overline{\text{DMA IN}}$ cycles can be used to load a program in memory starting at $0000. When the unit is placed in RUN, it will begin execution of the program starting at $0000.

Because of this static feature the 1802 can be operated without any ROM. This technique is used in the ELF II microcomputer which is one of the least expensive types offered. Using this technique along with a one-byte latching Hex keyboard and a two-digit LED display, an operating program can be entered sequentially. When the machine is set to RUN the program is executed. Compared to the dynamic processors, this static DMA technique is very powerful. DMA can be accomplished with a bare minimum of hardware.

Lines SC1 and SC0 are used to describe the current state of the machine to outside devices. The truth table is:

STATE	SC1	SC0
S0 - fetch	0	0
S1 - execute	0	I
S2 - DMA	I	0
S3 - Interrupt	I	I

These lines can be used to toggle DMA, etc.

The final line to be noted is the INTERRUPT line. It is used by outside devices to flag the request for an interrupt service cycle. This will be described in more detail later.

There are significant physical differences between the external operation of the 6800 and the 1802 which must be accounted for in the external hardware. Some of the physical features such as the reduced power consumption and the ability to operate without supply regulation are decisive factors in certain applications. Others such as the output device selection versus memory addressing of output have advantages and disadvantages. The ability to operate without ROM is an advantage mainly in the small single-board computer situation. Even there the greatest value is in reducing the cost.

Some other types of processors have made different tradeoffs on the address bus and the data bus and in the provision for multiple interrupts, etc. In most cases, the 6800 and the 1802 represent about the extremes of physical architecture among the general purpose chips.

INTERNAL STRUCTURE

By far, the largest differences in the architecture between the 1802 and the 6800 are in the internal organization. The construction of the 1802 is described as being register oriented, whereas the 6800 is a memory oriented machine. To understand the significance of this, refer to the diagram in Fig. 9-3. The columns on the left-hand margin are intended to represent the memory with the lowest addresses on the top and increasing addresses running downward. In about the center of the illustration is one of the most significant departures from the 6800 architecture. This is a block of 16 general purpose registers which are 16-bits wide. The usage of these registers represents the most significant difference in the operating scheme of the 1802 compared to the 6800.

Each of the registers represents two bytes which can be treated contiguously or separately. The registers are designated in the RCA COSMAC literature as R(0).1 and R(0).0 through R(F).1 and R(F).0. Suppose that register R(8) contained the address $ F1

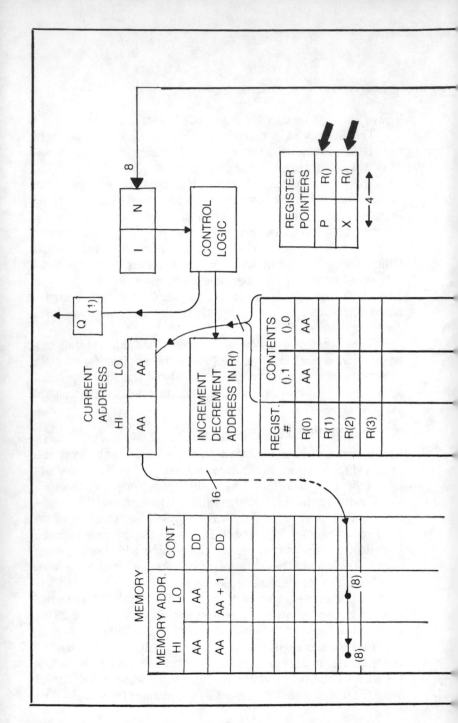

168

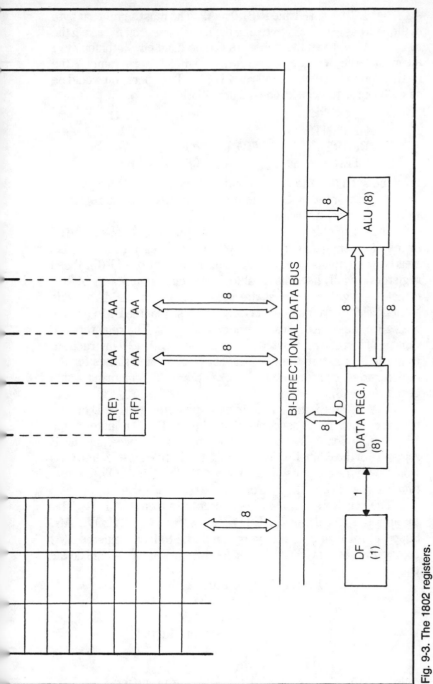

Fig. 9-3. The 1802 registers.

169

A3. Then R(3).1 = $F1 and R(3).0 = A3. The most significant byte of the address is in the .1 byte and the least significant byte is in the .0 byte. When I say the registers can be handled contiguously, I mean that they can be operated as a whole. For example, the instruction to increment register 4 is $14. The operation would be as follows for the conditions assumed below:

	R(4).1	R(4).0
CONTENTS		
BEFORE INSTRUCTION	00	FF
AFTER	0I	00

It can be seen that the carry required is automatically propagated from the low order byte to the high order byte and the registers were treated contiguously.

These registers can be used to assume the functions of the IX in the 6800 or the PC in the 6800; in which case they are also treated as contiguous registers. With the exception of R(0), these registers are fully interchangeable. The special significance of R(0) is that this register serves as the address register for DMA and it is automatically incremented on DMA cycles so that the DMA entries are written into successive memory addresses. The registers are capable of increment as noted and decrement with a 2N instruction. In the RCA notation the N in the above command stands for the register to be decremented. For example, a $23 command would decrement R(3).

The registers can be read in eight-bit bytes into the D or data register shown in the sequence that follows. The D register in the 1802 fulfills some of the same functions as the accA and accB registers of the 6800. For example the GET HIGH instruction (9N) would copy the contents of R(N).1 into D. The GET LOW instruction 8N would copy the contents of R(N).0 into D.

The registers can also be written into from the D register through the instructions: PUT HIGH; BN and PUT LOW; AN. Suppose, for example, that you would like to have register R(A) contain the address $ FCOO. The following sequence would do the trick:

COM	DATA	COMMENT
F8		ld imm. D
	FC	with $ FC
BA		Put high into R(A).1
F8		load imm. D
	00	with $00
AA		PUT LOW into register A

The registers can also be incremented with an instruction in which the register upon which the instruction is to performed is contained within the nibble in X. This instruction is $60.

The registers located along the right hand edge have a special function in the 1802 which is unlike anything in the 6800 or 6802. These four-bit or nibble-registers serve the following functions:

P Register

The nibble contained within the P register is normally the program counter designator. For example if P = 6 then R(6) is designated as the program counter and the current address in the R(6) is the address being read for the current program step. After each cycle, R(6) would be incremented for the address of the next instruction.

X Register

The nibble contained within the X register is the data destination register designator. For the increment via X instruction $60 mentioned above, if X = 7 it will be R(7) which is incremented. Suppose that X = 5 and R(5) = $ A431. If you had the program instruction $F0, which means load via X, the machine would go to address $A431, read the contents and write them over the bi-directional data bus to D: the data register. With the same contents in X and R(5), the command to store via X and decrement would have written the contents of D into $A431 and would have changed the contents of R(5) = $A430.

The contents of the X register can be established by the command SET X, which is EN. For example, to load $5 into X, the instruction would be $E5.

The P register can be similarly loaded by the command to SET P, which is DN. If the third register is designated as the program counter, the instruction would be $D3.

I Register and N Register

The I and N registers simply contain the most significant and the least significant byte of the current command. For example for the command $ D3: I = $D and N = $3. The command is fetched from program memory and latched into I and N. It is then interpreted in the control logic and executed.

The Q latch is described earlier with the instructions to set and clear Q. Note, however, that the current state of Q can be made the subject of a long or short branch or skip. This can be used in a toggle operation. On the first time through, a loop Q is tested for set; if not it is set. On the second time, the test finds it set and does the conditional operation. It also clears Q, etc.

This type of toggle instruction set is very useful with the 1802 and with a variety of other processors. Suppose that you want to operate a keyboard in a noisy environment and the keyboard itself is prone to bounce and not settle for something like 14 microseconds. In order to get a reliable entry from the keyboard, and only one entry, you could use the routine shown on the general flow chart in Fig. 9-4.

It is assumed that the processor enters the keyboard routine from other program such as display drive, etc. If it finds no key closed, it simply jumps out to node 4 and resumes other program execution. On the other hand, if a key is found closed, the processor sets the flag, stores the key identity and branches to a 20 microsecond delay and then back to node 1. On the second time through the machine will re-test the keyboard. If the key is still closed and the flag is set, it will test to determine whether it is still the same key. If so, it looks up the value of the key and writes it into the designated data memory. It also clears the flag.

Following this, it falls through node 2 into a routine which waits for the keyboard to open. The flag is again used to assure that two readings spaced by 20 microseconds agree upon the result. Only if two successive readings spaced 20 microseconds apart agree upon the key identity will the machine accept data, and only if 2 readings spaced 20 microseconds apart agree that all keys are open will the machine arrive at the conclusion that is safe to proceed to another program and then to another keyboard scan.

The program usage of the flag not only assures with very high probability that the right entry will be recorded, but it also ensures that one and only one entry will be made for each keystroke—even with a slow and noisy keyboard. Note that if the operator were to depress one key and then depress a second key while the first is depressed, (proceeding then to depress third and fourth keys, etc.) only the first would be entered unless the second was depressed within 20 microseconds of the first depression. The machine would be locked in the node 2 loop while the operator was fooling with the machine. This routine is even relatively free of errors when two keys are deliberately struck at the same time, since a human being can only occasionally make the two close within 20 microseconds of each other.

The Q output on the 1802 can also be used for serial data transmission. With the right software delays and lookup table, this

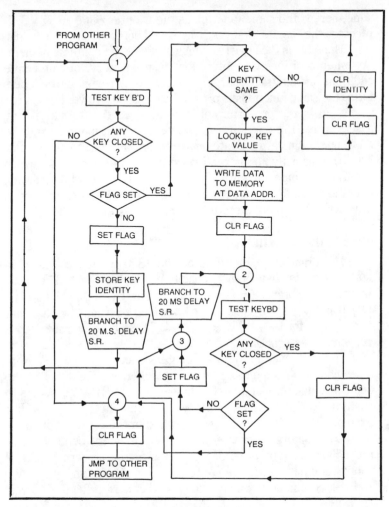

Fig. 9-4. Flag usage in a keyboard debounce routine.

line can be programmed to send Morse code, etc. On the ELF II, a single LED is hung on the Q line and is the only output indication supplied on this bottom-of-the-line development kit.

THE DATA REGISTER: ALU AND DF

The DATA (or D) register serves much the same function that the accA and accB registers serve on the 6800. When data is read from memory, it is read into D. Instructions like "add the contents of memory" add into D, etc. The DF register, which is only one bit

173

wide, serves the same function as the C of the 6800 HINZVC. It receives the results of shifts, carries and borrows on subtraction.

The ALU is the register which receives the contents of memory when additions or subtractions from memory, or immediate additions and subtractions, are performed. A register which performs the same functions is present in the 6800. However, it is not discussed in the programming manual since the manual simply assumes that the operation is done direct from memory and the ALU operation is a private and internal housekeeping matter. There are actually no instructions at the operators disposal which use the ALU independently. It is simply used to hold data during operations such as: add, subtract OR EXCLUSIVE OR, AND.—all of which are actually directed to the D register.

BRANCHING CONDITIONS

The branching conditions on the 1800 are more limited in some respects than branch conditions for the 6800. There are instruction to branch for $D = 0$ and $D = I$ for $DF = 0$ and $DF = I$ for $Q = 0$ and $Q = I$. There are also branch on zero and branch on one instructions for $EF-1$ through $EF-4$. These branches are used to respond to external inputs.

The difference in the branching instructions has both advantages and disadvantages. The rather richer branching set of the 6800 base upon the status of individual bits in HINZVC seems to make the 6800 much less clumsy for arithmetic operations. For example, if you wish to determine whether the contents of one of the accumulators is greater than some memory content or an immediate constant, the COMPARE instruction performs a virtual subtraction but leaves the contents of both the memory location and the accumulator unaltered. The result is reflected only in HINZVC.

By comparison, the same operation in the 1802 requires an actual subtraction and the contents of D and DF are subject to change. If these contents are to be used again, they must first be written to memory and the subtraction then performed. To me, this method is quite a bit more clumsy.

On the other hand, the EF1 through EF4 instructions are useful when sensing the state of individual input lines. Where there are four individual inputs to be read, the single instruction is much simpler and shorter than the 6800 routine which requires a read of PIA into the accumulator and a masking operation of the accumulator before the comparison can be made. However, if the inputs are to be read contiguously, that is if EF1 through EF4 = OIIO has a different meaning from either OIOO or OOIO, then the 1802 structure is very clumsy.

It is important to reiterate that what one programmer finds clumsy, another programmer might find very straightforward and clear. The requirement to write a multiple node program to decode EF1 through EF4 seems a bit clumsy. Most of the control applications I have encountered have had this type of decoding requirement. Where the meanings of EF1 through EF4 are independent of one another and can be treated as such, the single instruction format is both faster and requires less memory lines to program.

The 1802 has LONG BRANCHES and LONG SKIPS and SHORT BRANCHES and SHORT SKIPS. The short instructions are 2-byte and the long instructions are 3-byte. For example, a short skip skips a single byte and a long skip skips 2 bytes. The long branches only reset the lower byte of R(P), leaving the higher byte unaltered. Consider for example:

$$P = \$ A$$
$$R(A) = \$ 013F \qquad M(R(A)) = \$97$$

Then the instruction SHORT BRANCH IF DF NOT ZERO (32) when executed will yield if true: $R(A) = \$ 0197$ and program execution will continue from address $0197. If the test is false: $R(A) = \$0141$ and the program will continue in sequence, after skipping the contents of $0140. In either case, the contents of P and the memory are unaltered.

For the long branch instructions, two steps are skipped if false and both the upper and lower bytes of R(P) are loaded if true. The first byte goes into R(P). 1 and the second byte goes into R(P).0 The long branch instructions more or less correspond to the EXTENDED ADDRESSING MODE of the 6800. To show this, consider that both machines are performing some operation and you would like to have them jump to $ FC05 if the result is zero. See Fig. 9-5.

This shows one of the advantages of the 1802 instruction set. The 6800 has no capability for conditional jumps in extended addressing. All conditional jumps are relative addressed. Therefore, if a jump of more than 127 steps is required, the negative test must be used to skip over an unconditional jump. By comparison, the 1802 can long branch to any address in memory on the basis of a more restricted set of conditions. This saves 2 bytes of program. It should be noted that if the jump were less than 128 bytes, the 6800 could have come out ahead with the instruction $ 27, XX, where XX would be the offset.

The 6800 family has no direct counterpart for the short branch. Short skip instructions are really still DIRECT ADDRESSING instructions except that they are confined to addresses with the same high order byte. For example, all addresses $ AA xx are on Page $ AA.

The 1802 has no mechanism for relative or direct addressing. This has an effect upon *program portability*, which has come to be viewed as a desirable attribute. Suppose that you were to write a subroutine which contained only relative and direct addresses. If you place that subroutine elsewhere within memory, you could simply list it verbatim in the new address location and you would only have to change the call addresses which took you into the subroutine.

Conversely, since the 1802 features only *absolute addressing*, you would not be able to move a subroutine at will, since all of the addresses within the program would have to be rewritten. An exception to this exists. If all of the addresses within the subroutine are short branches or short skips and the program is moved an integral number of pages, the system would work. For example, a subroutine starting at $ 0134 could be transported to $0234 or $ AA34, etc. This can be a fairly stiff restriction on a system with limited read/write memory, since the machine might have no hardware memory on more than one page.

SUBROUTINES

Another significant difference in the 1802 is the manner in which subroutines are handled. I noted that the 6800 upon receipt of a call to a subroutine saved PC on the stack and incremented SP and then jumped to the subroutine. At the end of the subroutine, PC would be retrieved from the stack and SP set back. In the 1802, the mechanism is quite different.

Suppose that at the point in the program where the subroutine is required, $P = 3$ and that you have written the address for the subroutine into R(B). Instruction $ DB will establish register B as the new program counter by placing $P = B$ and the machine will resume operation in the subroutine. At the end of the subroutine, the instruction $ D3 will place 3 into P and the operation will return to the register 3 program counter. This works just like the branch to subroutine on the 6800. The first time through, however, it leaves the subroutine register B incremented to read the step after

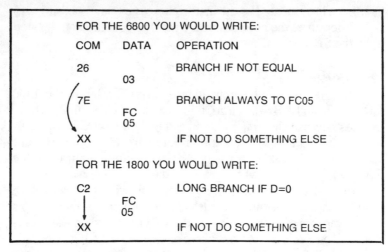

```
FOR THE 6800 YOU WOULD WRITE:

COM     DATA     OPERATION

26               BRANCH IF NOT EQUAL
        03

7E               BRANCH ALWAYS TO FC05
        FC
        05
XX               IF NOT DO SOMETHING ELSE

FOR THE 1800 YOU WOULD WRITE:

C2               LONG BRANCH IF D=0
        FC
        05
XX               IF NOT DO SOMETHING ELSE
```

Fig. 9-5. Extend addressing mode.

the last subroutine step. Before the subroutine can be reused it is necessary to reload register B. A little neater technique can be found for this.

Suppose that the subroutine begins at $FC10. Then you could write:

ADDR	COM	DATA	OPERATION
$ FC10	D3		set P = 3
11	xx		
	xx		
	xx		subroutine code
	•		
	•		
	•		
$ FCAA	30		shortbranch to $FC10
FCAB	10		

The entry address to the subroutine is FC11. This would have to be the contents of register B when the $DB call to enter the subroutine came up. Suppose that this were the case initially and you entered at $FC11. The machine would run through the subroutine until it reached the short branch instruction at $FCAA. Since the machine is operating in R(B), this would reset R(B) = $ FC10. The instruction at $FC10 would set P = 3, thereby transferring control back to R(3). At the same time it increments R(B) to $ FC11 and the subroutine is ready to run again. R(3) would of course have been incremented by the instruction to go to the subroutine ($ DB). Therefore, the program would resume operation on the step after the $DB call.

INPUT/OUTPUT DEVICES

A variety of input/output devices are provided in the 1800 COSMAC family. By and large, it is advantageous to employ these devices because they offer the advantages of CMOS power efficiency. In addition to this, the architecture of the devices are tailored to make use of some of the architectural features of the 1802 processor, such as the address data timing signals, etc.

In particular, the CDP 1852 is an 8-bit wide I/O chip which features three state outputs. Each of the eight output lines on this chip is capable of driving one standard TTL load when the chip is operated on 5V. It will either source or sink 1.6 mA when operating on 5V and 3.6 mA when operating on 10V. In general, you would not use current-hungry TTL when a CMOS processor had been selected for power economy. The 1852 draws only 100 microampere when it is in the quiescent state.

There are some significant architectural differences between the 6821 PIA and the CDP 1852. From the earlier discussion of the 6821, you will remember that there was an elaborate addressing procedure which allowed the 6821 to configure any individual line as an input or an output. Not so on the 1852. On this device the entire bank of eight lines is programmed as output by taking the MODE line to V+ and configured to input by taking MODE = 0. If the MODE connection is hardwired, the 1852 chips will of course be permanently set as inputs or outputs and cannot be made to change from input to output under program control. However, it should be noted that if MODE is connected to Q on the 1800, the 1852 can be reconfigured to either input or output under program control.

In cases where more than 8 inputs and 8 outputs are required, RCA also offers the CDP 1853 N-bit decoder which accepts TPA and TPB and decodes N0 through N3 to eight output lines numbered 0 through 7. With this chip, up to 14 I/0 devices can be selected under program control.

The 1852 has another pair of useful controls. When it is used with MODE line and the input configuration, the CLOCK line is used to strobe data into the register when CK = 0. The falling edge of $\overline{CK}$ sets the $\overline{SR}$ low on the 1852. This $\overline{SR}$ line is useful in signaling to the processor that the external device is requesting service. If $\overline{SR}$ is connected to $\overline{INTR}$ to provide an interrupt operation or to $\overline{DMA}$ to provide a direct memory access, both of these operations will stop the processor in flight and obtain immediate service.

On the other hand, if $\overline{SR}$ is connected to one of the EF1 through EF4 lines, the processor can read the interrupt when it gets around to that point in the program. It was noted earlier that the condition of the EF lines could be used for one of the conditional jumps or skips.

$\overline{SR}$ stays low until the chip is selected (CS2 = CS1 = I) and is cleared on the falling edge of (CS2 = CS1 = 0). This action can be used for a *handshake* operation with the external device. For DMA, after the required input is latched onto the eight input lines of the 1852 by the keyboard or external reader, the external device pulls CK low thus latching the data into the 1852.

When $\overline{SR}$ pulls $\overline{DMA}$ low, the processor goes into the DMA mode and writes the Byte into the memory address designated by R(0) and subsequently increments the address in R(0). If the DMA directly follows a RESET, the address in R(0) = \$ 0000. After the byte, the CS1 and CS2 clears $\overline{SR}$, which goes to I. The external keyboard device senses this and clears its own latch for the next data byte—thus using this line to signal the end of one cycle and the readiness for a new cycle.

When MODE = I, the 1852 is in the output configuration and the operation of CS1 is inverted and becomes $\overline{CS1}$ while the operation of $\overline{SR}$ is also inverted. If a 6N (N = 1 through 7) instruction is given to the processor, the memory byte addressed by R(X) is placed on the data bus and remains on the data bus before TPB goes high until after TPB returns low. If TPB is used for the 1852 CK, the data on the data lines is latched through the 1852 on the rise of TPB and SR is set to I.

If only one output chip is used $\overline{CS1}$ can be tied low and CS2 can be driven by the N0 or some other N line. The chip is deselected by taking CS2 low. This clears SR and places the chip in the high impedance state. It should be noted that many control applications require the latching action on the output lines rather than a simple strobe of data. Therefore, if the data word is required to stay on the output lines, it is necessary not to deselect CS2.

Provision for a latched output which might be required to hold a relay closed, etc. will generally require the use of additional hardware.

In a comparison between the 6821 and the 1852, it can generally be said that the self-latching and the ability to reconfigure the 6821 makes the 6821 more flexible. The larger number of programmable I/0 lines of the 6821 also serve to make it a far more powerful machine, serving functions which might require two or three 1852s, depending upon the I/0 mix. On the other hand, the 6821 requires the initialization routine which is not required by the 1852. Also, there sometimes can be a slight advantage in output execution time for the 1852, since it writes output direct from the memory location addressed by the R(X). By comparison, the same operation in the 6800 family requires a read of memory into accumulator and a write of accumulator to the PIA. For battery powered equipment, of course, the overwhelming advantage of extreme low quiescent drain goes to the 1852.

Like the processors themselves, the two I/0 parallel chips represent about the extremes in parallel I/0 architecture. The I/0 chips developed for other processor families generally will lie somewhere between these two in features and architecture.

PROMS

RCA does not offer any CMOS PROMs to go with the 1800 family. They do offer a variety of mask programmed ROM and a variety of Read/Write memorys. For PROM, you must go to the Harris 6611, which is organized 256 × 4. This is a CMOS blown fuse PROM which can be programmed only once. Because of the 4-bit width, at least two of the devices are required to generate the 8-bit control words needed by the 1802. The program for a typical application must be developed on another machine or by using read/write memory. Only after the program is written and debugged would it be blown into the PROM.

While the direct loading of program from the keyboard via DMA is possible on the 1802, this is a very clumsy mechanism for anything but a small bottom-end hobby device. The reason is that a program load starts always at addresses $0000 and works up one step at a time. By itself, DMA is not capable of showing any given step in memory or capable of editing any given step by any mechanism except walking through memory one step at a time until the desired step is attained. A small software program can be written which will serve these functions. However, that is a bit clumsy too. There are a considerable number of advantages to having an operating system in ROM or PROM so that the device will service the keyboard and display and permit any memory location to be loaded and read.

In control applications, the use of operating systems resident in ROM or PROM is just about manditory since you could not expect the baker to laboriously load the operating program via DMA every time the oven shut down. A TV game which required the operator to load the program every time would also not sell very well. RCA offers several pre-programmed ROM's which will perform the preload function and service keyboards for their development kits.

ARCHITECTURE SUMMARY

In this Chapter I have reviewed the contrasts between the 6800 memory oriented architecture and the register oriented architecture of the 1802 with an eye for the strengths and weaknesses of each. In the latest generation of processors from Motorola, a bow has been given in the direction of the register oriented architecture. The Motorola 6809 retains the technique of addressing all devices as memory, while it has added registers and enhanced the register manipulation instructions in an architecture possessing many of the features of the 1802. These changes, along with the ability to concatenate the accumulators for internal 16-bit operations have served to make the 6809 at least an order of magnitude more powerful than the 6800.

The Motorola 68000 has an architecture which looks even more like the 1802 in the large number of registers and the techniques for data handling. This 16-bit machine is capable of internal 32-bit operations. Through the use of relative addressing, it is possible to write fully transportable code. Furthermore, the width of the registers has made it possible to write certain instuctions in which the source, the operation and the destination of the operation are contained in the single instruction. These features have made the 68000 at least two and perhaps three orders of magnitude more powerful than the 6800.

It will remain to be demonstrated whether the 16-bit machines will eventually displace the 8-bit machines in most control applications. The wider memory required for these machines will tend to make them more expensive than the 8-bit machines at any stage in the price-learning cycle. In addition, the capabilities of the advanced 8-bit machines are more than adequate for most control applications. This tends to make the 16-bit machines seem like a lot of overkill for control applications which might be handled by 4- or 8-bit machines. In my opinion, the 16-bit machines are far more likely to take over the minicomputer general purpose market, whereas the single-chip micros in 4- and 8-bit widths will take over the dedicated control slots.

10 Interfacing to the Analog World

The real world in which we live is basically an analog sort of affair. If we rise in the morning to see the sun come up, it gradually sneaks up over the horizon a little bit at a time and the world gets gradually brighter. The sunshine makes it start to warm up a little bit at a time, reaching its greatest brightness at noon. The temperature follows more slowly and the peak temperature is usually not reached until well after noon. The same thing can be said about most of the things that human beings do and which the processor or microcomputer might be used to automate. For most of us, the operation of the foot throttle on an automobile is an analog or continuous thing. We do not slam the throttle to the floor when we want to start moving and do not floor the brakes when we wish to slow down.

However, the processor and the PIA are binary type devices. The individual input and output lines are simple on and off affairs. Therefore, a smooth control requires some technique to moderate between these extreme binary conditions. In this chapter, I will spend some time considering some of the ways in which a binary on/off type of machine like a binary microcomputer can be made to yield smooth variations in input and output functions.

The subject of controls is a whole topic unto itself and there are a great many things which must be considered which lie outside of the microcomputer box in most control applications. For a more specific treatment of these considerations refer to TAB book No. 929 *Solid-State Motor Controls*.

ON/OFF SMOOTHING

There are a great many automatic controls in common usage which are actually binary on/off affairs but which give a smooth finished performance. For example, the thermostat on your home heating furnace or on an electric baseboard heater is a straight on/off switch which generally uses a bi-metalic element. When the room temperature falls below the setpoint temperature, the contacts close and the furnace starting sequence begins or the current begins to flow through the baseboard heater. Because the room has a certain amount of thermal inertia, it does not heat immediately. The room gradually comes up to temperature. When the temperature rises through some slightly higher level, the thermostat opens its contacts and the heating process stops. The thermal inertia is used as a smoothing element in the system and the temperature of the room fluctuates only a few degrees about the point set in the thermostat. The thermostat can be made to turn on and off at lower and higher temperatures by turning the dial one degree or less at a time so that actual analog control is obtained of the room temperature even though the decision to turn the heat on is purely binary. This sort of arrangement is generally termed a duty factor control. When the weather is cold and the house is loosing heat more rapidly, the furnace stays on a little longer and it turns on a little sooner. Conversely, when the house is warmer, the furnace turns off more quickly and stays off longer.

In electrical controls performed with electronic devices, it has been common in the past to vary the average flow using just one of these mechanisms. In *pulse width modulation*, the repetition rate of the ON periods is held constant and the period that the power is

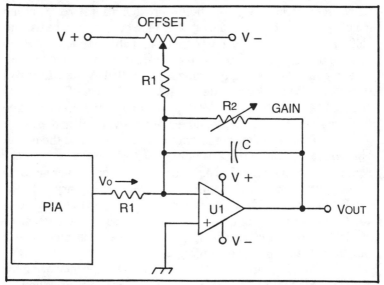

Fig. 10-1. The duty-factor analog-to-digital converter.

turned on is varied. In *pulse rate modulation*, a constant ON time is maintained and the rate of pulsing or the time between pulses is varied. In both cases, the *duty factor*, or the percentage of time during which the current is turned on, is the variable. In both cases, it is possible to vary the average power between zero (never on) to 100 percent (always on).

There are a number of techniques for introducing the equivalent of electrical inertia into a circuit. The circuit shown in Fig. 10-1 illustrates one of these. In this circuit, the op-amp U1 is shown connected to one of the output terminals of a PIA or some processor driven output. The op-amp is equipped with a capacitor in the feedback loop which reduces its gain toward zero for frequencies where the capacitor reactance is low compared to R1. If the offset voltage were zero and the PIA output were latched high, the output voltage of the op-amp would swing to within 95 percent of $-V_o$ in 3(R2 × C) seconds (where R2 is in ohms and C in farads). The value of (R2 × C) is referred to as the time constant of the circuit. In one time constant, after a step change in the input, the circuit will climb to −63 percent of the step value. In five time constants, it will settle to within −1 percent of the value.

With the circuit as shown in Fig. 10-1 with no offset voltage, clamping the PIA output low will take the output of the op-amp close to zero at the same rate.

It is often not convenient to have the analog output vary between two arbitrary points below ground. Therefore, a second control, the offset, is introduced. The offset control can be used to shift the quiescent point of the output either above or below zero so that the output of the op-amp can be made to swing above ground. The amplitude of the output swing is controlled by the DC gain of the op-amp, which is controlled by R2/R1. If you set R2 = 2.2 R1 and the PIA is operating on 5 Volts, the output of the op-amp can be made to swing between −5V and +5V or between 0V and +10V.

The above relationship is only approximate since the output high voltage and the output low voltage of the PIA is an *uncontrolled parameter* which is specified only to relatively loose tolerances. In order to make the relationship accurate, it is necessary to tweak the R2 and offset values. The device will also tend to be temperature sensitive and sensitive to changes in the supply voltage, since the PIA is not particularly designed to provide a constant value of output high and output low voltage.

The circuit in Fig. 10-2 shows a technique for improving the stability of the D/A by stabilizing the reference voltage. When the

184

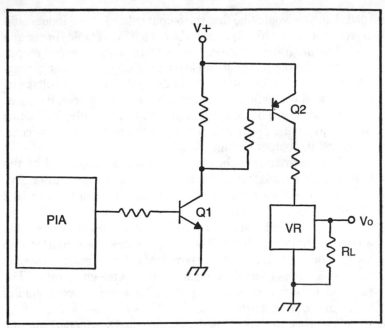

Fig. 10-2. Reference voltage stabilization.

PIA output goes high, transistor Q1 turns on thereby turning off
Q2. With the supply shut off to the VR, the output should go to
within a millivolt or two of zero. R1 is added to ensure this. When
the output of the PIA goes low, Q1, cuts off—thereby switching Q2
on in a saturated condition. In this case, the output to the A/D is
controlled by the precision voltage regulator VR. There are a
variety of types of these regulators which are accurately stabilized
for variation with temperature and supply voltage. The reason for
using the two transistors is that it is usually desireable to have V+
considerably higher than the supply voltage V_{cc} fot the computer
itself. Typically, $V_{cc} = +5V$ for an NMOS processor and PIA;
whereas a standard output swing for a D/A is 0 to +10V or −5 to
+5V. To accomplish the 0 to +10V swing, it is usually necessary
that V+ = 15V, since the typical op-amp will not swing closer than
a volta or two to the supply rails. This applys also to the negative
rail. Therefore, it is usually necessary to have a minus supply if the
op-amp is to go to zero volts output. If Q1 were eliminated, the
output high from the PIA would not rise high enough to cut off Q2.

    The software control of a D/A of this sort requires a little
thought. If a constant width output pulse were used for the ON

condition, you would find that the output related to the input could be very nonlinear. Ideally, the output of a PIA is stable, linear and fast. The programmer should be able to write a given output command into the program and know precisely the output voltage which will result. The output should also stabilize to that voltage as fast as possible. While a nonlinear relationship between the input and the output can be compensated by a lookup table, it is much handier to have a linear relationship between the program command and the output voltage.

This linear relationship is more easily accomplished by the pulse width modulation technique at a constant repetition frequency. The software routine shown in the flow chart in Fig. 10-2 illustrates such a program.

In Fig. 10-3 it is assumed that the object is to synthesize some arbitrary output waveform. The voltage samples are written into the memory in the form of successive table entries and the output is to be as nearly as possible a linear function of the entry value. The program is shown to run on a 6800. However, a very similar program could be written for an 1802.

The program starts at node 5 where the IX is loaded with the address of the first voltage sample. The output is loaded LO, the first sample is obtained from memory and the program reaches node 2. The loop at node 2 requires 6 microseconds for a circuit. Therefore, the D/A will be turned on for a period equal to the memory contents times 6 microseconds. When this is completed, accB is loaded with $ C8 = 200 and the contents of the memory is subtracted from this. If the intervening steps took no time, the program would be perfectly linear. However, it does take some time to do the second lookup and subtraction. After this is accomplished, the A/D input is tuned off by setting the output high. The second 6 microseconds loop is run at node three for 200-N cycles. When complete, the IX is updated and tested for completion of the table. If the table is not complete, execution returns to node 1.

The extra program steps add 12 microseconds to the ON time. Therefore, three no-ops and the test are used to balance the manipulation delays. If N=100 the D/A would be on for 112 microseconds and off for 112 microseconds. The duty factor would be exactly 50 percent giving a 5V output for the D/A. However, if N=1 it would still take 18 microseconds for the machine to find that it was supposed to shut off. The duty factor would be: $18/(200 \times 6) + 24 = 0.015$ duty factor. The linear value would have been 1/199

= 0.005. Therefore, the device and the program show a 1 percent deviation at the extreme ends of the scale. Note also that N=0 would produce a surprising result. Upon entering node 2, the decrement of 0 would load accB with $ FF. Instead of the voltage being low or zero it would be very high.

With this program, if there were no other errors in the D/A, the *resolution* of the D/A is determined by the smallest step. For

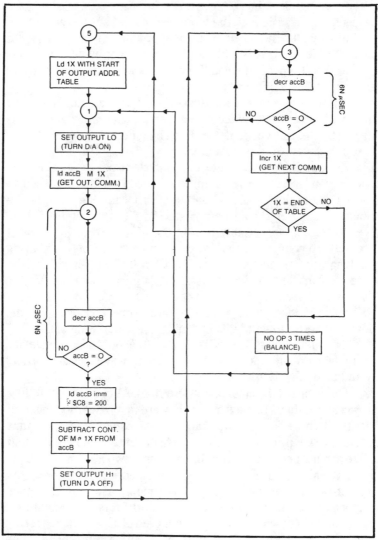

Fig. 10-3. Duty factor A/D program.

example, if N=99 you would have:

$$\frac{(99 \times 6) + 12}{(200 \times 6) + 24} = 49.5\%$$

The resolution is approximately a half percent; whereas the accuracy or linearity would be 1 percent. The terms *accuracy* and *linearity* are not synonymous. Suppose that the offset adjustment is in error so that all of the voltages on the scale are 0.2 volts high or 2 percent. At the scale end, the worst error would be the sum of the nonlinearity plus the offset error or approximately $1.5 + 2 = 3.5$ percent. The accuracy would then be 3.5 percent, while the linearity would be 1.5 percent since the voltages would be related to one another by the nonlinearity function as before.

These concepts are introduced in this example, however, they relate to all D/A devices. In general, the accuracy the linearity and the resolution are determined by different things and must therefore be separately specified.

For this D/A, a complete on/off cycle is set to require 1224 microseconds. Therefore, a limit is placed on the highest frequency of the device. As a matter of fact, the operation of the sluggish amplifier should be adjusted so that the output voltage does not droop appreciably during the off period of the longest cycle. If the voltage droop is to be no more than 5 percent during the longest off period, then $t/(R2 \times C) = 0.0513$. Therefore, the time constant of the device must be 1224 microseconds 0.0513 = 23.9×10^{-3} sec.

Since it takes approximately three time constants for the device to settle to within 5 percent, the settling time of the D/A would be specified as 71.6 milliseconds. At about 14 Hz, the device would be hard put to keep up with a square wave and the corners would be distinctly rounded.

This is one of the chief objections to a D/A of this type. If they are accurate, they are slow and if they are fast resolution must be sacrificed. If the base number had been 50 instead of 200, the unit would have been nearly four times as fast, but the resolution would fall to about 2 percent and the linearity error would climb to about 5.6 percent. Except for very low performance applications, this type of D/A converter is not very commonly used. Much higher performance can be obtained from other types, including monolithic single-chip designs which are relatively inexpensive. The example has been dealt with in detail as a mechanism for illustrating some of the performance tradeoffs and the sources of error common to D/A devices.

THE HIGH SPEED D/A

Whereas the previous example showed a D/A in which simplicity of hardware was optimized at the expense of software complexity, the high speed D/A is an example of a case where simplicity of software has been optimized at the expense of some hardware complexity. A few years ago, the hardware complexity was physically evident because a hardwired D/A could compromise one or more whole circuit cards. However, this D/A function is so commonly required that a number of the device manufacturers set themselves to the task of developing fast and accurate D/As which were easy to use in microcomputer applications.

To begin with, it should be obvious that the D/A performance could be immensely speeded up if the output voltage command were given in a parallel word instead of a time sequenced modulation. Figure 10-4 shows a circuit in a very simple form. In the circuit, the op-amp U1 is shown connected to outputs PA0 through PA3 of the PIA. The connections are made through a series of graded resistors such that PA3 is able to draw a current eight times as great as PA0. The action of the op-amp is such that the amplifier can very neatly drive the current at the inverting or summing gate to zero. In effect, the summing gate is at ground potential, held there by the amplifying action of the op-amp. In order to do this, the output voltage of the op-amp must rise to a level that forces a current through R3, which is equal and opposite to the sum of the currents being drawn from the PIA.

There are several things apparent with this setup. First of all, a command to latch a given output voltage onto U1 requires only a single write to the PIA. If you assume that U1 is infinitely fast and that there are no stray capacitances, then the command to a given voltage requires a load of the accumulator with the desired constant and a write to the PIA which takes only 10 or so microseconds. Since the PIA latches, that output voltage will be held until the next change and the processor is free to tend to another program.

If the PIA output high is 4.5 V and you want to limit the output current to 0.5 mA you would have to set R=9K ohm. This would mean that 8R= 72K ohm. If C stray were equal 20×10^{-12}F (20 pf) the RC constant would be 1.44 microseconds and it would take the unit about 4.3 microseconds to settle to within 5 percent. For the

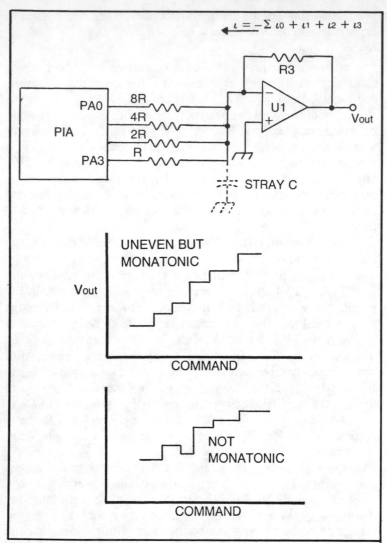

Fig. 10-4. A parallel addressed D/A Converter.

low resolution unit which can assume only 16 different levels (6.7 percent), the processor speed is still the controlling influence. However, an attempt to improve the resolution by adding a 16R and 32R input would result in a considerable slowing of the response time of the combination as a whole.

The outputs of the PIA are not sufficiently stable to support such an increased resolution. The same comments about stabilization of the outputs apply here as in the duty factor D/A. However, here it must be noted that every input must be stabilized. Suppose for the moment that the inputs are perfectly stabilized for voltage, but that the resistors have a 5 percent tolerance which is reflected in the current draw. The following conditions could be obtained:

PA	i nom	i actual
0	0.0626 mA	0.062 mA
1	0.125	0.119
2	0.250	0.238
3	0.500	0.525

It can be seen that the errors were assigned on the low side to PA0 through PA2 and high for PA3. If the PIA output word is $X7 the current would be 0.417 mA. A change in the output command to $X8 would raise the current to 0.525 mA, which is larger than one step bigger than $X7. The actual difference between the two is proportional to 0.108. This yields an output/input relationship which is uneven but monatonic. The errors can also build up in such a way that the output actually reverses at such a transition. In this case the device is said to be not *monatonic*. In order to guarantee monatanicity, the errors in all of the steps have to be less than one-half of the least significant step. If the most significant step gets to be much larger than 8 times the least significant step, this becomes difficult to do. This type of device is therefore usually limited to only eight steps in a group. For higher resolutions, other techniques are generally used. Another source of error in this sort

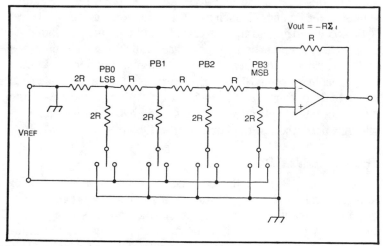

Fig. 10-5. The R-2R A/D converter.

of D/A stems from the fact that the output currents differ very widely from another. This makes it very difficult to regulate and compensate for the source drop since the most significant source might be supplying a milliampere and the least significant source might be supplying only microamperes.

Figure 10-5 shows another approach to the D/A involving an R, 2R ladder. The unit is shown with mechanical double-throw single-pole switches. However, the switching function can be implemented electronically. With the switch swingers in the left-hand position, the current from the particular mesh is shunted around the op-amp input and with the swingers in the right-hand position the mesh is on. If all bits except the most significant bit are off or grounded, the output voltage is $(-T/2R)$ times V ref. If only PB2 is on the output, voltage is one-fourth of V ref., etc. The R-2R network is popular since it is necessary only to use two resistance sizes with a 2:1 size ratio. For monolithic or deposited resistors, it is relatively easy to make the values track with temperature under these circumstances.

There are a variety of other techniques, many of which are proprietary to a given manufacturer, which stabilize the D/A. Note, for example, that each of the switches in the R-2R network carries a different current. In some of the monolithic converters, the emitter area of the switches is adjusted to be proportional to the current.

D/A SUMMARY

The design of a fast and accurate D/A converter is a rather sophisticated business if such items as temperature sensitivity are to be accounted for and any significant resolution is to be obtained. Monolithic D/A units selling for $4 are available in the 6-bit range and 8-bit units guaranteed over a commercial temperature range are available for about $15. At these prices, it does not make such sense to try to cobble up a homebrew D/A. For the most part, the microprocessor application will be served better with a commercial unit purchased to the correct specifications.

THE A/D CONVERTER

The other side of the coin is the conversion from analog voltages and currents to digital units so that the processor can accept analog outputs from various thermometers, strain gauges, etc. One of the more common uses for D/A converters is in the construction of A/D converters. Figure 10-6 shows a PIA, a D/A

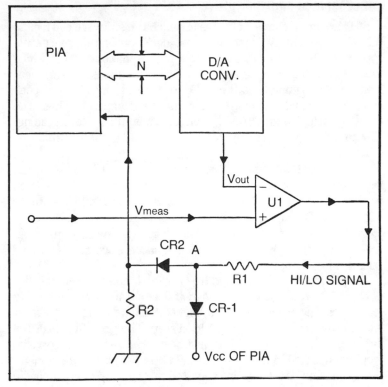

Fig. 10-6. An A/D Converter.

converter and a comparator U1. If the voltage to be measured exceeds the current setting of the PIA and D/A output voltage, the output of the comparator goes high. This can be sensed by the processor by a read of the PIA with perhaps a mask operation required to single out the comparator bit. When the voltage to be measured is less than the D/A output, the output of the comparator goes low.

The comparator can be especially fabricated unit in which the output is clamped within TTL levels or it can be some simple op-amp such as a microprocessor 741 operated without feedback. In the latter case, however, it is necessary to arrange clamping so that the PIA input will not be exposed to voltages higher than Vcc or lower than ground. The network consisting of the two resistors and two diodes assures this. R2 is also required as a pull-down on the PIA gate so that a solid low and not an open circuit is sensed when the comparator output is below ground.

SUCCESSIVE APPROXIMATION

There are a number of ways in which the software can handle this arrangement. One of the most common is the successive approximation technique. It is fairly obvious that one way in which the device could be programmed to make a voltage measurement would be to simply set the D/A to zero at the start of each measurement and then increment it until the comparator flips. The number latched in the PIA will then represent the voltage reading. The trouble with this measurement technique is the fact that it is slow.

Suppose, for example, that you have an eight-bit D/A. It can have 256 different output levels and in the worst case it would be necessary to try each of them. On the average, it would have to try 128 values. The mask, increment memory and test routine is liable to take about 16 microseconds. Therefore, the average measurement would take about 2 milliseconds and the worst case would take 4 milliseconds.

By comparison, you could first try the largest increment. If it is too large, you would take it out. If it is not too large you could leave it in. The program could then proceed to test the next largest and so on until you arrived at the least step. The result would be the same as before. After all bits had been tried, the voltage value would be latched in the PIA and could be read with a "read memory" command. If this routine required the same 16 microseconds, you can see that in the worst case, and for that matter in every case, you would only have to try 8 different commands; for a total of 128 microseconds. This amounts to a speedup of 32 times. For a 12 bit, A/D the advantage is even greater; amounting to $4096/12 = 341.33$ times speedup.

THE TRACKING A/D

The very same hardware used in Fig. 10-6 can be used in an even faster way if the voltage is a smoothly varying one over the time scale of a few readings. In the tracking mode, the processor can remember the voltage currently held. When a reading is called for, the processor could reduce the current reading by some "window factor." An example would be three times the LSB and begin incrementing the voltage in quantities of one LSB. On the average it would take only three steps and if the voltage has stayed within the window it would require only six in the worst case. For the 12 bit A/D, this would speed up the search by a factor of three to six times. If the voltage had drifted outside of the window, a successive approximation technique search could be used to find it.

The chief objection to the use of the tracking technique is that it requires extra software and the measurement period is variable. If the processor is doing nothing else and operating at the highest possible speed, this can be a disadvantage since the voltage readings will be unevenly spaced. However, if the processor is also

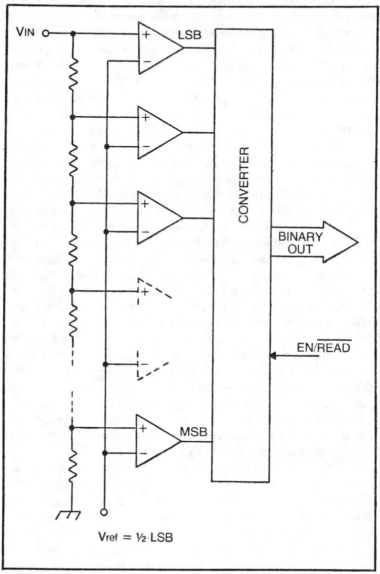

Fig. 10-7. A very high speed A/D converter.

occupied with other tasks, the variable length of the routine can be absorbed elsewhere or could perhaps be compensated by clever programming.

Conversion speed can be further enhanced by increasing the amount of hardware and the speed of the internal transistors in the D/A. If the algorithm for voltage measurement is hardwired into the A/D circuitry, the unit need no longer be driven by the internal software of the computer. In general, the hardwired functions can be made to function very fast and the speed advantage will always go to a hardwired logic solution as compared to a software driven routine. It should be noted, however, that the tradeoff between conversion speed and conversion resolution remains. It takes longer to test 12 bits than it does to test 8. Units which have both a high resolution and a high speed tend to be fairly expensive.

The converter type which shows the fundamentally highest speed is shown in Fig. 10-7. In this type of converter, Vin is divided across a string of resistors and compared to a reference voltage equal to ½ LSB. The unit closest to the source is the least significant bit and the unit farthest from the source is the most significant bit. In this type of A/D, all of the bits are tested in parallel. Therefore, the conversion time is limited only by the speed of the comparators and the speed of the converter. A/D converters of this type in high speed large scale integration chips are available with conversion frequencies up to 30 MHz, in resolutions to 8 bits.

The reason for the LSI implementation is the fact that there must be a comparator for every discrete level to be represented by the sytem. For an 8-bit machine, this means that 256 comparators and a 256-to 8-bit hardwired conversion logic is required. If attempted in discrete form, this would require several cabinets full of equipment. Obviously, the complexity in gates or devices on-chip of such a device would rival the count for the microprocessor itself.

The device is shown with a control line that enables the outputs when high and freezes the outputs when low. This permits the processor to read the data in a stable state.

Obviously, an A/D with this speed far exceeds the capabilities of microprocessors to absorb the data and it far exceeds the speed of most of the common types of RAM, even in DMA mode. In addition to this, the chips themselves are very expensive—running some hundreds of dollars. They are not in very common usage. However, there are also some chips on a smaller scale offering 6, 8, and 10 levels of comparison in linear or logarythmic weighting. These low cost devices offer speeds into the MHz region.

SPEED REQUIREMENTS

The stress placed on speed in the discussion of D/A and A/D devices stems largely from the applications for which the device is intended. Obviously, a system which need only monitor the temperature in an oven does not require the blinding speed of the parallel A/D or a parallel D/A which could as easily be constructed. If the process or the measurement itself is slow, then the instrumentation to monitor it need not be fast and expensive.

However, there are whole classes of measurements where speed becomes increasingly important. One of the most significant

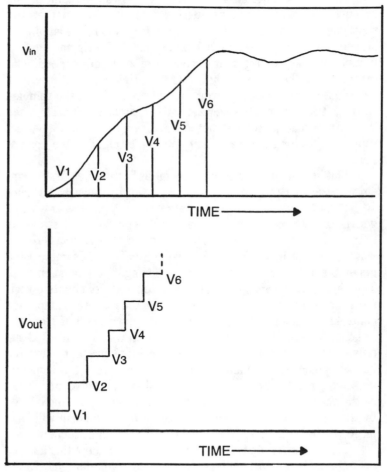

Fig. 10-8. The sampled waveform (top) and the reconstructed waveform (bottom).

of these is in waveform sampling and reproduction. Figure 10-8 shows a voltage waveform which has been created by some physical process like the sound of a human voice picked up by a microphone or the response of a photocell to the varying brightness it sees when scanning the clouds on earth from a satellite. In order to enter this data into a computer, it must be digitized.

As shown in the top portion of Fig. 10-8, this digitization can be performed by taking a series of readings which are equally spaced in time and digitizing this reading. After some transmission or storage process or some data manipulation process, it is usually necessary to reproduce the digitized data in analog form.

The bottom illustration in Fig. 10-8 shows the result of this reconstruction. The reconstruction is imperfect in that the waveshape has only been approximated. First of all, the amplitude proceeds along in a stepped fashion because the original digitization did not have either infinite resolution or infinite speed. The errors due to the finite resolution of the original A/D are termed *quantization noise* and the errors due to the fact that the samples were not taken at infinite speed is termed *sampling noise*. This uses the concept that the reconstructed waveform consists of a perfect replica of the original waveform and some added noise components.

This distinction is not as artificial as it might at first seem, since these noise contributions can be physically measured. Figure 10-9 shows a simplified representation of an apparatus in which a generator supplies an output to an A/D. The digitized stream is then sent over some transmission medium to a D/A where the wave is reconstructed. The reconstructed wave and a sample of the generator output are applied to the opposing inputs of an op-amp. The op-amp responds only the the differences between its inverting and non-inverting inputs. Therefore, if the phase and amplitude controls are adjusted to yield minimum power output from the op-amp, the entire generator signal portion will be cancelled and only the noise introduced by the system will be present. Obviously, this noise will contain the quantization noise, the sampling noise, any noise introduced in transmission, any noise introduced by the phase adjustment or the attneuator and any noise introduced by the op-amp. It should be fairly evident that the noise will have large components directly related to the sampling frequency.

Many years ago, Shannon introduced the concept that a signal could be digitized with no less than two samples per cycle of the highest frequency component. In actual practice, it is necessary to

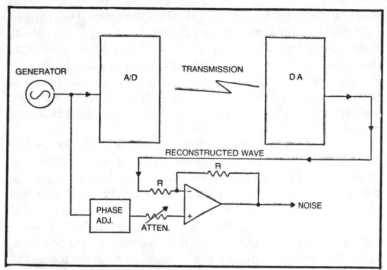

Fig. 10-9. Noise distortion testing.

sample at some multiple of the Shannon frequency if reasonable fidelity is to be obtained in the reconstructed waveform. For example, human speech on the telephone, which is filtered to limit the top frequency to something like 3KHz, must be sampled at 8- to 16-KHz in order to reconstruct the speech with reasonable fidelity. Because of the very wide dynamic range of human speech, the digitization is done on a logarythmic scale. Chips designed to digitize speech on an eight-bit log weighted scale and to reconstruct the waveform with antilog weighting are commercially available.

For the reproduction of high fidelity music, a similar log weighting is helpful. Most high fidelity equipment operates out to 20 KHz. However, the human ear generally gives up somewhere in the vicinity of 15 or 16 KHz. Therefore, the reproduction of the very highest frequency components is not required to be as precise as the midrange frequencies. Digitization at 60 KHz on a 16-level log-weighted scale provides for very good reproduction. Note that for transmission on a serial link, the bandwidth requirement has risen from 20 KHz to $60,000 \times 16 = 960,000$ bits per second without any allowance for start, stop and parity overhead bits. In general, the direct digitization of any information multiples the required bandwidth by a significant factor.

Commercial speed TV has a bandwidth of approximately 5 MHz. However, the major information is included within approximately 4.5 MHz for the picture and color information. Digitizing of a TV picture would require a sampling rate on the order of 15 MHz, with a resolution on the order of 10 bits. In the serial bit stream, this would require something over 150 MHz bandwidth.

Depending upon the type of radar, the video bandwidth can run from about 1 MHz for a search system, to 5 or 15. MHz for sophisticated gunfire control or track-while-scan high-resolution systems.

With the penalty in bandwidth which must be paid for digitizing this type of analog data, it seems logical to question just why there is such a considerable swing over to digital handling of the data. The answer comes in multiple forms. Probably first and foremost is the fact that all analog systems of transmission will gradually degrade the quality of the data. In any transmission medium, whether it be a TV or FM transmitter or a fiberoptic cable, the signal will attenuate on transmission. In the process of amplifying the signal, even the first equipment will subtly corrupt the information. If the information must be amplified many times in a relay system, the corruption of the information can become considerable.

In distinction to this, a digital system can amplify and regenerate the digital data in a manner essentially free from corruption. The regenerating equipment need only recognize whether each individual character was a 1 or an 0 and it can then regenerate the character with no corruption of the data. The errorless detection of an 1 or 0 depends upon the fact that the signal to noise ratio is above some threshold. There are even certain forward error correcting codes in which the receiving machine can locate and correct errors when characters become garbled in transmission. This is the reason that the various space probes and satellites send their data in digitized format.

Upon reception, the data from feeble signals which have travelled half way across the solar system can be reconstructed in an essentially error-free manner.

A second reason for the preference for digital recording of data is the fact that all analog storage media eventually degrade and contribute noise and distortion to the data. The old shellac discs used for music used to become granular and tapes get scratched and the general noise level rises with playing. More particularly, the pattern on the face of a storage oscilloscope will eventually bloom and the trace becomes indistinct. With digital storage, these effects do not occur as long as the medium is readable at all. The information is preserved without distortion or noise addition. All of the noise that is to be found in the data is introduced at the time of the initial digitization and at the time of reconstruction.

Particularly in the recording of one-time transients and other data, the use of digitization and digital storage is becoming increasingly popular. The ordinary oscilloscope is well suited to a display of rapidly repetetive data. For data that occur only one time, or very quickly with large periods of time between repetitions, the oscilloscope does not work very well. The storage oscilloscope is somewhat better in this regard. However, even here the length of time over which the data can be stored is very limited and the recording of slowmoving or infrequently recurring data is difficult. The digital storage scope has some very significant advantages in this regard.

Suppose, for example, that you want to record some sporadic phenomenon which occurrs only every few hours and lasts for something like 15 milliseconds. The digital storage scope can be set to continuously monitor the line, trigger on the event and cease writing perhaps 15 clock periods after the event. The data within the memory which has been circulating like an endless tape will then have a record of the data which preceded the trigger as well as the 15 clock periods which followed it. Furthermore, this data can be read back at any convenient viewing rate for a flicker-free display. The latter factor is particularly significant when viewing slow moving data. It is not very convenient to view a display which is being refreshed at rates less than about 25Hz. With digital storage, the display can always be operated at convenient rates. The availability of before-the-event data is particularly valuable in diagnostic work.

Another very significant advantage to digitization of data is the ability to have a computer massage the data to present it in more tractable or recognizable form. Suppose that the data is a measurement of the pressure within the cylinder head of an engine and that the transducer has a law something like: $P = kV + V_o$. With the aid of the processor, you can subtract the offset voltage V_o and divide the voltage read by a factor k such that the instrument will display P in pounds per square inch. Alternatively, a different value of k will yield a display reading newtons per square meter and the instrument can jump from one type of display to another at the push of a button or the receipt of an electrical command over the interface bus. Most of the "smart" instruments being sold today have processors included inside for just such purposes.

Another common example of the use of digital data processing is found in the "false color" displays shown in satellite photographs, etc. An example is the infrared weather maps shown on the nightly weather reports. Before presentation, the processor scans the entire picture data and locates the coordinate of all points having temperatures between say 68 degrees F and 72 degrees F. In the presented picture these areas are colored blue. The next higher temperature range is colored yellow and the highest red. Before the advent of computer processing, someone would have had to carefully trace the readings on the map and draw the outlines by hand.

A yet more sophisticated level of information processing is also practiced. For example, it has been shown that the human eye perceives shapes and objects by the detection of edges where the shape or the reflectance has a boundary. The clarity of a presentation can be greatly enhanced by a computer program which is designed to enhance the edges on a picture which is originally gray and fuzzy.

The performance of this form of *image enhancement* on pictures which have been blurred by atmospheric haze, camera motion or even an out-of-focus exposure is truly remarkable. Objects can be seen and interpreted and signs can be read after this form of processing has been done on the picture.

Digitally recorded music is another remarkable advancement. Since the final product is in no way dependent upon the homogeniety of the tape, truly remarkable signal-to-noise ratios are attainable and the distortion free dynamic range using logarythimic decoding is impressive.

In the field of communications, the additions due to digital processing are similarly remarkable. A normal telephone system is usually referred to as being a *duplex channel*, which means that both parties can speak simultaneously if they choose to. Actually, the two parties rarely speak simultaneously. More often, one talks and one listens. Sophisticated communications make use of this fact to provide what seems to the two parties in any given contact as a full duplex channel. Actually the systems swipes one channel during the pauses when it is not in use. When cleverly done, this technique can yield an effective increase in system capacity on the order of 40 percent. In general, the faster the A/D conversion is, the more things can be done with it.

Transcribers 11

Within the past decade or two, we have been progressing in the direction of making all physical measurements electrical in process. The devices for converting these physical properties into electrical signals are referred to generically as *transducers*. A transducer is a mechanism for transforming one sort of energy into another. However, the term is usually reserved for devices which change physical phenomena into electrical energy or which transfer electrical energy into something physical. For example, the barium titanate block which transforms the electrical output of a sonar transmitter into a burst of sound in the water is a transducer. The same block can convert the returning sonic echoes in the water into a feeble electric impulse for the sonar receiver.

The term transducer is seldom applied to a loudspeaker or a microphone even though they perform a very similar function. The older name persists due to popular useage.

In this chapter, a variety of transducers and techniques for transforming some physical phenomenon into an electrical signal which can be used in either instrumentation or control through a computer, are examined.

It is noteworthy that at the transducer interface, many of the devices used in common measurement and control applications are fundamentally analog in nature and not digital. Until the last decade or so, the measurement field was almost entirely an analog field with very little digital instrumentation present. Even at this writing there are certain fields where analog instrumentation is to be preferred. For example, in any situation where something is being tuned or adjusted to find a maximum or a minimum value, the analog presentation of the output is to be preferred since a change in the direction of motion of a needle is much easier to pick out than the peak reading of a digital decimal presentation. The latter requires a mental arithmetic process, whereas the former is a built in property of the human eye. Eventually this will change as well with the introduction of digital bar-graph and pointer displays with no moving parts.

TEMPERATURE MEASUREMENT

Temperatures can be translated into electrical signal in a variety of ways. However, the first with which I will deal is the use of a temperature sensing diode. The reason for this order of selection is not the fact that the diode is the most commonly used temperature sensor or transducer, but rather because it tells us something about the behavior of electronic circuitry and some of the things which have to be considered when developing other transducers.

THE DIODE THERMOMETER

The fundamental property which makes the silicon diode useful as a temperature sensor is that a forward biased silicon PN junction carrying a constant current exhibits a forward voltage drop which varies linearly with temperature from about −40 degrees C to about +125 degrees C. The linearity is a very nice feature since it permits an even calibration of the instrument. Also, in most diodes the variation seems to stay constant with age.

The voltage variation is approximately 2mV/°C with the forward drop increasing with temperature. However, the 2mV is not one of the fundamental constants of the universe. Even among diodes taken from the same batch, the variation might run from 1.6 to 2.2 mV/°C. The diode must therefore be calibrated against known temperature standards.

Another point worthy of notice is that the current must be held constant since the forward drop also increases with increasing forward current. If this is not done, an increase in current due to increasing bias supply can be misread as an increase in temperature.

The circuit in Fig. 11-1 a typical circuit. Q1 and Q2 are depletion mode junction FETs. These devices have the property that the current through the load connected to the FET drain is determined almost entirely by the value of R3 and is nearly independent of the value of V+ over a very wide range. With values on the order of R3 = 1.2 K ohm and R4 = 2 M ohm, these devices will supply a current to the drain load that runs from I = 0.834 mA at V+ = 4V to 0.836 mA at V+ = 10V. The diode current is therefore stabilized against changes in supply voltage.

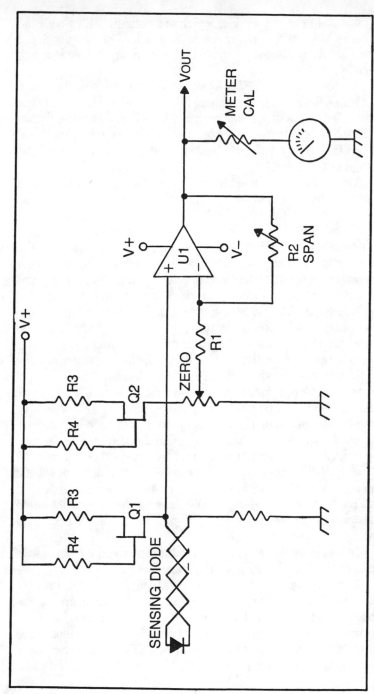

Fig. 11-1. The silicon diode thermometer.

Constant current diodes, which are actually FETs with the resistors built in and packaged in a two lead diode pack, are commerically available and would probably be preferable in a high precision thermometer.

The current through Q1 flows through the sensing diode and then through a resistor to ground. The current of the FETs is not entirely independent of temperature either. Therefore, the second FET, Q2, is used to derive the bucking voltage. To the extent that the FETs are identical, the bucking voltage will vary with the voltage in the diode leg.

The op-amp U1 is used to amplify the change in forward drop across the diode to a more useable level. The gain of this amplifier is determined by the ratio R2/R1.

To calibrate the unit a container of icewater is required along with a container of boiling water. The diode is first placed in the icewater and the potentiometer marked zero is adjusted for a zero volt output. After this, the diode is placed in the boiling water and the span control is adjusted to yield the desired reading—for example + 10V. The diode is then returned to the icewater and the process repeated. After a few tries, settings will yield stable and repeatable readings for the icewater and the boiling water. If you want to be a purist about the whole thing, the boiling water reading should be reduced to account for the altitude above sea level and the barometric pressure at the time of the calibration.

The diode can be any silicon diode, such as 1N914, etc or some other small signal switching diode. It can even be a bipolar transistor with the base and collector tied together.

With a proper calibration, the unit will read temperature at the rate of 0.1V/°C. The output will be zero V at 0°C and 10V at 100°C. The accuracy will be within a degree or so across this range. If a 1mA meter is used, a setting of 10K ohms for the meter calibration resistor will give readings which track with the meter calibrated scale.

In this example I went to some rather substantial lengths with the inclusion of a bucking voltage source which would approximately track the variations in the diode current and the supply voltage variation since the temperature would be measured at the diode and not within the box. Secondly, the instrument contains a mechanism for adjusting both the axis crossing and the slope of the output in the form of *zero* and *span* controls. This is characteristic of electronic transducer circuitry.

It is a characteristic of most electronic transducer circuits that they must be protected against variation in supply voltage, temperature variation and must be provided with zero and span adjustments. Furthermore, they must generally be calibrated against outside known good references.

The device as illustrated in Fig. 11-1 is equipped with a meter for local reading. However, it should be obvious that an A/D could be used to load the temperature readings into a computer or controller.

OTHER TEMPERATURE MEASUREMENT DEVICES

There are a number of other techniques which can be used for making temperature measurements. The resistance of a coil of platinum wire varys in a remarkably linear fashion with temperature. Platinum coil sensors are the sensors of choice for very low temperature measurements because of their remarkable stability. The circuit is capable of being calibrated with a platinum resistance sensor since the voltage across the sensor varies linearly with its resistance if the current through the resistor is held constant. With a platinum sensor, attention would be paid to the temperature coefficients of the various resistances within the circuit because of the greater precision which is attainable with the more expensive sensor.

Platinum coil sensors are usually supplied with a calibration curve of resistance versus temperature. The instrument could be calibrated by substituting known precision resistors for the platinum coil without any requirement for hot and cold baths.

Thermistors are also usable for temperature measurements. However, resistance variation with temperature is very nonlinear, has only a limited repeatability and will vary as much as 10 percent from unit to unit of the same nominal specifications. Thermistors have the advantage of being much more sensitive than any of the other types. They are often used when differential temperature measurements as small as 0.1 degrees C are required by comparing the resistance of a matched pair.

Thermocouples are the sensing measurement unit of choice for temperatures from 0 degrees C up to several hundred degrees. Thermocouples are also nonlinear and they must be compensated for the junctions where the thermocouple is attached to the measuring circuitry. Compensation tables prepared by the National Bureau of Standards are available for all common types of thermocouples. The use of the thermocouples is a rather complex subject and far too lengthy for inclusion here. Compensation tables can be written into ROM in a processor based instrument, thereby automating and adding precision to the temperature readings.

Several semiconductor manufacturers have begun to offer integrated circuit temperature sensors which have been accurately calibrated and compensated and are housed in a tiny T0-18 or T0-92 package so that they look like tiny transistors. In general, the smaller the sensor, the lower the thermal inertia of the temperature measurement. Faster response usually means less waiting for readings and more accurate control of devices.

LINEAR TRAVEL MEASUREMENTS

In a great many control applications and in some measurement applications, it is necessary to have an electrical readout of the position of mechanical pieces. One of the simplest ways in which this can be accomplished is with the linear potentiometer. A number of manufacturers offer potentiometers in which the tap slides straight back and forth on the straight-line resistance card, rather than being turned around a circular resistance card by a shaft. For these devices, if the near end is held at some voltage and the far end held at another voltage, the tap voltage is a linear function of the shaft motion between the ends.

This is a very simple arrangement to use. For example, if the near end is at ground potential, the far end is held at 10V and the total shaft travel from minimum to maximum voltage is one inch, the tap output voltage will have a sensitivity of 10V/in or 10mV/ 0.001". This can be read directly with an A/D converter.

An example of the use of a device of this type is shown in Fig. 11-2. In this device a bellows is connected to a system whose pressure is to be measured. The bellows expands linearly with internal pressure and drives the slider on the potentiometer. V_{out} is linearly related to the pressure. Suppose that the output is zero volts for zero pressure and 10V for 25PSI. Then the sensitivity is 10V/25PSI = 0.4V/PSI. It should be noted that the pressure sensitivity in this case was tailored to the standard 10V full-scale reading, which is common in A/D converters. This is somewhat of a common practice since the processor can easily be programmed to interpret the reading. If the voltage is to be +2.5 volts at 25PSI, the sensitivity would have been 0.1V/PSI. This would be easily readable by a human being but would have sacrificed a quarter of the resolution of the A/D.

One of the failings of a device of this type is that the slider on the potentiometer drags on the resistance card. The slider fingers must be made of a springy material to take up tolerances in the slider/card spacing. The net result of this is that the slider tends to lag behind the pressure a little since there must be a certain amount of pressure change to make the device move at all. The result of this is shown in the curve at the bottom of Fig. 11-2. If the pressure is increasing, the V_{out} follows one curve and if the pressure is decreasing, it follows one curve and if the pressure is decreasing, it

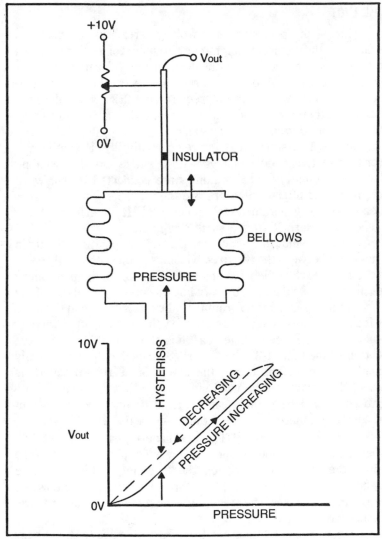

Fig. 11-2. The linear potentiometer pressure gauge.

follows a slightly different one. The difference is termed *hysterises*. This is the difference in V_{out} obtained at a given pressure if that pressure is arrived at by increasing or decreasing pressure.

Many measuring devices show some hysteresis, which is the equivalent of *backlash* or *lost motion* in a mechanical linkage or gear train. The amount of hysteresis is generally quoted in the specfications for gauges.

THE LVDT

One of the principal causes of hysteresis in the previous example is the requirement for a certain amount of friction between the slider and the card due to the need for the slider to exert some pressure on the card to obtain a reliable electrical contact. Obviously, a device which did not require such friction would slide easier and therefore reduce the hysteresis. One such device is the *linear voltage differential transformer*.

Figure 11-3 shows this device schematically. Essentially, it consists of two fixed windings with a single movable winding between them. The fixed windings are connected to half wave rectifiers and filter condensers and the movable winding is connected to an ac generator. A frequency of 2 KHz is commonly used. This can be derived from a small oscillator.

When the movable winding is pushed to a position exactly in the center between the two fixed windings, it induces exactly equal voltages in each of the windings and $Va = Vb$. As the mechanical push rod pushes the movable winding off center toward one of the fixed windings and farther from the other, the voltage in the fixed winding, which is closer, rises and the voltage in the other winding falls. The difference voltage, $Va-Vb$ is shown in the curve at the bottom of the Fig. 11-3. The curve is S-shaped with an essentially linear center section. If only the linear (or nearly so) section is used, the device can be used simply as a linear device. With a processor, a lookup table can be used to linearize the output readings and therefore extend the range of the LVDT.

The friction of the LVDT can be made a great deal lower than the friction of the potentiometer. However, it cannot go to zero since the connection between the traveling winding and the generator is generally brought out through a pair of flexible wires. Also, in most cases, the traveling winding and the push rod are supported on sliding bearings.

In terms of resolution, the LVDT can be made to have a very high sensitivity. Units with a sensitivity of 0.1V/0.001″ are availa-

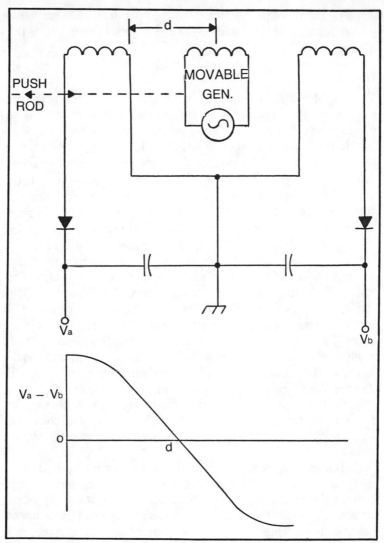

Fig. 11-3. The LVDT.

ble with a travel of 0.125″. A unit of this sort can easily be read through an amplifier to a resolution of 10 millionths of an inch. By itself, the unit has very little hysteresis. However, the friction of moving the sliding coil can produce hysteresis in the device being measured. There is also the matter of the temperature sensitivity of the diodes and the windings, as well as the spacing of the windings due to the expansion of the case. On any measurements going down to millionths of an inch, temperature stabilization is generally required since even tool steel expands several parts per million per degree centigrade.

THE NON-CONTACT GAUGE

The ultimate in low friction comes from the non-contact gauge which does not touch the piece being measured at all and has no moving parts. Figure 11-4 shows a gauge of the *eddy current* type.

In this device, a balanced ac bridge is made up of two resistors, a dummy coil L2 which has the same reactance as the probe coil and the probe. The bridge is excited by a generator. If the bridge is perfectly balanced with the workpiece a great distance from the probe, the voltage between points A and B is zero since the voltage drop between point A and ground and point B and ground is identical. As a conductive workpiece is brought toward the probe, eddy currents are induced in the workpiece which effectively reduces the inductive reactance of the probe. This causes the voltage drop from point A to ground to fall and a voltage exists between A and B. The curve at the bottom of Fig. 11-3 shows the approximate response obtained. The response is in the form of an S curve which has some approximately linear section. Gauges of this type can be made to demonstrate sensitivities on the order of 0.1V/0.001″ or more and measurements down to millionths of an inch are possible with this type of unit.

Since the probe does not touch the workpiece, there is no force or friction hysteresis whatever. There is a completely negligable electromagnetic repulsion, which does not enter the picture at all.

The eddy current gauge in general has a very limited range and it is sensitive to the nature of the conductive material. It will show a different calibration on tool steel than it does on aluminum or brass. The calibration can also vary as a function of the temperature of the workpiece. Since it is sensitive only to conductors, it will read right through dielectrics like paper or a cellophane bag or a film of cutting oil which would give erroneous readings with a contacting gauge like the LVDT.

If the generator frequency is high enough, the response time of the gauge can be made so fast that it can read on turbine blades flashing by or it can be used as a vibration amplitude sensor. The last point is particularly interesting in some cases since unlike a normal accelerometer, which has to be stuck to the piece being measured, it does not alter the resonant frequency of the piece

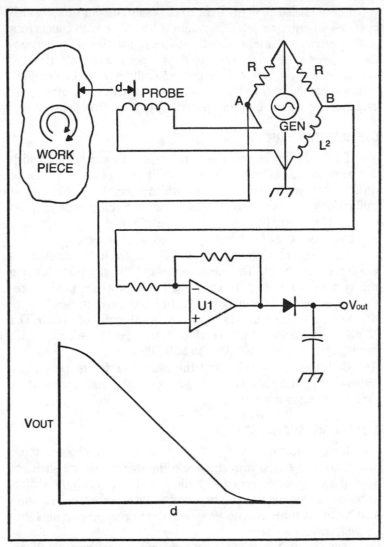

Fig. 11-4. The eddy current gauge.

being tested. Furthermore, it does not have a steep nonlinear slope of output related to frequency.

Because the eddy currents do not flow in a tiny spot, the eddy current gauge averages the reading over a spot about twice the diameter of the probe coil. This can be an advantage when reading on sandblasted or knurled surfaces and a disadvantage when trying to read on small pieces or in a corner.

There is also an equivalent to the eddy current gauge which operates on capacitance. This gauge will read on both conductors and dielectrics and is less sensitive to the properties of the conductors. However, it is sensitive to the properties of dielectrics.

Both of these types of gauges generally have to be provided with a span and offset or zero control and both must usually be calibrated using some other contacting type instrument.

OTHER LINEAR GAUGES

There are a variety of other types of linear gauges in use which can be read and calibrated down to millionths of an inch. One of these is the *quartz ruler* type in which a highly precise set of calibrations is etched into what amounts to a ruler made of fused quartz. The quartz has a very low coefficient of linear expansion and the ruler is read optically by a photocell scheme.

The laser interferometer is the class item in the category of linear measurements. The measurement of distance is made using the very precisely known wavelengths of two lasers. Measurements can be made of distances from fractions of inches to hundreds of feet with accuracies measured in millionths of an inch. The principle objection to the laser interferometer is the cost, which tends to run between $30,000 to $50,000.

Both the quartz ruler and the laser interferometer can be obtained from the manufacturer equipped with a digital readout for direct loading into a computer.

ROTARY MEASUREMENTS

Rotary measurements generally fall into two classes; those which are concerned with the angle through which the shaft has turned and those concerned with the speed with which the shaft is turning. The simple angle and speed measurements are sometimes combined. At times it is necessary to determine other things such as angular acceleration.

The simplest form of rotary sensor is the rotary potentiometer. Precision rotary potentiometers equipped with ball bearings are available from a number of sources. The operation of these devices for angle sensing is exactly as described for the linear potentiometer shown in Fig. 11-2. The advantages and disadvantages also follow the same arguments.

Rotary potentiometers are available for either continuous rotation or limited rotation through multiple turns. These sensors are frequently used on analog positioning servomechanism such as chart recorders. Linearities of one-half percent are common and higher linearities are available.

THE SYNCRO OR SELSYN

The syncro or selsyn is the rotary equivalent of the LVDT in that it has relatively lower hysteresis than the potentiometer. It is capable of continuous rotation at relatively high speeds and does not have a "dead spot" at zero degrees.

Figure 11-5 shows a typical selsyn pair installation. The selsyn is actually wired like a wound rotor induction motor. The stator generally has a three-phase winding and the rotor has a single-phase winding which is brought to the outside world through a pair of slip rings. If the rotor of each selsyn is energized from an ac

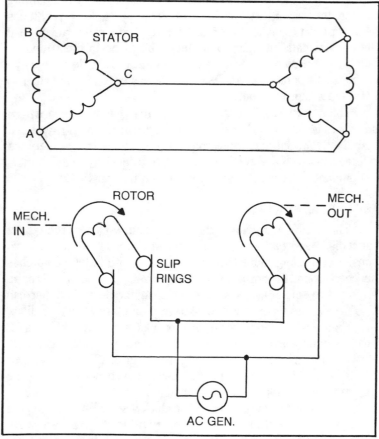

Fig. 11-5. The selsyn link.

source, the voltages induced in the field will have a specific magnitude and phase determined by the angular position of the rotor. When a pair of selsyns are wired together as shown, rotation of the shaft of one will cause an equal rotation of the shaft of the second unit. In a physical sense, the action is just as if the two shafts were mechanically coupled. If the leads to any pair of terminals, say A and B, are exchanged, the direction of rotation of the slave unit is reversed. In the larger size units, the torque which can be transmitted is considerable and quite comparable to the torques developed by a motor of the same size. The finite torque of the devices make them act as if the "mechanical shaft" were a little bit springy.

For many years, selsyns were used as a substitute for mechanical shafting in applications like radar antenna position sensors, etc where it would have been difficult to carry the shafting through the various articulations. In recent years, however, it has been common to make use of a selsyn-to-digital converter to load the angular data into the computer to be found in most modern radars. These converters are a bit sophisticated and lie beyond the scope of this book. Like A/Ds, they are easier to just buy and use than to attempt to build.

The selsyn is still used in a great many applications where precise angular measurement is required. Units which have been optimized for accuracy rather than torque stiffness are sometimes referred to as *resolvers*. These units are frequently found in inertial guidance platforms, autopilots and similar applications.

THE OPTICAL RESOLVER

The optical resolver is the rotary counterpart of the quartz ruler discussed earlier. In the simplest form, these devices can consist of nothing more than a metal disc with holes or notches punched around the periphery and one or more photocell LED pairs arranged to sense the passage of an opaque object. The disc can also be a photo or evaporated pattern on a glass or quartz disc.

Figure 11-6 shows a simple form of resolver which has 8 opaque and 8 transparent areas masked onto the disc. Photosensors A and B are shown in their relative positions. The waveforms illustrate that due to the relative placement of sensors A and B, the direction of rotation of the disc can be sensed.

When the disc is rotating in the clockwise (CW) direction the squarewave generated by the B sensor will lead the square wave generated by the A sensor by 90 degrees in phase or one-quarter of

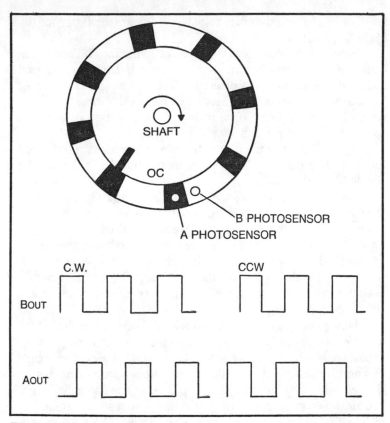

Fig. 11-6. An optical resolver.

a full period. In the CCW direction, the opposite condition occurs and B lags A. Once a revolution C outputs a pulse indication, the zero degree location.

If the only object is to determine the speed of rotation of the shaft, then a simple frequency counting routine will suffice and only a single sensor is required. However, if a measure of the angle through which the shaft has been rotated is desired then a somewhat more sophisticated routine is needed.

The flow chart in Fig. 11-7 shows a program which will realize this angle measurement. The program is entered at node 1 and tested to see whether the register should be reset for zero. In the node 2 loop, first the A and B flags are tested and then A and B themselves are tested. If the disc is rotating clockwise, flag B will be set first and the program then tests for A being set. When A is set, the program looks for B clear and A set. If this is satisfied, the machine increments the angle register and clears the B flag and the cycle begins anew.

However, suppose that the disc is oscillating a bit and in the course of oscillation it just barely tickles A on and then turns around and heads back in the CCW direction. The second test of A assures that this will not be counted since when B goes low in node 4, if A is not still set, the B flag is cleared and the test is started over. The CCW test is a mirror image of the CW routine.

A "cold" start of the unit will not read angles correctly until the first clear due to C. However, thereafter the angles will be correctly tabulated.

Obviously, this type of sensor must be accurately mounted on the shaft for concentricity if high accuracy is required and a relatively large number of teeth on the disc are required. Interestingly, a sensor of this type can be very inexpensively constructed using a fine toothed circular saw blade. The sensors can be photointerruptor modules available for less than a dollar. The modules contain both the LED light source and the photo transistor detector in a single slotted package.

On a given size disc, there is obviously some lower limit to the accuracy which can be obtained due to the size of the photo interruptor beam, etc. There are several techniques for getting around this problem. One of these is the *moire pattern* so named because of the resemblence to moire silk. Suppose that you had a disc which had 100 lines on it and superimposed this upon a second stationery disk with 101 lines on the same size circle. The pattern seen viewing the superimpsoed discs would show a dark band that represented an area where the lines and spaces of the discs were out of phase. This would shade around to a light band where the lines and spaces were aligned or in phase. Rotation of one of the discs through 1/100 of a revolution would send the dark band racing a full turn around. A series of detectors spaced around the fixed disc could be used to resolve the 1/100 revolution period of the dark band into perhaps 10 equal parts. This would permit reading of the angle to a thousandth of a circle or about 20 minutes of arc.

For the moire pattern resolver, one of the chief problems is zeroing the reading with the same accuracy that relative angles are read. Like the simple optical resolver, the use of these units generally requires a bi-directional counting technique. Most often, the inital zero is loaded into the system by some other technique with suitable accuracy or else the resolver is used only for relative angle readings.

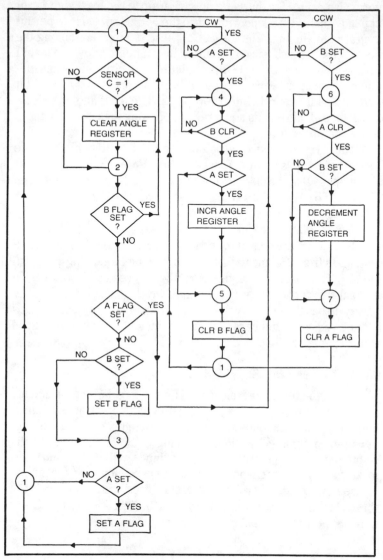

Fig. 11-7. An optical resolver routine.

THE ABSOLUTE OPTICAL RESOLVER

For applications where it is neccessary to be able to read absolute angle right from the start without rotating the device to some zero setting, there are a variety of optical disc devices in which the actual angle is directly encoded upon the disc in as many digital bits as required. These disc devices are usually larger than a

219

moire disc device for the same precision since the least significant bit must still have a stripe wider than the optical spot size to permit accurate functioning. The largest of these devices are among the most accurate mechanical measuring instruments known to man. I have used discs with an 18-bit readout for positioning a missile-guidance radar antenna. To put this in perspective, and 18-bit readout divides a circle into 256K parts. The least angle readable on a device of this type is equivalent to one-fourth inch at a distance of one statute mile.

This type of device is seldom encoded with a binary code because of the possibility of large errors. For example, on a 7-bit disc suppose that the disc is stopped exactly on the border between 255 and 256. The binary representation for this is:

0 1111 1111 = 255
1 0000 0000 = 256

Exactly on the crossing, the six lower order bits would still be reading Is from 255 and the seventh bit would be reading an I from the 256. Therefore, the device would briefly read all Is or 511. To prevent this form of gross error, a *gray code* is usually used. The gray code has the property that not more than one bit ever changes between adjacent numbers. This minimizes the errors possible on a border line reading.

BACK TO LINEAR MEASUREMENTS

All of the techniques described for the angular measurements in the optical resolvers are just about equally applicable to linear measurement techniques and each of techniques described is represented in commercial linear gauging equipment. Some of the commercially available measuring machines called *coordinographs* make use of a rotary encoder driven by a precision rack and pinion. These machines will typically measure the location of a point in three dimensions with an accuracy of 0.0001 inches by simply moving the carriage and pointer to touch the object.

THE STRAIN GAUGE

Another mechanical engineering measurement which is frequently required is the measurement of the strain or elongation of a structural member. It is frequently required to determine the extent of the forces acting on a landing gear, a shaft, a bolt, etc. The measurement could be made by actually cutting the member and inserting some sort of force measuring gauge. However, this is generally impractical or expensive. The most common technique for this form of measurement is the use of a strain gauge. The strain gauge is generally a metal film resistor whose resistance changes with stretching. The resistor itself is usually bonded to a piece of paper or plastic, which is in turn glued to the member to be tested. With the load applied, the member stretches—thereby stretching the strain gauge. The change in resistance of the strain gauge is a measure of the elongation of the member. Strain gauges are also subject to change in resistance due to temperature change. The gauges themselves are therefore usually constructed with two elements in the form of a cross or four elements in the form of a box. The gauge is cemented to the member so that one set of legs will be stretched and the other set of legs will be at right angles to the stretch. The stretched and non-stretched members are used in a bridge circuit so that the changes due to temperature will cancel.

For computer usage, strain gauges are usually read with an amplifier to raise the unbalance voltage to a reasonable level and an A/D. One example of the use of a strain gauge in a daily application is the thrust indicator used on jet aircraft.

CURRENT MEASUREMENT

One of the most common types of measurement used in engineering of scientific work is the measurement of electric current. Many of the measurements in chemistry and physics can be reduced to an electric current which can be monitored by a computer. For example, the output of a monochometer or the output of a gas chromatograph are typically a small current measured in microamperes. These currents must be converted to a form suitable for digitization if the computer is to be employed.

The type of circuit shown in Fig. 11-8 is commonly used when the requirement is to measure the magnitude of a current which would normally flow to ground.

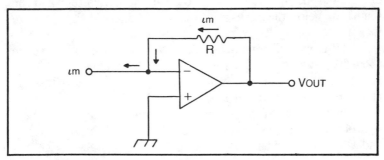

Fig. 11-8. The voltage to current converter.

With the non-inverting input referenced to ground, the normal action of the op-amp is to drive the total current at the inverting (or summing) gate to zero. For a current of either polarity, the output terminal of the op-amp will rise to a voltage such that i in = − i m. In effect, the inverting gate will be driven to ground potential. The output voltage will then be equal to i m × R.

Suppose, for example, you would like to have the output of the op-amp be +10V when the input is 0.001 A. The required value of R = 10V/0.001A = 10K ohm.

In a great many cases, however, the current to be measured does not flow to ground and it is too large to be handled by the op amp directly. In such cases, it is the practice to measure the current by measuring the voltage drop across a resistor through which the current is flowing. A standard value for high current meter shunts is to assign a size to the resistor such that 50 mV is developed across the shunt or resistor when the current is at the rated value. In such cases the shunt might not be in the ground leg of the circuit and both ends of the resistor might have some *common mode voltage* which is larger by far than the 50 mV drop you are seeking to measure.

The circuit shown in Fig. 11-9 is designed to handle just such a situation. U1 and U2 are a set of identical op-amps should preferably be of the type where they are both on the same chip so that the temperatures are identical. If N=2 and that A=20V and B=20.010V, the output of Op-amp A will rise to 10 volts in order to drive the current on the inverting input of U1 to zero. However, note that through the CMR BAL pot, U1 will also supply enough current to the inverting input of U2 to balance out 20V worth of signal at B. For this reason, the output of B will only need to shift enough to balance the slight difference between A and B. With a small adjustment of the CMR BAL control to remove slight second order differences, it is possible to tie A and B together and run them from below the minus rail to above the plus rail without more than a few microvolts swing at the output of U2.

This circuit will operate to reject common mode voltages up to about N(V supply − 1.5V). If N is greater than 1, U1 and U2 are operating at less than unity gain. U3 is provided to restore the gain and to permit zero and span adjustment.

The precision of the common mode rejection depends almost entirely upon the precision of the matching of the resistors for U1 and U2. With ordinary op-amps such as the 5558, it is easily possible to obtain common mode rejection ratios as large as 70db at

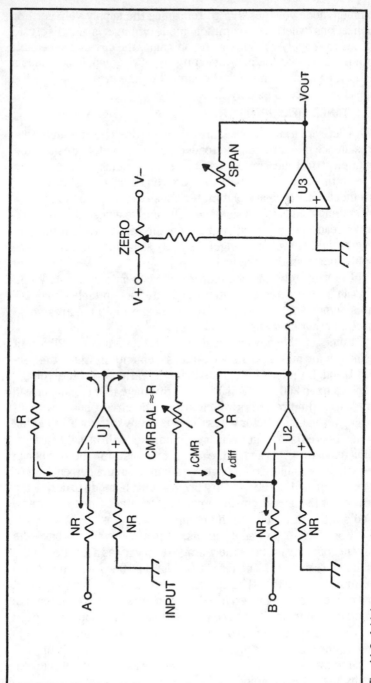

Fig. 11-9. A high common mode rejection amplifier.

223

common mode voltages five to ten times the supply voltage. For applications where the common mode voltage is not likely to exceed the supply voltage for the op-amps, the circuit can be built with the inputs on the non-inverting leg of the amp. This yields a higher input impedance for the amp. For the circuit shown, the input impedance is exactly 2NR.

RESISTANCE MEASUREMENTS

There are a number of applications in which it is required that a resistance measurement be loaded into a computer. Besides the usual electrical measurements, there are a number of pressure, temperature and conductivity sensors requiring a resistance measurement. The ordinary ohmmeter usually consists of a meter, a battery and a midscale resistance. The unit is adjusted so that the meter reads full-scale current when the leads are shorted and progressively lower and longer currents as higher resistances are applied between the terminals.

Unfortunately, the ohmmeter scale is very non-linear. While this can be corrected with an appropriate lookup table, it contributes significantly to errors and the lookup table requires some space in program memory.

Some of the newer precision meters employ a different technique for making resistance measurements in which the current through the unknown resistance is varied until the voltage drop is a fixed 200 mV. This has the advantage that resistance can be measured on resistors which are on the circuit board without turning on semiconductor gates. This is handy for troubleshooting circuit boards since an ordinary ohmmeter will usually turn on semiconductor gates and the reading of a resistor in the circuit can become impossible. D/A converters which have a current output are common and can be used in a programmable mode to derive the current for the measurement. A precision voltage reference can be used set the threshold for the comparator.

For many of the applications, it is worthwhile to have the current constant and have the voltage drop vary as a function of the unknown resistance. The circuit in Fig. 11-10 shows a technique for implementing this. The op-amp is driven on the inverting input by a constant current reference diode. In order to drive this gate to ground, the output of the op-amp rises to a voltage sufficient to put the cancelling current through the unknown resistance which is used as the feedback resistance. Therefore, V_{out} is linearly proportional to the resistance. The resistance is passing only the current set by the reference diode.

224

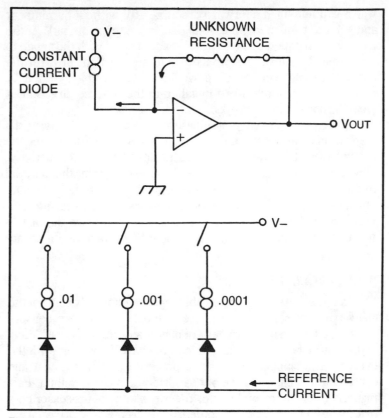

Fig. 11-10. The constant current ohmeter.

The range of such an arrangement is obviously limited. If the reference current is 0.001 ampere, then a 10V output will be attained with a 10K ohm resistor and the range of the instrument will be from zero to 10K. If higher resistances are to be measured, the current must be reduced. An instrument with range switching can be constructed if more than one constant current diode is supplied—as shown at the lower portion of the illustration. The voltage drop due to the steering diodes does not degrade the accuracy of the measurement since only the current is important. Alternatively, a current output A/D can be used as the current source. In this case, the device can be operated in either the constant voltage or the constant current mode under program control.

One note of caution is in order concerning this form of device. There are certain solid-state devices such as light-emitting diodes which will not stand a forward drop like 10V without burning out and will not take an inverse voltage of more than about 3V. If the LED were installed in the forward sense, that is with the anode to the output terminal, the device would simply light up with the current and the voltage drop would be something like 1.75V. However, if the diode were installed in the reverse direction, it would probably be destroyed.

In certain chemical type measurements, the conductivity of a material is monitored. For example, it is possible to determine the amount of salt in water by a measurement of the conductivity. However, if the polarity is left fixed in one direction, the material in the solution will begin to plate out on the electrodes in minute amounts. This will cause eventual errors in the reading. For readings of wet solutions, it is usually better to have the instrument reverse polarity with the reading being taken on a square wave.

TRANSDUCER SUMMARY

In this chapter I have been able to touch upon only a few of the many types of sensors which are available. There are sensors obtainable for the measurement of nearly any phenomenon. Many of these have been very expensive in the past. However, with the ever growing application of microprocessors to instrument and control situations, the price of the various sensors is falling. Particularly in the automobile field, the acceptance of processor control hinges upon the development of extreme low-price large-volume sensors. These will become increasingly available in the future.

Keyboards, Displays and Multiplexing

12

While a great many microprocessor applications have no operator access, there are also a great many like the electric clothes dryer and the microwave oven in which a principal feature is the presence of a keyboard for data entry and a display to show that entry. In this chapter, I will examine some of the facets of these displays and keyboards to see how they influence the overall system.

DISPLAY MULTIPLEXING

Probably the most common form of display in use today is the seven-segment light-emitting diode display. There has been a fairly widely accepted standardization of the reference used to describe each section of the display. This is illustrated in Fig. 12-1. The seven individual bars are called segments "a" through "g" and the decimal point is generally called "h." Table 2-2, describing hexadecimal notation, showed the formation of all of the hexadecimal characters using the segments. In addition to this, there are a number of other characters which can be formed from the segments. For example, it is possible to form:

	Error
or	STOP
or	End of run
or	HELP

The characters are not necessarily standard, but they are readable. Also, a choice between upper case and lower is not always available.

The display is not said to be fully alphanumeric since all of the letters in the alphabet cannot be formed. For example, you cannot form a K or an X.

The reason for multiplexing becomes fairly obvious when you consider the logistics of servicing even a pocket calculator display.

227

Suppose that you want to drive a 10-digit calculator display. The display diodes which light up the segments generally draw too much current to be driven from the MOS calculator chip if they are larger than one-eighth inch high. Therefore, it might be necessary to have a switching transistor for each segment of eahc digit. This would amount to 7 segments times 10 digits = 70 transistors. Adding the 10 decimal points would give a total of 80 transistors and 80 connections required between the calculator chip and the display. If the current drain did not flatten the battery, you would still have the problem of stuffing all of the connections into the calculator package. Furthermore, the calculator chip would have to have 80 pins devoted to the display alone—let alone servicing the keyboard. Obviously, something more efficient is required.

If you pick up the calculator and move it rapidly back and forth before your eyes you will see that the display is actually flashing or blinking rapidly. With an oscilloscope, you would find that there is only one character turned on at a time and that the display is rapidly scanned from one end to the other. The scan is fast enough to prevent the central vision of the eye from following it. Therefore, the characters all seem to be on at the same time. The flickering is often detectable in the peripheral vision which has a faster response.

Figure 12-2 shows the manner in which this scanning is accomplished. For simplicity, only one segment driver and one digit selector is shown and only three display digits are included. The LED digit is shown as a common cathode type, however, common anode units are also available.

As shown Fig. 12-2, all of the "a" segments are tied together. Each segment of each digit is the anode of a LED. Within the digit package, the cathodes of all the segment diodes are tied together. When the SEGMENT DRIVE line is taken low, all of the "a" segments (in this case) are connected to V+ through Q1 and R. The calculator then designates which digit is to display the information by taking the appropriate DIGIT SELECT line high. This completes the circuit to ground through Q2 and any driven segments will light. Eight segment drive switches are required (including the decimal point) and as many digit drivers are required as there are digits. For the 10-digit display, you would need eight segment switches and 10 digit select switches—for a total of 18 rather than the 80.

The purpose of the resistor R in the segment drive line is to limit the current through the LED. In the bottom half of Fig. 12-2,

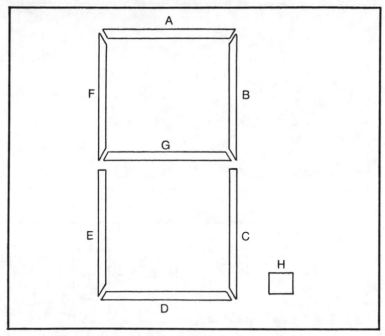

Fig. 12-1. The seven-segment display.

the voltage current curve of a typical LED is shown. Up to a certain voltage, the LED draws little or no current and then the curve breaks up and the current tries to climb to infinity. A LED actually makes a fairly good constant voltage source and can be used for a voltage reference for a constant current transistor circuit. It has the advantage that the forward voltage climbs with the temperature at about the same rate as the emitter/base drop of a bipolar transistor. The purpose of R is of course to limit the current that the LED can draw, to prevent burnout. A LED should never be operated without some current limiting device.

There is an interesting property of the LED which makes scanning not only attractive but also advantageous from an efficiency standpoint. A LED which is operated at 10 mA for 10 percent of the time will actually deliver about 1.5 times as many photons as the same unit operating on 1 mA continuously.

For typical LED displays, the following currents are required for each lighted segment:

⅛ inch high	2 to 5 mA
⅜ inch high	15 to 25 mA
⅞ inch high	50 to 150 mA

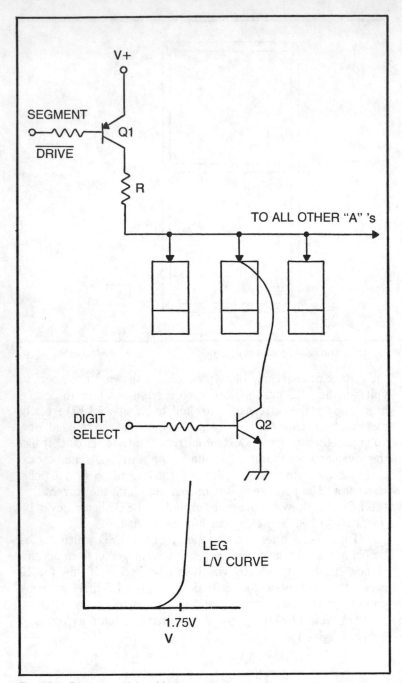

Fig. 12-2. Display multiplex drive.

230

As you can see from this table, there are significant differences in the efficiency of LED displays. As a matter of fact, obtaining digits with a uniform brightness was somewhat of a problem.

It has been experimentally determined that an ON period of about 25 milliseconds will produce a good display up to about 10 characters in width where the total display is updated four times per second. Beyond 10 characters, the small ON time begins to produce noticeable dimming. For ON times less than 1.0 microseconds, there is generally some turnoff problem and the characters can start to smear noticeably. Data from adjacent characters tends to "leak" in. Peak current limitations tend to hold the scan to about 10 digits since the peak current cannot be increased indefinitely.

There is another human factor limitation on displays. From a series of experiments performed on instruments using digital displays, I have found that it is inadvisable to update a display more often than once a second since few people can follow the change of the data. In particular, there is the problem of creating gross reading errors. For example, suppose that the instrument is receiving data such that the average reading is midway between three and four on the least significant digit. If there is any noise on the measurement, the instrument will sometimes display a three and sometimes display a four in the least significant digit. If the switch is rapid, the three superimposed upon the four can be read as: Shown in Fig. 12-3. In a similar fashion a five on a six will be read as an eight. A two on a one will be read as a b or a backward six. If the display is not updated more than twice per second the eye can separate the oscillating characters.

If the display must be read and evaluated, it is not wise to allow less than a half second per character for a four digit number and something closer to one digit per second as the display climbs to 10. If the number must be accurately copied, these factors should be increased by 5 times to allow for an initial reading of the

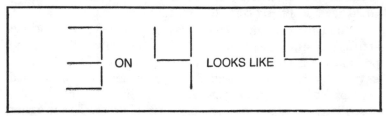

Fig. 12-3. Superimposed digital display.

digits and a verification of the copy. Any briefer presentation of the data will result in errors and aggravation on the part of the people using the unit.

KEYBOARD SERVICE

Many of the same arguments which applied to the need for multiplexing the display apply to the keyboard as well. On the simplest calculator, keys are required for the numerals zero through nine, a decimal point, add, subtract, multiply, divide and clear—or 16 keys in all. It would be possible to organize the keyboard into a 4 × 4 matrix using only eight lines rather than 16. However, on most calculators, advantage is taken of the fact that the digit select lines must be supplied for the display in any event. This can be reflected in a reduction of the number of I/O lines required.

Figure 12-4 shows one possible arrangement. In this arrangement, digit lines D0 through D3 are also used for column selection of the keyboard. If you depress key three, then every time that the machine selected D0 there would be a pulse on K0. If the closed key is CLR, the selection of D0 would have placed the pulse on K3. Since in the example there are 10 digits, it would have been possible to get by with only two key lines in an 8 × 2 matrix instead of the 4 × 4 used here. The tradeoff would involve the question of the number of total connections into the keyboard versus the minimization of the number of pins required on the calculator chip.

Obviously, the number of keys required is a function of what the machine is going to do. If full alphanumeric entry is desired, then the choice would probably go to a full typewriter keyboard which might run to 64 keys by the time punctuation, space and other functions are added. On the other hand, if the keyboard is intended to make a general purpose computer of minimal configuration out fo the processor, then the 16 hex keys plus a few more functions such as enter, stop, advance, reset, (which would come to 20 keys) is a fairly common selection.

The actual definition of the keys is determined by the machine software or firmware. A lookup table is generally built in by the programmer in order to interpret the key closures. Therefore, the keyboard wiring can be routed for maximum convenience and perhaps for human factor reasons. The keyboard on the Commodore PET is arranged in simple alphabetical order. This is easier for a non-typist to hunt-and-peck on. However, it will drive a typist

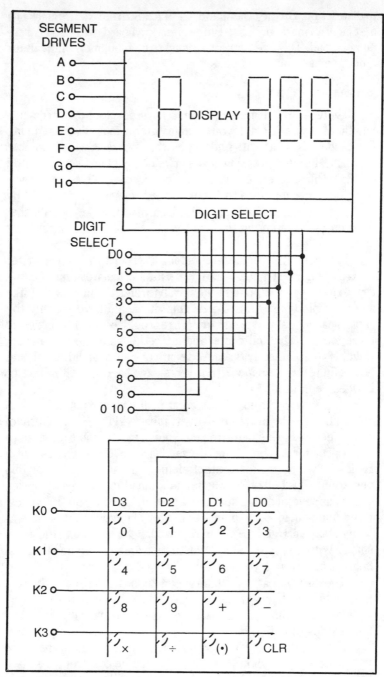

Fig. 12-4. Multiplexing keyboard and display.

to distraction. On the other hand, the TRS-80 from Radio Shack has a standard (more or less) typewriter keyboard with a separate numeric pad. This is easier for a typist to use, but more difficult for a non-typist to hunt-and-peck.

KEYBOARD MECHANISMS

There really are more mechanical systems for keyboards than you can shake a stick at. If you examine the various advertisements for keyboards, you will find types that operate with a simple mechanical bridge pressing across two contacts and sophisticated examples like Hall effect switches under each key which operate by bringing a magnet close to them or reed relays also operated by bringing a magnet alongside. One can also find keyboards that function by interrupting the light path in a LED/phototransistor pair.

In general, the requirements for a keyboard with a typewriter design are more stringent than those for a calculator type. On the typewriter keyboard, people generally prefer the unit to feel like an electronic typewriter. To do this, it should have roughly the same spacing as a typewriter. That would be on the order of three-fourth inches on centerlines. The keys should also have a travel of approximately three-sixteenth of an inch and there should be a definite *tactile feedback*. The key should have a "feel" or kick to it when depressed.

People will put up with a great deal less sophistication in a calculator type keyboard. However, most will favor some form of tactile feedback. One of the most common mechanisms for giving a thin calculator keyboard tactile feedback involves the use of a Belleville washer as the contact element. Figure 12-5 shows this operation. The belleville washer is a small dome-shaped spring which has several stable states. At rest, the dome is up. However, when sufficient force is applied to the top of the dome, it buckles in with a sharp snap action. When released, it snaps back to the dome shape. With this type of key, you always know when an entry has been made because you can feel the washer spring.

The disadvantages to this type of keyboard stem mostly from the fact that the keytop must be placed through a hole in the cover. Coffee or ice cream spilled on the keyboard will make it gummy and the keytops can stick in.

For applications where this represents a problem, there are two different types of keyboards which can be constructed so that they can be easily washed and kept completely waterproof.

234

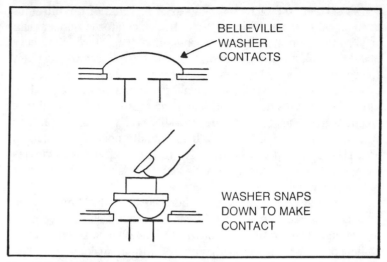

Fig. 12-5. The bellville washer keyswitch.

The conductive elastomer keyboard is constructed with the two contacts positioned in the center of a hole in a stiff insulating board. A layer of rubbery conductive elastomer is stretched above the top of the hole and covered with a waterproof jacket which has the key identification printed on it. When the key is pressed, the elastomer stretches down into the hole and makes the contact between the elements. This type of keyswitch usually has a relatively high ON resistance but it has little bounce and is actually cleanable with soap and water. In my opinion this sort of keyswitch is not very satisfying to use since the switch simply mushes down into the hole and you cannot tell by feel alone whether you have actually made an entry or, for that matter, whether you have made several. Some other form of feedback is required.

The second type of keyboard consists of nothing more than a pair of printed capacitor plates under a very thin dielectric cover on which the key identification is printed. The control or device used with this type must sense the change in capacitance caused by the presence of your finger. This requires a fairly sophisticated analog sensor. This type of keyboard is absolutely rigid and has no feel whatever.

In order to provide some feedback to tell the operator that he has made an entry, there are several gambits used with this form of keyboard. If the unit is equipped with a display, the display can be blanked whenever a closed key is sensed. You know that you have hit the key because the display goes out.

A second type of feedback is used in some of the ultrathin calculators. In these devices, the entire calculator is thinner than the keyboard on a belleville washer unit. Therefore, the short travel technology must be used. Many of these calculators contain a very tiny beeper which beeps every time a key is depressed.

The third type of feedback makes use of a small solenoid on the back of the board itself. Every time that a key is closed, the solenoid gives the back of the board a sharp rap which can be felt by the finger depressing the key. It is actually possible to make a board feel as though more expensive tactile feedback keyswitches were used by this technique. However, it consumes a fair amount of power and takes space.

Obviously, there are places where the individual types cannot be used. For example, a capacitive touch board would not be good for typing since the lightest touch is registered as an entry. You could not rest a finger on the board without making an entry. However, for a kitchen appliance where someone might be making entries with fingers covered with flour or maple syrup, the washability of the capacitive board could be ideal.

KEYBOARD USAGE

The trend in modern appliance and machine design is toward the use of a keyboard for all entries. There are a series of fairly compelling reasons for this. First of all, the functions and facilities are becoming more diverse as processor based controls are added. Once the processor is in, the addition of bells and whistles becomes fairly inexpensive. For example, on a microwave oven it becomes simple for you to specify the time that the dinner is supposed to be ready. You then enter the cooking and defrost cycles. The machine can calculate the time to start by itself. To do the same functions using mechanical timers would have required several expensive dial controls. The processor, display and keyboard can accomplish the sophisticated control function at less cost and with a less cluttered panel.

Because of the economics and marketing appeal it seems unlikely that more and more controls will be built using keyboard entry rather than dial and switch type devices.

THE UNION JACK DISPLAY

One type of alphanumeric display which has found a certain amount of popularity is the *union jack* display, so named because of its similarity to the stripes on the British flag. This display type is capable of displaying a full alphanumeric range. Figure 12-6 shows this display and some of the relatively awkward characters. It is capable of producing the full English alphabet in upper case characters as well as numerals from zero thru nine. The display has 16 segments as shown in the illustration. These characters are generally made in small sizes using light-emitting segments. However, liquid crystal versions have begun to appear.

In general, this display is used with a ROM lookup table to identify the character. However, there are some manufacturers who provide displays of this type which will decode parallel ASCII code and latch the character to the display so that no scanning is required. The unit has built-in ROM for the decoding and usually features four characters per hybrid assembly. The characters are addressed sequentially.

The 64-word subset of ASCII covers all the upper case English letters and numerals zero through nine as well as certain punctuation. Displays of this type are commonly used where short messages of 12 to 30 characters are required. Since the coding is latched into the display, the processor can ignore the display until a change or update is required.

Fig. 12-6. The Union Jack alphanumeric display.

Some of these devices appear as though they could be fitted directly across the memory bus of an eight bit processor and addressed as memory. Unfortunately, some of the very early units were quite slow and had a very elaborate timing protocol for sequencing the digit select, write and data lines which could not be accommodated on the standard memory bus. Before using one of these decoding displays, it is wise to check the timing requirements to determine whether a PIA is required or whether they can be addressed as memory.

The use of a latched display is worth noting. Most of the time the processor will have other things to do besides servicing the keyboard and the display. Therefore, it is handy to have some arrangement whereby you can write to the display and have the data remain latched while the processor attends to other business. If a 6821 PIA is used for the display interface, this latching is accomplished automatically since the 6821 latches all outputs and stays latched until a new write command is directed to that register. However, not all output chips have an automatic latching feature. It is therefore worth an investigation of the particular chip properties when a display must be serviced while other things are going on.

THE DOT MATRIX DISPLAY

One of the more common and relatively high quality types of display is the dot matrix display. If you stop to examine the photographs on the front page of a newspaper with a magnifying glass, you will find that the entire picture is made up of a series of tiny dots. The dots are all equally black since the paper uses only one color of printers ink. However, you will find that the lighter areas in the paper have very tiny dots with a white surrounding. The dark areas have larger dots and correspondingly less white. Obviously, it is possible to generate nearly any shape if you use enough tiny dots.

A similar close inspection of a color TV screen will show that there are tiny clusters of dots of three colors which are also used to produce the picture seen on the screen. The trick also works for full color pictures.

The main question which comes up in using this sort of a technique for a computer display is one of economics. In a solid-state display, each dot can be represented by a LED or a neon or other gas discharge in a tiny cell. However, each of these cells must somehow be addressed and driven. If a full half-tone presentation is to be made, then the cell must be given some output magnitude control as well. Each of these things costs money and uses power. The question therefore becomes how few dots are required to make up a usable display.

Figure 12-7 shows a 5 × 7 dot matrix which is generally considered to be the fewest number of dots which can be used for a full alphanumeric display. The individual dots have been represented by Os.

Lighted dots are connected by a heavy black line to indicate which of the elements are lighted. It is possible to make some

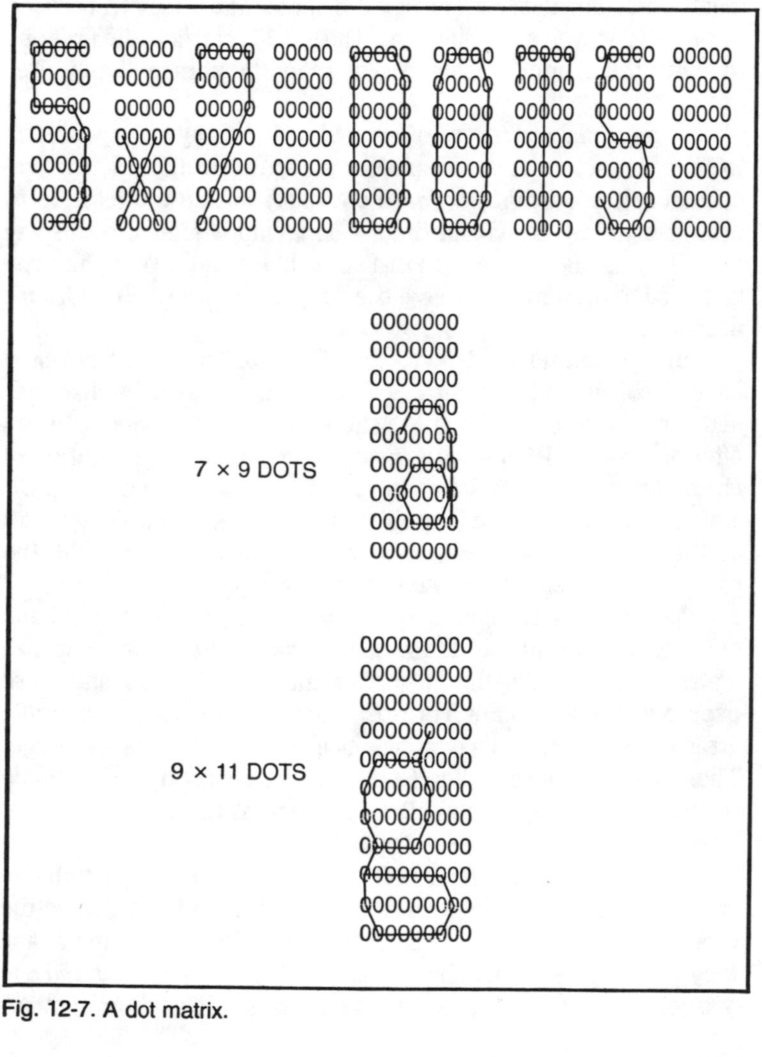

Fig. 12-7. A dot matrix.

reasonably good quality characters with the 5 × 7 matrix in upper case only. The 5 × 7 matrix is usually used with the 64-character subset of ASCII code.

The second illustration in Fig. 12-7 shows the 7 × 9 dot matrix which is generally considered to be the smallest capable of producing both upper and lower case characters in the full 128 character ASCII set. The lower case characters in several of the FONTS (sets of type) are a little nonstandard but quite readable.

The 9 × 11 matrix is the one shown at the bottom of Fig. 12-7. This matrix is the first one to allow the generation of fully formed fonts—including descenders on g and q, etc. The dot matrix is used on printers as well as on displays. The 9 × 11 matrix is the first one to which the printer manufacturers apply the phrase "typewriter quality."

Several manufacturers offer the blank display chips with one to four characters and a character select as well as a row and column select on-chip. It would obviously not be too feasible to bring out the 35 individual diodes on a chip designed to display three-eighths inch characters in a stackable fashion. With this type of device, it is common to have the dot patterns stored in ROM for decoding.

In a column selected device, the ROM for a 5 × 7 matrix would have to consist of 5 columns of 7-bit words times a 64 character set—or a total of 2,240 bits. There are several manufacturers offering masked ROMs with a variety of codes for generation of characters direct from the code. The most popular code is ASCII and the 6-bit ASCII word is applied to the address lines along with a 3-bit column or row select. Rather than build a special ROM, the pattern is masked into a 512 × 8 standard part.

The ROM can be obtained in either a row selected or a column selected version in the different fonts and for the different size matrices. Obviously, the larger the matrix the larger and more expensive the ROM. For a printer, the little needles are generally arranged in a vertical column which is swept across the page. Therefore, a colum selected ROM is generally used. On a cathode ray tube or TV type display, the spot generally scans from side to side. Therefore, a row select scheme is generally used.

A few manufacturers are offering selfdecoding chips with five characters or so. These need only be sent the 6-bit code and the character select. They are rather expensive. However, in volume they probably save enough external hardware to justify the $75 to $90 cost. The principal use of these displays is in desktop computers where a single line of perhaps 30 characters is to be displayed. If the display is made much larger than that, it begins to pay to simply include a cathode ray tube.

There are also some multiline displays offered by a few manufacturers which will display a number of lines of dot matrix characters. Burroughs offers these under the trade name Self-Scan® and provides the support electronics to go with the display. The gas discharge multi-line displays are really not economically competitive with a cathode ray tube but they offer the advantage of being relatively flat and shallow so that they can be used in places where the cathode-ray tube cannot be fitted. They are also capable of operating with great brightness so that they can be used in high levels of ambient light where a special high-brightness CRT would be required. The LED displays have been improved, but most do not have enough brightness for use in direct sunshine as on a gas pump, in an airplane cockpit or other outdoor applications. In some of these applications, incandescent seven-segment or union jack displays are employed.

THE CATHODE-RAY TUBE DISPLAY

The cathode-ray tube has been around the longest of any type of display and is probably the best of any display technique. While the solid-state devices have made some inroads, it still seems likely that the cathode-ray tube displays will be with us for some time. Despite some of the difficulties with the CRT, it still represents the cheapest form of display if anything like a full typewritten page of information is to be displayed.

The drawbacks of the cathode-ray tube are relatively obvious. It is big and heavy and it requires a very high voltage to drive and to operate the anode. There are some other features about it which also bear some attention. From the engineering practice of television, it has been found that it is necessary to scan the screen at approximately a rate of 30 times per second to present a display which does not flicker. If this 30 per second rate is combined with the standard 525 lines used in TV, you obtain the horizontal scan rate of 15,750 sweeps per second. To further reduce flicker, the scan is operated in an *interlaced* manner. One scan, which requires 1/60 second, covers all of the odd numbered lines and the second scan covers all of the even numbered lines.

Large screen CRTs are generally easier to build in short neck, compact designs using magnetic deflection rather than electrostatic deflection. They also require fewer internal parts and therefore are cheaper to build. However, they are also harder to deflect. To minimize the deflection problems, they are usually used in a *raster scan* mode rather than in a more or less random access mode such as can be obtained in a lab oscilloscope where the spot can be deflected in any direction by applying appropriate voltages to the X and Y amplifiers.

For the raster scan, a 60 Hz sawtooth current wave is applied to the vertical deflection coils and a 15,750 Hz current sawtooth is applied to the horizontal deflection coils. Figure 12-8 shows that the beam path goes across the screen with a slight tilt. Whenever the screen is required to show a dot, the *video amplifier* applies a pulse to the grid of the tube. This increases the current and brightening the spot on the screen.

In Fig. 12-8, scan line five is represented as having just gone through the top row of the five and seven of a message to be displayed. Note that the proportions have been exaggerated so that they will show in the illustration. There are several points worthy of note on this display. First of all, the fifth sweep has to display the top row of cells of all of the matrices on that line. This means that the memory has to jump from character to character as the spot flies across. The second point is that the next trace must go through the third row of every character because of the interlace action.

Suppose that you would like to have the screen display 25 characters across. Allowing for a one cell gap between matrices, there are $6 \times 25 = 150$ cells which must be scanned on every trace. Since the beam is scanning horizontally at 15,750 times per second, the video system has to handle $15,750 \times 150 = 2,362,500$ cells per second. Multiplying this by two for Shannon's criterion at a bare minimum, you find that a video bandwidth of 4.725 MHz is the minimum that is required without some smearing of the dots. This is the cutoff frequency of a standard TV. Therefore, a display of 25 characters is the top limit achievable with a standard TV screen.

The memory itself will have to access $15,750 \times 25$ characters $= 393,750$ characters per second or one character every 2.5 microseconds. This is far too fast for a read from memory and write to output cycle on 8-bit machines of the 6800 generation. Therefore, some other approach must be used.

One technique which is successful is to have the CRT equipped with its own memory. This can be a serial access affair. If you assume that a two cell spacing exists between lines of characters,

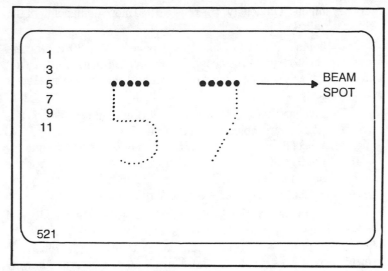

Fig. 12-8. The CRT raster display.

then nine cells are required for a single character and the display
will be 521/9 = 57 characters high and the memory would have to
have 57 × 25 = 1425 characters. In actual practice it has been found
that the screen is easier to read and the borders work out better if
the display is limited to 25 lines of text vertically with 20 characters horizontally which will fit into a 512 byte memory.

A second technique has been gaining favor recently. In this
approach, the memory access is by DMA and the processor and the
video display alternate cycles of memory, thereby sharing a common memory.

The sweep circuits on a display are an analog sort of arrangement and they require something to keep them synchronized with
the digital data. This action is usually accomplished by using a 3.57
MHz color burst crystal and dividing it down to obtain the 15,750
horizontal sync pulse and the 60Hz vertical sync pulse. There are a
number of manufacturers currently supplying CRT management
chips for this purpose and to handle the video processing.

WORD PROCESSING

One of the common usages for digital processing is the word
processor or electronic correcting typewriter. In this machine, you
can type in text, view it on the screen, edit it, transpose paragraphs, etc. When the text is ready, a touch of the GO button will
cause the printer to type out error-free copy at 150 to 600 charac-

ters per minute. Obviously, there is a little more demanding of the video terminal.

To begin with, a normal typed page is not 20 characters across, it is 80 characters across. Secondly, the characters are not all upper case. It is necessary to present both upper case and lower case characters.

This means that a 5×7 matrix will not suffice. The 7×9 matrix is the least usable. If you assume that a 7 column and two space matrix of 80 characters is to be presented, the dot frequency is $15,750 \times 9 \times 80 = 11,340,000$ and a usable bandwidth for the high resolution terminal will be about 22 MHz. The memory will have to present a character every 0.7 microseconds.

This is the reason that high quality text-editing terminals tend to be expensive. Relatively high speed memory is required and a fast video processor is also needed. A typical high resolution terminal will present 25 lines of up to 80 characters—thereby requiring 2K bytes of memory. The 25 lines represent about the same text distribution as double spaced typing. In actual typing practice, the margins of the page cut the number of characters on a given line to about 60. The 25×80 suffices to present about the same amount of information on the CRT screen as a full page of double-spaced typing.

Reasons for the popularity of the text-editing or electronic typewriter systems are that they can be used for editing and new copy generation, form letters, contracts, standard contract paragraphs and other repetitive material that can be stored on a floppy disc or a tape and summoned up without alteration. It is possible to have the machine stop for the manual insertion of names, addresses, etc. so that the finished document does not resemble a form letter even when it is a form letter. Certain of the mail-order houses have taken to having the front cover of a catalog printed with some blank spaces left for the insertion of a name. The printed form is then fed through a computer-driven printer and your name and address are typed on and your name will be typed into several gaps left in the text. The effect is somewhat hokey, but it does seem to give a personal touch if you don't look too closely and realize that the personal references were taken from a computer file of your account number and printed by the computer without human intervention. The effect of the letter produced on the same machine is much greater. However, the cost would be prohibitive if the computer were to produce all of the cover text.

KEYBOARD DEBOUNCE

If you were to use one of the fast digitizing techniques to examine the waveform of the keys, you would find that a mechanical keyswitch does not smoothly make the circuit or break the circuit. Figure 12-9 shows this effect. On the microscopic scale, the surface of the contacts is made up of mountains and valleys and tiny wiskers which resulted from previous sparking. As the keys are pressed, the contacts are usually designed to wipe over one another. This scrubs off the oxide and corrosion that is present in microscopic amounts. During this scrubbing action, the actual contact is established in high and low resistance configurations many times before the switch settles in the closed condition. If the keyswitch actually toggles parts together under spring tension, the mechanical impact of the contacts might actually result in a mechanical bounce before contact is established. The effect is generally referred to as *bounce*.

Figure 12-9 shows the response attained from a relatively common type of keyswitch. On closure, the intermittant contact can persist for as long as 14 milliseconds. On the break operation, the bounce is usually only about a third as long. However, on occasion some switches will show a late bounce on opening due to a mechanical resonance in the swinger.

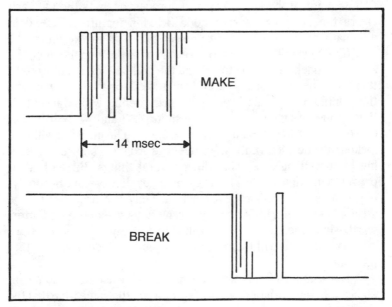

Fig. 12-9. Keyswitch bounce effects.

On expensive keyswitches, gold plating is often used on the contacts to minimize the oxidation. Bifurcated or serrated contacts are also used. The electronic keyboards where a Hall effect magnetic sensor is used or where a light beam is broken by depression of the key are usually free of bounce. These keyswitches are expensive—running as much as several dollars per key. Probably one of the biggest differences between an inexpensive pocket calculator and a "good" pocket calculator is the quality of the keyswitches. Far more pocket calculators fail because of sticking or bouncing keys than for electronic reasons. It is very annoying to try to enter a digit and discover that the calculator absorbed five of them. Relatively inexpensive keyswitches can be used on processor based equipment when a proper debounce routine is included in the software.

Figure 12-10 illustrates a keyboard debounce routine which has N KEY ROLLOVER. This routine us a slight expansion upon the initialize routine of Fig. 8-8. The program is entered through node 1 and the keyboard is tested for a key closure. If no key is closed, the processor exits the routine. If a key is closed, the processor next tests to see whether the key flag has been set. On the first reading, the flag will not be set and the program loops back to node 1, after a delay of 14 milliseconds to allow for key bounce. At this point, if the key is open the processor exits the loop and clears the key flag through node 3. This feature is useful in eliminating false keying due to noise spikes on the key lines.

If a key is still closed on the second pass through the loop, the key is decoded, the data stored and the node 2 loop is entered. In this loop, the keyboard is reread and tested for a key open condition. Until the keyboard is open, no further entry will be accepted. For example, suppose that you push key #3 and while it is still down you push key #4 and then key #5, etc. The machine will stay locked in node 2 loop until all of the keys are open before proceeding to something else. This does several things. First of all, it prevents multiple entries from a single key depression. Secondly, it provides the n-key rollover action. Only the first key that is struck is entered no matter how many keys are depressed afterward while the first key is still down. Only when the entire keyboard is open will the machine proceed to node 3 and another program.

A variation of this scheme has proven useful in some instances. In this variation, at the first entry at the same time that the key flag is set, the key data is also recorded in a temporary storage.

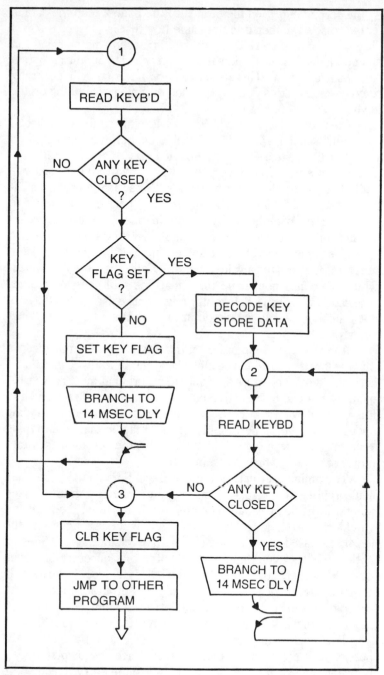

Fig. 12-10. Keyboard debounce routine.

At the second entry, on the branch to the node 2 loop the data is tested to see whether it is the same key that is closed. If it is a different key or if more than one key is closed, the machine can clear both entries and the key flag and proceed to another program or signal an alarm. This precautionary program will generally prevent false entries due to someone dropping something on the keyboard, etc.

The program as shown in Fig. 12-10 will ensure a good solid single entry action with any reasonable quality of keyswitch. It is very difficult to "tease" it into a double entry. If someone deliberately stabs a finger at side-by-side keys it will give a nonsense multiple entry on about one in 10 tries. For a calculator, an instrument or a point-of-sale terminal where the operator is expected to be cooperating with the device, it is quite adequate. For a vending machine or other device where the public will be using the machine or where someone might have something to gain by defeating the program, the test for a valid single-key entry is probably worthwhile. This also holds true for a machine tool control or other application where an invalid entry might cause damage. If they are not watching, people will sometimes strike two keys simultaneously.

A few words are in order on the delay. The 14 milliseconds that the key is required to be closed and the 14 milliseconds that it is required to be open are adequate to assure that most reasonable quality keys will have settled out. But this is not slow enough to limit the rate of data entry. The timing is adequate for a typing speed of 428 words per minute. This is faster than even typing "bursts" as in typing "the" or "is" where the instantaneous rate might reach 250 words per minute.

The timing need not be simply wasted. For example, the delay could represent a display scan or some other program of fixed length. If the delay is only a do nothing timing loop, the keyboard will blank the display at every entry and will not relight until the key is released. This is sometimes handy since it provides an optical feedback informing the operator that an entry has been made. However, not all people will like this feature. If the delay is actually made up of a display scan and other program operation the program as shown will display the entry instantaneously upon the key depression. This is the way that most calculators behave.

For vending machines and other devices to be used by the public, it is sometimes worthwhile to place the display update between the exit from the node 2 loop and the entry to node 3. In

248

this case, the display will update upon release of the key. This provides a form of "human factor" toggle action which encourages the user into a push-the-key and release-the-key action.

Preferences differ widely and the display itself can be a subject of controversy. For example, should the entries start at the left and march to the right as on a typewriter:

$$1$$
$$12$$
$$123$$

or should they start at the right and march to the left:

$$1$$
$$12$$
$$123$$

Hewlett Packard feels that the first technique is best. Texas Instruments thinks the second is best. You could probably summon evidence to prove that either technique is better.

On any new product which has a display and a keyboard, these items and the operational procedure of their use are the portions which are the most visible to the public. They are also the hardest points to settle within any organization since there will probably be as many opinions about the "right" way to organize them as there are people involved with the product. Deciding these items will often be the largest hurdle in the initial product development.

13 Power Devices

For many of the applications in which a processor can be used, it must be interfaced to outside devices which have to operate at voltage and power levels which are beyond the capabilities of the processor or the PIA. The purpose of this chapter to show some of the more common techniques for doing this.

DC SWITCHING

Since the processor itself is a binary on/off type of device, it lends itself to on/off switching applications. The input/output devices usually supplied with a processor are generally restricted to voltages no greater than the supply voltage and currents of usually less than a milliampere or a mill and a half. If relays, lamps, switches or motors are to be operated, the I/0 will require some help.

Transistors operating in the switching mode can handle a great deal more power than they can when operated in the linear mode. For example, a 2N2222 switching transistor will easily turn a 28V supply on and off and will handle currents of 0.2 amperes. In the saturated condition, the transistor will have a forward drop of less than a volt and the power dissipation at 0.2 amperes will be less than 0.2 watts. This tiny T0-5 cased item can dissipate this with a clip-on finned heatsink. In the off condition, the drop will be 28 volts but the current will be negligable and the power dissipation will be near zero. The device will be turning on and off a load of 28V × 0.2A = 5.6 watts.

However, suppose that the transistor did not get turned on to saturation and that it reached a condition where half of the supply voltage appeared across its collector at the same time that it was passing 0.1 A. In this case, the transistor would be dissipating 14V × 0.1 amperes or 1.4 watts. In this case, the transistor would rapidly heat and probably eventually be destroyed in a very short period. It is therefore important that the transistor have enough base drive to pull it into saturation in switching mode operation.

If you assume that the transistor has a beta of 100 you can see that a 200 milliampere collector current will require something on the order of 2 mA of base drive. This is likely to exceed the output characteristic of the PIA. For this reason, the use of darlington amplifiers on output switching applications is common.

Figure 13-1 shows a typical darlington switch. Transistor Q1 is used only to amplify the base drive to Q2. In effect, the beta of the assembly is the product of the beta of Q1 times the beta of Q2. The four-thousand ohm resistor in the base will limit the base current of Q1 to about 1 mA. If Q1 has a beta of 200 and Q2 has a beta of 50, the drive is adequate for switching 10 amperes. The darlington can be fabricated from discrete units or purchased as a packaged unit. Packaged darlingtons with a beta guaranteed at 10,000 minimum are commercially available.

An important feature of the switch is the presence of CR-1. If the load has any significant amount of inductance, there can be a large surge of voltage developed during turnoff. The voltage de-

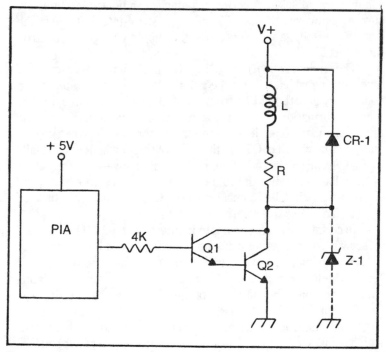

Fig. 13-1. The darlington dc switch.

veloped by the inductor is L di/dt. The current can be as much as 10 amperes. The turnoff time for a darlington is on the order of a microsecond. Therefore, di/dt can easily reach values like 10^7. The voltage is actually reversed in polarity compared to the supply. Therefore, when the transistor turns off, the current can "free wheel" through CR-1 and prevent destruction of the transistors.

An alternative is the inclusion of the zener diode directly shunting the transistor. This prevents the voltage from rising above levels that the transistor can tolerate and protects against reverse polarized surges as well.

Both of these techniques tend to slow the collapse of the field in the inductor and thereby to limit the voltage developed. They do, however, slightly slow the operation of the circuit load.

THE INPUT LEVEL SHIFTER

Often the problem calls for the processor to sense a binary input from a source which has a much higher voltage than the processor supply. For example, on automotive systems, the outside voltages being sensed might be 15 volts or 24 volts on trucks and military vehicles. A series resistance can be used to limit the current. However, if the PIA input goes tri-state and opens the circuit, the voltage will rise above the supply voltage and destroy the device.

The circuits shown in Fig. 13-2 illustrate some techniques for level shifting which will handle relatively high input voltages and completely isolate the PIA from the voltages while conveying the binary information. Both of these circuits invert the data. The diodes clamp the input level to the transistor base between ground and V+. The circuit of Q1 will fire on a low input whenever Vin falls below V+ and will cut off when the Vin rises above V+. The circuit of Q2 will turn on when the value of Vin rises above ground and will cut off when Vin falls to near ground. Both circuits are protected against large negative values of Vin.

In certain cases, for example in interfacing to PMOS, the case arises where a processor using positive logic must be interfaced to a device having logic levels running from ground to some negative level. The lower circuit shows one technique for accommodating this conversion. When Q2 is cutoff due to a ground level Vin, then the resistor chain R1 R2 and R3 is proportioned to bring the base Q1 to ground or just below ground. This cuts off Q1 and the PIA senses a high input. When Q2 is turned on by a low level (negative) on Vin, then the R2 R3 junction rises to ground level and Q1 turns on

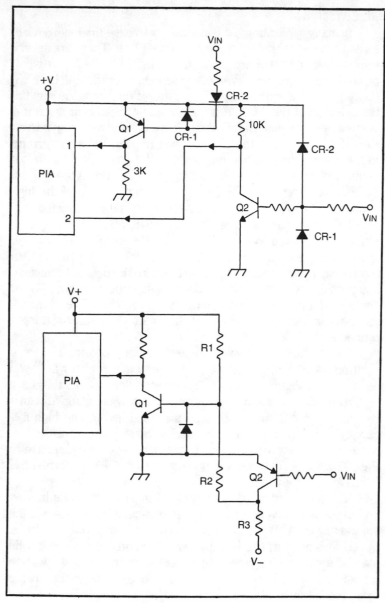

Fig. 13-2. Logic level shifters (top) and negative logic levels (bottom).

hard—thereby presenting a low input to the PIA. The base of Q1 is shown with diode protection. Diode protection could also be used on Q2 if required.

AC SWITCHING

In many applications, it is necessary to have the logic devices switch devices on and off of the ac 120 volt line. There are several things about this that are problematical. First of all, you would probably prefer to have even the ground side of the line have any contact with the logic ground. There are several reasons why this is advisable. If the AC line is carrying any significant amount of current, it is not unusual to find that it is a volt or two removed from the safety ground on a three wire power line due to heavy currents in the return line. In addition, there is the possibility that a load connected without a three-wire safety plug could have the leads plugged in in reverse. This would raise the chassis of the logic system to 120 VAC above ground with the attendant shock hazard.

The second reason that it is adviseable to have the logic completely isolated from the line is that the line is noisy and can cause the logic to malfunction. The very action which you intend to control can make enough line noise to cause the device to misfire. You probably went to great lengths to isolate the power supply for the logic from the ac line with a transformer. Therefore, it makes sense to provide high levels of isolation on the output and input connections.

A few years ago this was somewhat of a problem. The usual solution was to build a high frequency oscillator which was keyed on for a I and shut off for a 0. The oscillator was coupled through a high frequency isolation transformer, which was equipped with a rectifier on the output to restore the logic level. The high frequency signal would couple through a transformer whose inductance was two low to permit any significiant reverse coupling from the 60 Hz line. For a good isolation protection, the transformer had to have very good insulation.

The photo isolator has eliminated most of the complication and expense involved in the fast acting oscillator isolator and the slow acting relay. Photo isolated switches are commonly available. Space does not permit a lengthy exposition on the subject of solid state ac switching. However, the circuits which follow show some workable designs for ac switches and serve to illustrate some of the principles of available solid-state relays.

In Fig. 14-2, the circuit shown is a full wave ac switch. The PIA drives transistor Q1. When the PIA output is in the low state, Q1 turns hard on—thereby lighting the two LEDs. The light from the LEDs triggers the two photo SCRs—thereby permitting the line current to flow through the load. A high level on the PIA will turn the line current off at the next zero crossing of the load current. This is a natural action of the SCR. After the SCR has been switched on, it stays latched on until the anode current falls to zero—even after the gate drive has been removed.

In ac applications, this is an advantage since the SCR does not attempt to interrupt a high load current, thereby causing large transients as were noted when the DC transistor switch operated. It is the nature of SCRs that they turn off "easy" with little disturbance.

The photo SCR assembly shown in Fig. 13-3 is available from General Electric in the H211C which is a single 14-pin DIP. The two SCRs can be used in either two different half-wave circuits or in a single full-wave circuit as shown. These units are capable of switching a 120VAC line and will carry 0.3 amperes. The 330 ohm resistor is required to limit the current drawn by the LEDs. In addition, the gates of the two SCRs have been tied to the cathode to prevent spurious firing in high ambient temperatures.

For applications requiring something a bit more robust in the SCR department, the circuit at the bottom of the Fig. 13-3. The photo SCR package brings out the anodes, cathodes and SCR gates to separate pins. Therefore, the small SCRs can be used to trigger much larger SCRs which are capable of handling nearly any load current. In this circuit the LEDs can be tied in series as in the circuit above. SCRs capable of handling hundreds of amperes can be fired with gate currents of less than 100 mA. Therefore, the small IC is capable of driving arc welders and the like.

Since the only connection between the ac circuit and the logic is through the beam of infrared light the LED emits, the isolation between the ac circuit and the logic is complete. Packaged units with isolation ratings beginning at 1500 volts are common and isolations into the 15 KV region are commercially available. A number of manufacturers make these photo SCR and photo transistor isolators in packaged form. Bottom end unit prices are less than $1.

While the SCR alwys turns off easily with minimal transient generation, the same cannot be said of the turn on operation. At any time that the SCR gate is triggered, the SCR turns on with a rise time which can be less than a microsecond. If the line voltage happens to be at peak at the instant the turn-on command is given, the voltage is liable to be changed at a rate of 150V/microseconds. This gives a sharp click or pop in nearby radio equipment unless great pains are taken to filter and shield the load and the power line.

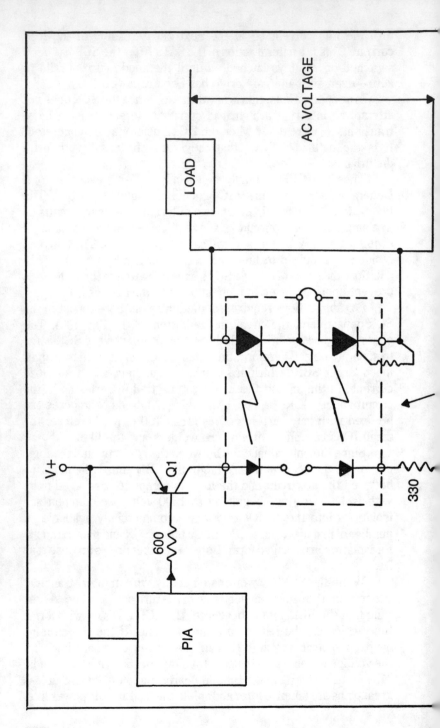

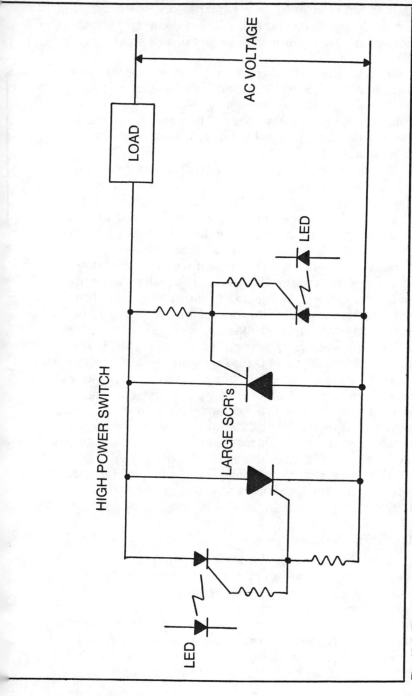

Fig. 13-3. The photo isolated ac switch.

This is known as radio frequency interference or RFI and it is generally illegal. Furthermore, the RFI can be a real nuisance in your logic and cause all manner of nasty malfunctions and runaway of the processor.

RFI supressors are a story unto themselves and they generally add considerable expense to the device. Fortunately, there are ways to minimize RFI by preventing this noise pollution from coming into being in the first place. The simplest of these is to prevent is near zero. This will make the turn-on as smooth as the turn-off which comes with the SCR.

The circuit shown in Fig. 13-4 represents a zero-crossing firing technique. Across the ac line is a voltage divider which supplies a small sample of the line voltage to a pair of opposed LEDs. The LEDs are protected by diodes CR1 and CR2 from inverse voltage which would destroy them. The LEDs are part of photo transistor isolators. The waveforms shown in Fig. 13-4 represent the currents and the equivalent photon output of the two LEDs. The phototransistors PQ1 and PQ2 are OR wired through a load resistor to V+ of the logic. Only during the period when the line voltage sample is below the forward firing voltage of the LEDs are both transistors turned off—thereby allowing Ea to rise to V+.

The PIA is not directly connected to the photo SCR switch, but rather passes through a D flip flop. This device clocks on the rising edge of the Ea pulse, thereby passing the data from the PIA to the switch. Since this happens only on the zero crossing of the line voltage, the SCR switch can turn on or off only at the zero crossings. The nature of the SCR switch is to stay on until a zero in the current occurs. With an inductive load, this will be a fraction of a cycle after the PIA gives the off command.

This type of device offers the quietest operation of any ac line switch since both make and break occur on zero crossings. The RFI is therefore minimized and no special line filtering will be required.

ALTERNATE CYCLING

When driving magnetic loads such as transformers, or motors, a peculiar phenomenon occurs. Suppose that the last cycle which passed through the unit was positive-going. There is always a small amount of hysteresis in the magnetic material and the core will be slightly magnetized with a given polarity. If the next turn on takes place at the start of another positive going cycle, the unit will already be slightly magnetized. Since this magnetization is in a direction to aid the field being forced by the line, the unit will

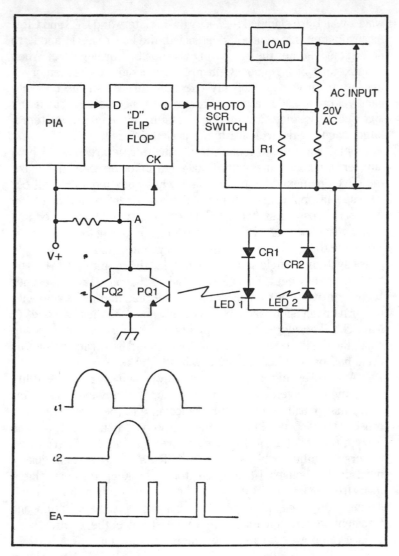

Fig. 13-4. The zero crossing turn-on photo isolator switch.

probably saturate and draw an excessive current for the first half-cycle. This is the reason that the refrigerator will sometimes dim the lights more than others on startup.

The circuit shown in Fig. 13-5 shows a technique whereby this form of starting transient can be eliminated. The transformer samples the line voltage. Rectifiers CR1 and CR2 rectify half-waves which are clamped to V+ by the resistors and CR3 and CR4. At any instant that a turnoff is signaled, the PIA reads I1 and I2 to determine whether the last swing was positive or negative. When the next turn pin is required, the processor examines its memory of the last turn off flag and only executes turn on in the opposite half-cycle. This adds a bit of hardware to the system, but it can significantly reduce turn on transients in the electrical system if large magnetic devices are being cycled.

Solid state photo isolated switches for ac are offered by a number of manufacturers in packaged form for prices which make the developement of homebrew switches questionable in all but very special applications. Most of these devices are also available with zero crossing switching. The zero crossing sensor used in a single phase load can actually serve for a number of load switches. The same thing is true of the alternate cycling sensor. In any single phase system, a single sensor will provide the required data for any number of devices. The zero crossings happen 120 times per second or every 0.0083 seconds and the read memory cycle with the turn on decision takes a total of only about 25 microseconds (1 MHz ck). Therefore, there is plenty of time for the processor to make the decision whether the device should be turned on on this cycle-half or whether it should wait for the next.

At the present time, there is usually no penalty from the utility company for waveform mutilation or surges. However, it seems likely that penalties might be forthcoming in the near future because of the disparity between the utility construction rates and the growth rate of electrical usage. At present, most industrial customers are billed only for peak load. Therefore, the main goal of most of the industrial load regulators is to keep too many large loads from operating at the same time. In the future, however, it seems likely that price penalties for waveform mutilation and transient generation migth be imposed since these effectively reduce the power capability of the installed plant.

SAFETY CAUTION NOTE

Whenever large electrical loads are handled, the question of safety arises. In addition to the usual electrical and mechanical considerations concerning large loads or moving machinery, the processor adds several new dimensions which must be considered. For example, what happens if the processor runs excessively due to a transient or other malfunction? Does the garage door suddenly start coming down? Does the crane suddenly start to travel, or

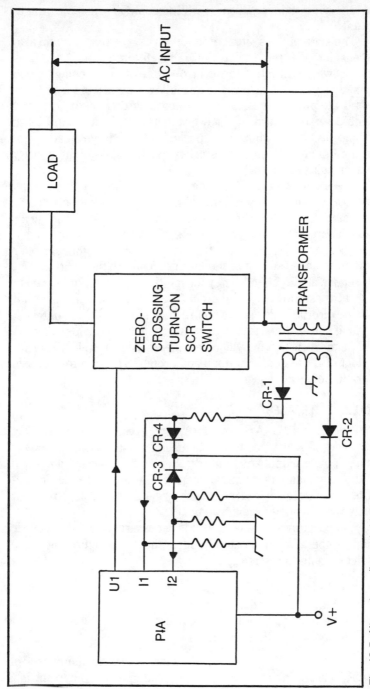

Fig. 13-5. Alternate cycling switching.

261

does the oven suddenly turn on while people are inside trying to clean it?

The state of the system at initial turn on or reset should also be considered. If the line current is briefly interrupted and then returns, what will all of the controlled devices be doing? Good engineering practice demands a careful examination of these questions if the processor is to control anything that could present a possible safety hazard. This would naturally include any large moving machinery which is exposed and any large heating apparatus. It might also include smaller items such as high intensity or laser lights, etc.

The study of this sort of thing is termed *failure mode analysis*. A device is said to *fall safe* if in failure it goes to a safe condition. For instance, the air brakes on a train are arranged so that the air holds the brakes off. If there is a leak, the system fails safe in that the brakes are applied and the train stops. A traffic light controller must be arranged so that in the event of a failure the lights cannot be green in all directions. They must either all go out or fail red in all directions. Similarly, an automobile engine control cannot fail with the throttle wide open; a failure must stop the engine or take it to idling speed. American courts have begun to consider that the firms and even the individual engineers can be held liable for neglect of these considerations and proper provision for fail safe operation of any product.

ANALOG INTERFACES

The use of the A/D and D/A have been discussed earlier. However, these devices are, in themselves, usually capable only of limited power output and limited voltage output—usually in the 0 to 10V range and a few milliamperes. The processor can be required to operate devices with much larger power requirements or much higher voltage requirements.

Suppose, for example, that it is necessary to test the electric window operator for an automobile. The manufacturer of these devices wants to test:

—No load speed and current.
—Full load speed and current.
—Stalled rotor torque and current.
—Communication waveform.

The no-load speed is a measure of the magnets in the motor as well as the bearing friction. etc. The full load speed and current is a measure of the gearing in the device. The stalled rotor torque and current is a measure of the resistance of the windings. The commutation waveform determines whether all of the windings have been properly welded onto the commutator bars. All of these tests are actually performed under computer control in a period of about 5 seconds. They require analog control of 12 volts and currents up to 15 amperes.

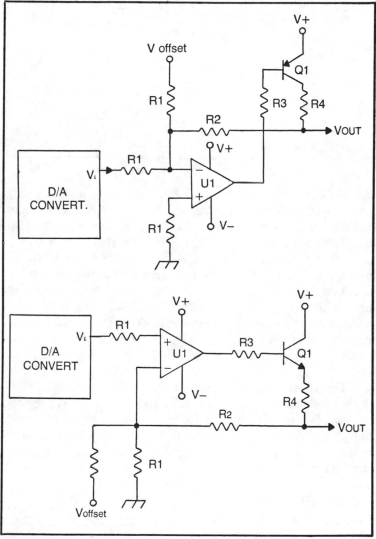

Fig. 13-6. High power or high voltage digitally controlled analog circuits.

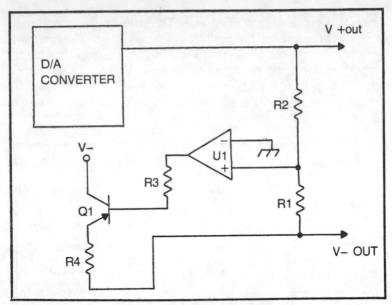

Fig. 13-7. The regulated negative supply or voltage inverter.

The circuits shown in Fig. 13-6 represent techniques which can be used to obtain an increase in range or a larger power capability from a processor controlled D/A converter. In both cases, the ratio of R2/R1 controls the closed loop gain of the system and the output voltage is: V out = R2/R1 (V i + V offset). Resistor R4 serves to limit the maximum output current that the circuit can deliver into a short circuit. This resistor can be used to monitor the current being delivered. Obviously, the voltage developed across R4 has a high common mode voltage which must be ignored by the monitor circuit. This can be done with either the single op amp or with the high CMRR circuit, as shown in Fig. 11-9, to drive an A/D converter.

The power deliverable from a circuit of this type is controlled by the dissipation capabilities of Q1 which will require good heat sinking. The temperature sensor as shown in Fig. 11-1 and a comparator can be used for thermal overload protection. The processor can periodically test the thermal overload bit and shut down the unit if it is overheating.

THE VOLTAGE INVERTER

Sometimes it is necessary to generate a negative voltage which is related to a positive voltage. The circuit as shown in Fig.

264

13-7 will perform this trick. The output is given by: V– out = –V+ out (R1/R2). Suppose that V– out goes too negative so that the junction R1 and R2 goes negative with respect to ground. The output of U1 will go negative causing Q1 to draw less current; thereby making V– go more positive, thus restoring the equilibrium.

R4 serves the same purpose as before and can be metered in the same manner. With a modest op amp, such as a 741, V– can be made to track V+ within a millivolt or so. This is a handy property since certain tests are more easily performed if equal positive and negative voltages are availalbe.

VOLTAGE TO CURRENT CONVERSION

There are a great many tests in which it is handier to provide a constant digitially controlled current and then measure the voltage drop or other activity of the device under test. For example, in testing the drop on zener diodes or light emitting diodes, it is handier to set the current and then measure the voltage. In relays and current sensing solenoids it is usually necessary to determine

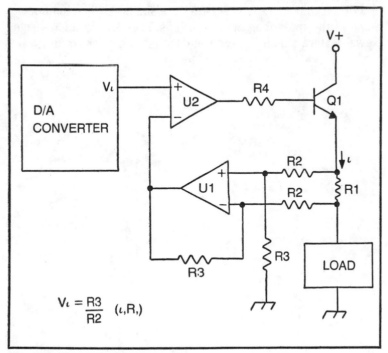

Fig. 13-8. The programmable voltage to current converter.

the current at which they will pull in and the current at which they will drop out.

The circuit shown in Fig. 13-8 illustrates one technique for obtaining a programmable current source. Suppose that the current through the metering resistor R1 is higher than programmed. The common mode rejection amplifier U1 will see this as a more negative voltage on its inverting input which will drive its output to be more positive than the value of V i. This will drive the output of U2 in the negative direction, thereby causing Q1 to draw less current and restoring equilibrium. As V i rises, it takes more and more current to drive the output of U1 up to the value of v i. This design is not as simple as some. However, it has the advantage that the current can be driven to zero and that the current is directly proportional to the output of D/A converter.

OTHER CIRCUITS

The National Semiconductor application notes for linear ICs is an excellent source of neat circuitry for control and application metering circuits for use with microprocessors. In addition, several of the chip manufacturers produce similar application notes. Some of the trade magazines, such as EDN (Electronic Design News) feature a monthly section devoted to similar circuitry.

Microprocessor Arithmetic

14

One of the many advantages of the use of the microprocessor in instruments and controls is the ability to do precision arithmetic on the data. The diode thermometer shown in Fig. 11-1 has a forward voltage drop of the diode with the function:

$$Vo = V1 + 0.2T$$

where
$V1$ = the forward diode drop due to the bias current at 0°C.

T = Temperature in degrees C

In the example an op-amp offset is used to subtract V1 and to do the multiplication 0.2T. However, it should be noted that there were some temperature bath adjustments that were required to make the amp precisely track the real world. Suppose that you wanted to monitor a number of diodes, each of which had a different V1 and a different temperature coefficient. As the number increased, it would become increasingly attractive to simply use an analog switch to connect the diodes one at a time to the A/D converter and do the offset correction and the coefficient correction mathematically in the processor.

This example is not a singular one. A great many measurements of physical paramaters follow an offset linear law like that shown above and require mathematical massaging before the readings can be presented in meaningful physical terms.

Another physical example is the measurement of very low frequencies. Suppose that you wished to measure the frequency of the power line to six significant figures. Since a counter is accurate only to ± one count this would mean that we would have to count a million cycles to achieve the desired accuracy. This would require 16,667 seconds or 4.63 hours. Not only would the length of time be intolerable, but the measurement would be misleading. Averaged over four hours, the power line frequency would probably turn out to be accurate to one part in a million. However, a measurement of a single cycle would tell us something quite different. Suppose that instead of measuring the frequency of the power line directly, you instead measured the number of cycles of a precision 1MHz clock during a single cycle. In most locations you would find that the measurement could jump from 0.016598 seconds to 0.016736 seconds over a span of a few seconds. This corresponds to a frequency span of 60.25 to 59.75 Hz which is obtained by taking the reciprocal of the time.

Several of the modern frequency counters offer the option of using the period of a low frequency wave for measurement. Some of the most modern feature an internal processor so that the frequency can be directly displayed with the internal processor doing the arithmetic of determining the reciprocal. This is a division problem, which is quite common in processor based instruments.

In Chapter 2, I touched upon the binary number system and binary addition and subtraction and noted that most second generation eight-bit machines do not offer an instruction for either multiplication or division. Some newer machines, such as the Motorola 6809, do offer an 8-bit by 8-bit multiply and divide. However, this is useful in only some cases when the limited precision is satisfactory. In this chapter I will touch upon some reasonably fast algorythms for some of the *number crunching* operations which might be required in instruments and controls.

PRECISION REQUIREMENTS

The requirement for precision in measurement and control work is a function of what is being measured or controlled. For example, most voltage and current measurements are made to a precision of 8 or 12 bits corresponding to accuracies of ± 0.39 percent and 0.024 percent. Only under special circumstances are measurements made with much greater accuracy in voltage, current or resistance. The required instruments and procedures are very special. On the other hand, frequency and time are frequently measured to accuracies of 1 part in 10 to the sixth and in special cases to 1 part in 10 to the fifteenth or 10 to the seventeenth.

It is fairly obvious that an 8 × 8 multiply or divide would be useful in some cases for voltage and current measurements. But it would be useless in most frequency measurements, unless a way is found to extend the accuracy of the operation.

MULTIPLICATION

One of the earliest *algorithms* for digital multiplication was the shift and add algorithm. An algorithm is defined as a mechanical procedure which will, if followed, always yield the answer to the problem. In the shift and add algorithm, the multiplicand is shifted one place and stored if the bit under consideration in the multiplier is a I. For example, consider the problem:

$$
\begin{array}{r}
9 \\
\times\ 12 \\
\hline
=\ 108
\end{array}
\qquad (\$C)
\qquad
\begin{array}{r}
I00I \\
\times\ II00 \\
\hline
0 \\
0 \\
I00I \\
I00I \\
\hline
II0II00
\end{array}
$$

or $64 + 32 + 8 + 4 = 108$

The algorithm has the advantage that only one bit of the multiplier is considered at a time and it works very well in a serial machine which considers the addition one bit at a time. However, it is unnecessarily slow in most modern machines which will perform a parallel addition on a single instruction.

The flow chart in Fig. 14-1 shows 8 × 8 multiply algorithm in a form which takes advantage of the 6800 Rotate memory instruction. On rotation, the carry bit is inserted into the spot vacated by the rotation. This is eventually propagated through the following registers. The routine will actually run about 20 percent faster if direct rather than indexed addressing is used. It takes about 74 microseconds for a pass where addition is required and about 44 microseconds for a pass where it is not. At most, the problem will require .016 × 74 = 1.18 microseconds and on the average it will require 1.06 microseconds.

This operation is called a *double precision* operation since it operates on words twice the width of the processor word. The extention to greater precision is fairly obvious. Each of the registers is extended by the proper amount. Both the multiplicand register and the result register have to be twice the width of the number being multiplied. The clear of carry after node 2 is not

269

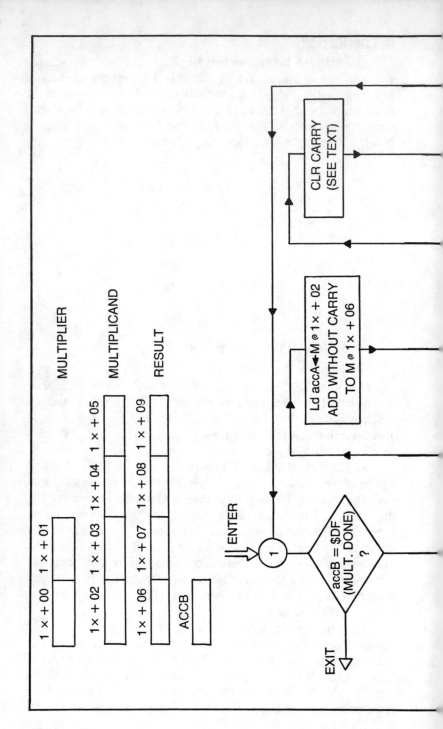

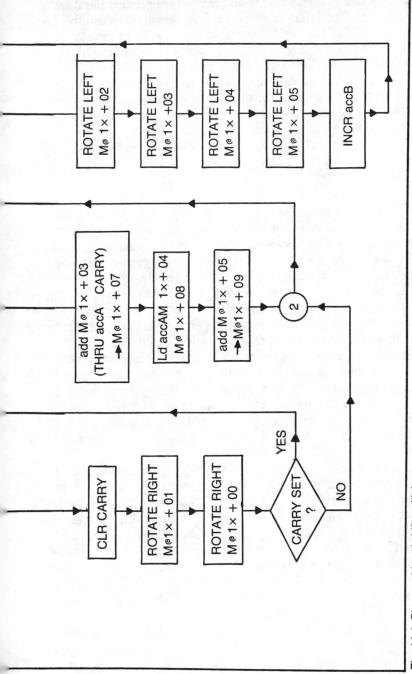

Fig. 14-1. Binary add and shift multiply.

271

actually needed since the result can never overflow the double width result register. However, it was shown for clarity of the program. With increasing precision, the algorithm runs slower since there is not only an additional add and two additional shifts required but the loop must run eight more times for each byte added. A triple precision multiply will run about twice as long. For a 6-byte by 6-byte multiply, the loop running time grows to about 174 microseconds and 48 passes will require a worst case running time of about 8.35 milliseconds. This is a very large binary number, equivalent to 2.8×10^{14} in decimal notation. The accuracy would be suitable for nearly any engineering calculation.

BCD MULTIPLICATION

BCD multiplication is somewhat longer and slower than binary multiplication because of the need to continually adjust the multiplier, the multiplicand and the result for the unused codes in BCD. Most of the processors of the second generation have a decimal adjust command which operates immediately after an addition. However, this tends to make the process slow and a bit clumsy. For example, consider the problem of multiplying 145 × 16 = 2,320. As in the previous case, perform the multiplication by addition. However, the shift band and add algorithm does not work for BCD. Therefore, add the multiplicand to itself as many times as the multiplier number. Decrement the multiplier until it goes to zero. Each memory register contains two BCD digits. Therefore, the maximum contents of a register will be 99. For the example on a 6800, place the multipler in accB and do the arithmetic in accA since only accA is equipped with the DAA or decimal adjust command ($ 19).

The flow chart for a long BCD multiply routine is too lengthly to permit its inclusion here. However, the general operation of the described algorithm is illustrated in Table 14-1. AccB is tested for zero. If it is not zero, the entire multiplier is added, register by register, into the result register—with a decimal adjust being performed on each addition. In steps seven and 14, the decimal adjust propagates across the result register. The decimal adjust from the least significant register must be decimal adjusted in propagation to the next more significant register since it can cause an overflow into hexadecimal.

This is a very slow algorithm since it requires a complete loop for each value of the multiplicand. With large numbers, this can be rather slow. If the multiplicand is larger than 99, you must load it

Table 14-1. BCD Multiplication.

step	Multiplier Reg.	AccB	Result register		
	$145 \times 16 = 2320$				
0	01 45	16	00	00	00
1	01 45	15	00	01	45
2		14	00	02	90
3		13	00	03	BD
	after decimal adjust		00	04	35
4		12	00	05	80
5		11	00	06	AD
	after decimal adjust		00	07	25
6		10	00	08	70
7		9	00	09	9D
	after decimal adjust		00	0A	15
	after decimal adjust		00	10	15
8		8	00	11	60
9		7	00	12	7D
	after decimal adjust		00	13	05
10		6	00	14	50
11		5	00	15	95
12		4	00	16	C2
	after decimal adjust		00	17	40
13		3	00	18	85
14		2	00	19	B2
	after decimal adjust		00	1A	30
	after decimal adjust		00	20	30
15		1	00	21	75
16		0	00	22	A2
	after decimal adjust		00	23	20
	ANSWER				

from the memory register and decrement it to zero. The next more significant register is then tested and if it is not zero it is decremented and accB is reset to 99 and the loop resumed.

This is by no means the fastest possible algorithm for an 8-bit binary machine, but it is easier to explain than some of the faster ones and it is relatively easier to program than some of the more sophisticated ones. It is relatively obvious that the smaller of the two numbers to be multiplied is the one to decrement if the operation is to be speeded up.

BINARY TO BCD CONVERSION

In most control and many instrument applications it is faster and easier to do all of the data manipulation in straight binary notation and then do the conversion only at such time as BCD is required. The simplest and most straightforward technique for accomplishing this is to decrement the binary code and perform an addition followed by a decimal adjust. An algorithm to perform this operation is shown in Fig. 14-2. It should be noted that in the 6800 it is necessary to perform an addition in order to have the decimal adjust function. Storing or wiring to memory does not reset the HINZVC. Therefore, a carry left over from the decimal adjust will remain. It is also noteworthy that the carry is always set by the result of the decimal adjust. Therefore, it is not necessary to clear the carry provided that accA and the memory are added without carry. The node 1 loop takes about 32 microseconds of running time. Therefore, a maximum conversion takes $32 \times 255 = 8.17$ microseconds/byte.

In a processor like the 1802, which does not have a decimal adjust, the count can be softwared by incrementing the count and testing to see whether it has reached $ XA. When it does, the least significant nibble is set to zero and the next significant nibble is incremented. The most significant nibble is then tested to see whether it is an A and the increment propagated. This can happen twice at counts of 100 and 200. The increment into the next byte need never be tested for overflow since it can happen only twice.

BCD TO BINARY CONVERSION

BCD to binary conversion presents something of a different picture since the BCD byte can never overflow a binary byte. On the other hand, it might be necessary to perform a borrow from the next more significant registers in order to fill the binary result register. For example, 02 55 = $ FF. The conversion might require the propagation of the borrow across the full set of BCD registers as when converting $65,535 = $ FFFF. The carry in the binary must also propagate in this example. The speed, including testing, is approximately equivalent to the binary/ BCD conversion and of course is a function of the actual data being converted.

In many control and instrumentation functions, the principle source of BCD data is keyboard entries and the principal requirement for BCD otuput is display or printer operation. If all of the intermediate measurements and data manipulations are handled in binary, it generally speeds operation and takes less code in ROM if an initial BCD/ binary conversion is done on entrys and a binary /BCD conversion is done on output with all of the remainder of the data handling being done in binary.

On the other hand, if the device to be developed is a point-of-sale terminal or a cash register, or other device which principally interfaces with human entrys and requires human displays , it can be preferable to operate directly in BCD.

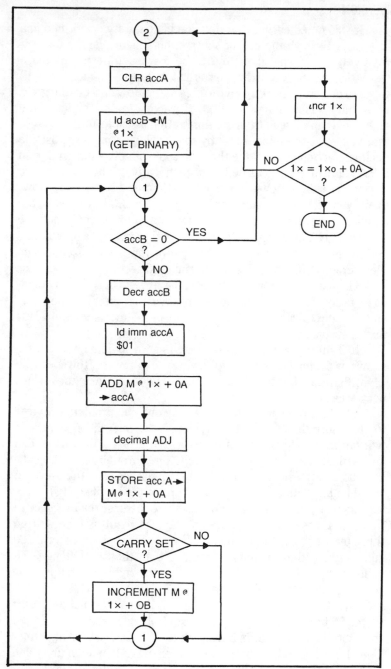

Fig. 14-2. Binary to BCD conversion.

DIVISION

It was noted earlier that division is generally performed in a processor through the use of subtraction which tends to make it relatively slow. The algorithm to be discussed here runs much faster than a simple subtraction routine, but it is a bit more complicated to program. Here again the size of the flow chart is too great to permit its inclusion in the text. However, the principles of the algorythm can be seen from the illustration in Table 14-2. Suppose that you want to divide 9,990 by three. Neglecting any possible decimal fraction you can see that you could simply subtract 3 from 9,990 until the result turned zero or negative. The count of the number of subtractions, 3,330 would then be the answer. However, you would be going through the loop 3,330 times. If the number to be divided were to grow to a million, you would be subtracting 333,000 times. If the subtract, propagate a borrow and increment with a carry propagated routine ran 14 microseconds on the average 333,000 cycles would run 4.66 seconds. If the divisor is 0.3 instead, the problem would run 46.6 seconds. This is obviously fairly slow if large numbers are divided by small numbers. A small pocket calculator will do the same problem in something less than a second.

In Table 14-2 a faster technique is shown. The numbers are shown as decimal for ease in following the example. However, the algorithm runs faster in binary since the decimal adjustments are not required.

The first item on the agenda in any division problem is to test to make sure that you are not dividing by zero. A division by zero will run an infinite amount of time. With this done, the minuend is larger than the subtrahend. In steps one through four, the subtrahend is successively shifted until it is larger than the minuend and then backed off one step. A record of the number of shifts is kept so that you will know where to write the first result. Since in this case three shifts are required, the first result will be written three placed to the left of the binary or decimal point. After three subtractions, the minuend is smaller than the subtrahend. The subtrahend is then shifted one place to the right and the process continued as at step eight and step 12 and at step 16.

In actual practice, the subtrahend is subtracted and the result tested for being negative; if it is the subtrahend is added back in and the subtrahend shifted. In binary, the shift can be a byte at a time. The shift can continue until the subtrahend is less than unity and finally falls off the end of the register or until the minuend is exactly

Table 14-2. Division Speed Up Routine.

STEP	Minuend		Subtrahend		Result		
1	99	90	00	03	00	00.00	00
2	99	90	00	30			
3	99	90	03	00			
4	99	90	30	00			
5	69	90			10	00.00	00
6	39	90			20	00.00	00
7	09	90	30	00	30	00.00	00
8	09	90	03	00			
9	06	90	03	00	31	00.00	00
10	03	90	03	00	32	00.00	00
11	00	90	03	00	33	00.00	00
12	00	90	00	30			
13	00	60	00	30	33	10.00	00
14	00	30	00	30	33	20.00	00
15	00	00	00	30	33	30.00	00
16	Halt						

zero as in this case. The progressive shifting can fill in any number of decimal or binary places. In binary, this algorithm would run in about 22 microseconds per loop. For the problem shown, the running time would be about 302 microseconds including the initial test for zero. Of course, an extension in the number of significant figures extends the running time. If the problem had been 9,991/ 3.037, the running time would have been about eight times as long.

In operating the problem in BCD, the nibbles must be tested for overflow with each operation, which tends to slow the operation. Using this technique for four byte numbers, a binary division can usually be performed in a few tens of milliseconds. The BCD operation of equivalent size will require the best part of a second. In control and instrumentation applications, if the same constant is to be used as a divisor very many times, it is usually practical to take the reciprocal once, store it and multiply to obtain the result.

TRANSCENDENTAL FUNCTIONS

Transcendental functions such as Sin, Cos, Tan, Ln can be calculated in a variety of ways, but most of them are rather slow. Sin function for example can be calculated by:

$$\text{Sin } X = X - \frac{X^3}{3!} + \frac{X^5}{5!} - \frac{C^7}{7!} \quad \ldots\ldots\ldots$$

where X is the angle in radians. As was shown earlier, multiplication is slow, division is slower and this series requires a multiple series of these operations in each term of the series expansion.

For the Sin and Cosine functions, a much faster operation can be obtained by the use of a lookup table, if the limited accuracy is sufficient. Some enhancement in accuracy can be obtained by use of interpolation.

At first glance, it might seem that a simple 8-bit table would give in 255 entries the value of the sin of an angle to one part in 255. However, the sin is a very nonlinear function and it gets very crowded around 90 degrees. For example, the sin of various angles in binary, considering that the binary point is at the far left is shown in Table 14-3. It can be seen that if our angle were confined to a single byte, then a one byte lookup table would be accurate to a half degree only 73 degrees.

One approach would be to make the table have only single byte entries below 73 degrees and have double byte entries above this level for every half degree—thereby adding 16 entries to the table. A somewhat better breakpoint might be 69 degrees since the breakpoint here would occur at an even angle. Sine 69.002 = IIIO IIII. This would add 22 entires to the table. To use this, the lookup algorythm would have to sense whether the angle was 69.5 degrees or above and then go to the double precision table. This table represents a fairly good compromise since the sin 89.68° = IIII IIII IIII IIIO. Below 69 degrees, all entries could be read to the nearest half degree.

Aside from the errors due to the granularity of the table, and interpolation scheme will work fairly well if the calculation is carried out with sufficient precision. For instance, suppose that you want to determine the sin of 45.25 degrees and you know the values of the sines of all angles to a 10-digit precision:

$$\sin 45 = .707106781$$
$$\sin 45 = .719339800$$
$$\text{difference} = .012233019$$
$$\sin 45 + 0.25 \times \text{diff} = .710165036$$
$$\sin 45.25 = .710185376$$
$$\text{error} = .000020340$$

Such a scheme is of little value if the original table errors amount to several tenths of a degree. The split table scheme has errors on the order of .16 degrees in the vicinity of 69 degrees and a gain near 89 degrees. The precision could be improved to about 0.1 degrees with interpolation if the table contained byte and nibble

Table 14-3. The Sin of Various Angles in Binary.

Angle	Sin		
90°	I	0000	0000
84.93°		IIII	IIII
82.83		IIII	IIIO
81.22		IIII	IIOI
79.85		IIII	IIOO
78.66		IIII	IOII
77.57		IIII	IOIO
76.57		IIII	IOOI
75.63		IIII	IOOO
74.76		IIII	OIII
73.93		IIII	OIIO
73.14		IIII	OIOI
72.39		IIII	OIOO
71.66		IIII	OOII
70.96		IIII	OOIO
70.28		IIII	OOOI
69.64		IIII	OOOO

entries below 69 degrees and double bytes above with two bytes and a nibble above about 86 degrees.

An accuracy of 0.1 degrees is probably sufficient for most navigation triangulation problems, but not sufficiently accurate for celestial navigation where angles have to be subtracted. It is probably also accurate for some classes of optical triangulation but not for surveying. Beyond the double byte level, it is probably not worthwhile to pursue the lookup table procedure because the table becomes so long.

In measurement and instrumentation problems, it is frequently necessary to take either natural logs or Naperian logs in order to solve certain classes of problems. In general, this problem is somewhat alleviated by the fact that the quantity whose log is to be taken lies within a rather restricted range. For example, to determine gains in decibels, the actual readings of the two levels probably both come from an A/D converter which has a range of only 0 to 10V. If scale changes due to autoranging are included, these are usually fixed quantities like 20 db or 40 db, etc. Therefore, it is only necessary to take the log of the A/D output over the single range. The nonlinearity of the logarithms also suffers from the granularity problem similar to the trig functions and lends itself to the same form of solutions. A lookup table with 255 entries will probably suffice for most db calculations.

SUMMARY

In this chapter I have attempted to show some of the simpler algorithms for mathematical manipulation of data using a microprocessor. In general, it has been noted that increased precision comes only at the expense of increased operating time and that the handling of data in BCD format nearly always carries a penalty in running time and program complexity.

After an examination of the algorithms required for relatively simple data manipulation, it can be seen what power some of the third generation processors such as the Motorola 6801 or 6809 bring to bear upon the manipulation of data with the offering of 16-bit binary and BCD adds and subtracts and 8 × 8 multiply and divide.

Serial Interfaces and Communication

15

It might be observed that the modern art of electrical engineering began with the concept of serial communications. The way in which this came about can be briefly summarized as follows. In 1820, Hans Christian Oersted showed that an electric current can produce a magnetic field which will deflect a compass needle, and furthermore that the deflection of the needle was proportional to the current strength. This discovery was very significant for several reasons. First of all, it showed that electricity and magnetism were somehow related; a fact that led to the scientific investigation of the relationship. Secondly, it provided for the first time a mechanism for the detection of electrical current which did not rely upon some slow chemical reaction. Here at last was a technique for building a reasonably fast meter to measure electrical current at low voltages such as produced by voltaic piles. It also provided the basis for electrical machinery.

By 1825, William Sturgeon had shown that wires wrapped around an iron bar would turn the bar into an electromagnet. If the iron is soft, the magnetism seems to begin instantaneously with the onset of the current and to cease instantaneously when the current is stopped.

In 1790, a French inventor, Claude Chappe, established a visual telegraph system across France and into Spain. Operators on towers spaced about 20 km would read and relay messages sent by semaphore arms on the tower. This system was an instant success with businessmen and government officials who wanted to follow political and commodity market news. Alexandre Dumas immortalized this system in his novel "The Count of Monte Christo" in which the hero, Edmund Dantes, brought financial ruin to several of his enemys by bribing the semaphore operator.

The seemingly instantaneous reaction of the electromagnet led to a number of investigations into the possibility of using the new inventions in the construction of a system which would duplicate the performance of the semaphore without the dependence upon good visibility. In 1837, William F. Cooke and Charles Wheatstone patented a telegraph in which magnetic needles were deflected to point to letters printed on circular cards. In the initial arrangement, 26 wires were required for the letters and 10 for the numerals for a total of 36 wires. Obviously this was an expensive system to construct because of the large number of wires and it was relatively slow. However, it was a financial success because it was so very much faster than messangers on horseback. The Cooke-Wheatstone telegraph was used in England until 1870.

An American painter, Samuel F.B. Morse, heard about the experiments with the telegraph in 1832 while studying in Europe. Upon returning to the United States, he began a series of experiments in telegraphy and completed his first telegraphic device in 1836. Morse learned about the improvements in electromagnets developed by the American physicist Joseph Henry and improved his telegraph so that on Sept. 4, 1837 he was able to send signals over 1700 feet of wire.

The original Morse telegraph operated by swinging a pen to make V-shaped marks on a strip of paper driven by clockworks. However, the Morse telegraph differed from the Cooke-Wheatstone telegraph in that it required only 1 wire to connect the sender and the receiver. This was an obvious advantage from a financial and construction viewpoint. Very shortly after his first success, Morse came up with two other important improvements. The first was the invention of the relay which would receive a relatively feeble current from a distant sender and re-key the message from a local battery. With this addition, the telegraph could be made to operate over virtually any distance on land.

The second important invention was the Morse code which equated the letters with strings of dots and dashes in a formal and recognizeable manner. It was Alfred Vail, an assistant to Morse, who recognized that with a little practice, you could learn to read the clicks of the Morse code by ear far faster than the sluggish pen or embosser could follow and that the operation of translating the chart record into English could be eliminated. Vail designed a telegraph sounder in which a heavy bar clicked against the bottom of the frame when the current was turned on and against the top of the frame when it was turned off. A dot was read as click-clack and a dash as click — —clack. Within a very few years, operators were sending "Morse" regularly at 20 words-per-minute and a few "lightning slingers" would crank their speed up to 50 words-per-minute until the operator at the far end begged for mercy. In 1843, Congress appropriated $30,000 to build a telegraph line between Washington D.C. and Baltimore, Maryland. On May 24, 1844 Morse sent the famous message "what hath God wrought" (Numbers 23:23) to Vail in Baltimore and Vail relayed the message back to Morse in the Supreme Court Building in Washington. The telegraph was an almost immediate success and within a year the newspapers began to feature "telegraph news."

This first serial communication technique was more or less binary in nature except that it did not lend itself very well to machine decoding. With the audible reception in mind, the original morse code was arranged more or less so that the vowels and the frequently sent letters were shorter. It remained for a Frenchman, Emile Baudot to develop a true binary code in which each character was represented by a five-bit binary word. With the Baudot code, the machine can easily tell when a character is complete because all characters are five bits long. This development in 1880 paved the way for successful printing telegraphs or teletype machines.

ASYNCHRONOUS COMMUNICATIONS

The technique used in most of the original teletypes is termed asynchronous communication since there is no synchronizing clock signal sent along with the data. In the typical teletype loop, a current of 20 mA or 60 mA (there are two standards) is maintained in a loop containing two teletype machines. Either machine can open the circuit and interrupt the current.

Through the use of a tuning fork or the 60 Hz power line, the machines can be adjusted so that they sample the current in the loop at the same rate. However, you have no assurance that they are synchronous, or sampling the current at the same instant in time. Furthermore, the adjustment on the machines is never perfect. Therefore, the one machine could eventually drift with respect to the other. How do they manage to get the two devices in step?

On the simple teletype system, this is accomplished by sending a *start bit*. At the start of a character, the line is taken to zero current for one period. The receiving machine recognizes this start bit and prepares to decode. The next five bits are interpreted as zero or one, depending upon whether the current is low or high during the center third of a *bit cell*. After the five-bit cells are sent, the sending machine returns the loop to the high condition for one,

one-and-one-half or two bit periods for the *stop bit*. There are three standards for the stop bit. The longer stop bits are generally used in radio teletype applications where static or radio noise is likely to be present. The loop can be held in the high or stop condition for any period of time.

Figure 15-1 shows the general layout of this form of start/stop type of transmission. In the illustration, the sampling pulses are shown operating at a rate somewhat different from the transmission. The system will tolerate sampling errors which are small enough so that the receiver does not lose synchronism during the six-bit periods including the five data bits and the stop cell or bit. In this day and age, it is very easy to control the sampling rate to a few parts per million using electronic components and a crystal clock. However, it must be remembered that some of the standards for teletype transmission were set at the turn of the century when the sampling devices were made up entirely of gear trains and mechanical switches. The use of the center third of the cell for sampling is due to the fact that the mechanical switches used on early teletype machines tended to dirty and burn the commutator switch making the transitions from 0 to I and I to 0 very noisy and uncertain. In the center third of the cell, it was usually presumed that the arcing and bouncing had settled out.

For the usual TTY circuit an I is sent as a high and an O is sent as low (full current and zero current respectively). The single-stop bit is rarely used except in very low noise circuits. The timing is for a nominal 60 word-per-minute circuit. The timing is for a nominal 60 word-per-minute circuit. The dot cycles are sent at a rate of 1/22 microseconds = 45.45 Baud (in honor of Baudot) The single character would take 154, 164 or 176 microseconds depending upon the stop bit width. These would correspond to 389.6, 365.85 or 340.9 char per min. If a word is assumed to be five characters in length plus a space character, this would correspond to 64.94, 60.98 or 56.82 words per minute. At this time amateur radio and the computer hobbyist represent the largest usage of the five level baudot code, due principally to the availability of surplus teletypewriters.

The 20 mA or 60 mA loop standards, the start/stop standard and the timing have nothing to say about the content of the code. In theory, you could use any code by assigning any meaning to a given character string. However, one thing should be noted. The use of a five character string allows only for the assignment of 32 characters. This is not sufficient for the 26-letter English alphabet and the

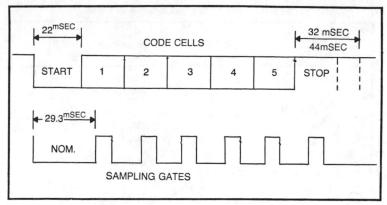

Fig. 15-1. Start/stop transmission with 5-bit code.

numbers zero through nine. In addition to these, it is usually necessary to provide for characters to give necessary functions such as punctuation, line feed, carriage return, space, etc. In order to provide for these, the teletype is fitted with a shift key similar to a typewriter. Upon receipt of the Baudot character "FIGURES = IIOII" (note most codes are sent lsb first, i. e. B1, B2, . . . Bn). The machine would shift and apply a whole new set of definitions to the following code. The new definition would be kept until the machine received "LETTERS = IIIII" when it would shift back to the first definition. If the machine is in the "LETTERS" case, an error on a punched tape could be corrected by punching "letters" over the erroneous character which would punch all five holes. In the "NUMBERS" case the error could be eliminated by punching "LETTERS"—"NUMBERS".

Table 15-1 shows the 5-level Baudot code in both the letters case and the figures case along with a MOORE ARQ code.

ERROR CORRECTING CODES

Once the machine printing of telegraph messages and radio teletype began to take hold, it became apparent that there were certain circumstances in which it would be desirable to have the machine able to detect its own errors. A human operator handling a plaintext message could request a repeat of the transmission if a character became garbled. However, the machine could not sense whether the message was garbled or not. The garbling could arise from static or an interfering station on the radio circuit. On land lines, the garbling could arise from magnetic storm, power line interference or slight malfunctions in the multiplex circuitry which

Table 15-1. The Baudot and Moore ARQ Codes.

Character LETTERS case	NUMBERS case	Baudot 54321	MOORE 7654321
Blank	Blank	00000	1110000
E	3	00001	0001110
Line feed	Line feed	00010	0001101
A	-	00011	0101100
space	space	00100	0001011
S	"	00101	0101010
I	8	00110	0000111
U	7	00111	0100110
Car. Ret	Car Ret	01000	1100001
D		01001	0011100
R	4	01010	0010011
J	Bell	01011	1100010
N	,	01100	0010101
F		01101	1100100
C	:	01110	0011001
K	(	01111	1101000
T	5	10000	1010001
Z	+	10001	1000110
L	)	10010	1010010
W	2	10011	1010010
H		10100	0100101
Y	6	10101	1010100
P	0	10110	0101001
Q	1	10111	1011000
O	9	11000	0110001
B	?	11001	1001100
G		11010	1000011
Figures	Figures	11011	0110010
M	.	11100	1000101
X	/	11101	0110100
V	=	11110	1001001
Letters	Letters	11111	0111000

permitted the transmission of multiple telegraph messages on the same line. An obvious technique for detecting a garbled character is to add *redundant* or extra information to the character.

The MOORE ARQ code is such a code developed for radio transmission. In the MOORE code, every character consists of precisely 4 zeros and three Is. If the receiving machine is equipped with a counter, any error which made the code depart from this format could be recognized and an automatic request for repeat (RQ) could be sent and the character repeated until it was correctly received. Most modern codes have some error detection mechanism included in the code. Some have a very eleborate mechanism in which all single-bit errors can be detected and corrected and some have the ability to detect and correct multiple bit errors.

One of the simplest and most widely used techniques for error detection (with no correction) is the *parity* technique. In this technique, if the initial character has six bits, the seventh bit can be arranged to make the total count of Is in the character either even or odd. In a 7-bit code, the eight bit can be arranged to fulfil the parity assignment. For example, the USACII code for a = II0000I. If even parity is to be used, the string has three Is. Therefore, one I would be added. If odd parity is used, an 0 would be placed in the parity slot which is usually just before the stop bit. The character above is written MSB or LSB. However, it would be sent LSB to MSB. Therefore, with even parity a = I0000III.

Table 15-2 is the code which is most widely used in present day equipment. It was adopted in 1967 by the USA Standards Institute and goes under the title "Recommended USA Standard Code for Information Interchange (USASCII) × 3.4-1967—for use on tape." The code has the advantage of offering a total of 128 characters. Not all of these characters are printable, particularly those in the 00XXXX and 0IXXXX range which contain various device controls, linefeeds, carriage returns, etc. This code obviously takes longer to send than Baudot, by the ratio of 11/8 if parity is used and a double stop bit is used. However, it is richer in content and provides both upper and lower case plus a variety of punctuation symbols and device controls which can be used to remotely enable punches, printers, etc. For most modern equipment, USASCII is the code of choice.

In some cases, a G-bit is subset consisting of IIXXXX, I0XXXX, 0IXXXX and 00XXXX is employed when only upper case letters and numerals and some punctuation will suffice. This subset is used on most home computers which employ a TV screen for readout and also on Union Jack alphanumeric decoding displays. The subset can be obtained from the full set by simply deleting bit 7, provided that the original text was edited to eliminate or not make use of most of the control characters. This permits most 7-bit messages to be read on a 6-bit decoder with a few surprises in store. For example, a DEL (delete) becomes a?. Note also tht the subset does not contain a carriage return or a linefeed. If these are required in the application, they are generally swiped from the punctuation column. You might find that a 7-bit * causes a linefeed and a - causes a carriage return.

If you begin to get the feeling that the phrase "accepts standard ASCII code" does not necessarily mean that the given device will always do exactly what you except it to do, you are copying me correctly. Devices thus designated in advertising will frequently be found to have non standard responses to certain of the codes. For example, certain digital tape recorders have had to swipe some of the ASCII characters in order to produce functions, such as fast forward, stop, fast rewind, etc. Plotters will be found to have swiped characters for pen up, pen down, home, etc. Only be a detailed reading of the specifications and perhaps the unit manual can such departures from "standard" be detected.

SINGLE LINE INTERFACES

All of the codes and material thus far discussed are distinguished by the fact that they can be sent on a single conductor (and ground). In an actual working system, if there is any significant distance to be covered, the transmission medium might prove to be coaxial cable. In any event, it is inadvisable to use the power line ground or other earth connection to provide the signal return. This caution becomes all the more important as the pathlength between the units becomes longer.

For a relatively short haul 20 or 60 mA loop, a circuit arrangement of the sort shown in Fig. 13-8, the programmable voltage-to-current converter can be employed as a transmitter. If the D/A is eliminated, the V/i converter can be adjusted so that the TTl levels on any output port can be made to provide 20 or 60 mA into the loop for a I and zero current for a zero. A photo insulator at the far end of the line for detection will serve to eliminate ground noise from the system and can be readily made to provide TTL level inputs for any of the input ports.

If the transmission line begins to become longer than a few tens of meters, it becomes increasingly necessary to use a transmission line with better RF properties. The most common and the cheapest medium to use is twisted pair wire in which a pair of insulated conductors is tightly twisted together. Because of the twisting, the signals from nearby power lines or other signal lines will tend to cancel and the system will remain relatively noise free.

The current loop type of circuit is generally used for relatively slow transmission of serial data and because it consumes a fair amount of power it is generally relatively free of noise on short to medium length loops. However, if the loop gets to be more than a few miles in length, substantial amounts of voltage may be found on

Table 15-2. The USASCII Code.

BIT NUMBERS				COLUMN →	0	1	2	3	4	5	6	7
b4	b3	b2	b1	ROW ↓	$0\,0\,0$	$0\,0\,1$	$0\,1\,0$	$0\,1\,1$	$1\,0\,0$	$1\,0\,1$	$1\,1\,0$	$1\,1\,1$
0	0	0	0	0	NUL	DLE	SP	0	@	P	`	p
0	0	0	1	1	SOH	DC1	!	1	A	Q	a	q
0	0	1	0	2	STX	DC2	"	2	B	R	b	r
0	0	1	1	3	ETX	DC3	#	3	C	S	c	s
0	1	0	0	4	EOT	DC4	$	4	D	T	d	t
0	1	0	1	5	ENQ	NAK	%	5	E	U	e	u
0	1	1	0	6	ACK	SYN	&	6	F	V	f	v
0	1	1	1	7	BEL	ETB	'	7	G	W	g	w
1	0	0	0	8	BS	CAN	(	8	H	X	h	x
1	0	0	1	9	HT	EM	)	9	I	Y	i	y
1	0	1	0	10	LF	SUB	*	:	J	Z	j	z
1	0	1	1	11	VT	ESC	+	;	K	[	k	{
1	1	0	0	12	FF	FS	,	<	L	\	l		
1	1	0	1	13	CR	GS	-	=	M	]	m	}
1	1	1	0	14	SO	RS	.	>	N	^	n	~
1	1	1	1	15	SI	US	/	?	O	_	o	DEL

NUL Null, or al zeros
SOH Start of heading
STX Start of text
ETX End of text
EOT End of transmission
ENQ Enquiry
ACK Acknowledge
BEL Bell, or alarm
BS   Backspace
HT   Horizontal tabulation
LF   Line feed
VT   Vertical tabulation
FF   Form feed
CR   Carriage return
SO   Shift out
SI   Shift in
DLE Data link escape

DC1 Device control 1
DC2 Device control 2
DC3 Device control 3
DC4 Device control 4
NAK Negative acknowledge
SYN Synchronous idle
ETB End of transmission block
CAN Cancel
EM   End of medium
SUB Substitute
ESC Escape
FS   File separator
GS   Group separator
RS   Record separator
US   Unit separator
SP   Space
DEL Delete

the conductors. The open-circuit voltage can run as high as 75 volts with transients on the order of 150 volts occurring with moderate frequency. On a nominal 20 mA loop it is not unusual to find the equipment designed to accept anything in excess of 16 ma as a I and anything less than 4 ma as a 0. On outdoor lines it will generally be necessary to provide protection from lightning surges and the use of photoisolators on both the transmitter and receiver is highly advisable to avoid difficulties due to ground current loops.

The circuit shown in Fig. 15-2 shows an arrangement suitable for lengths on the order of a few miles. The transmitted data from PIA-1 operates photoisolator PI-1. The output of the phototransistor is changed into an 10/20 mA or 0/60 mA current by a source capable up to 75V on open circuit. The current then flows through the twisted pair to the receiver end. At the receiver end, a surge protector is hung across the line and a resistor chain R1 and R2 divides the voltage such that a current in excess of 16 mA will fire the LED in PI-2. A current less than 4 mA should not provide enough voltage drop to fire the LED. The output of the phototransistor is sensed by PIA-2 and the received data can be read by the second processor.

There are several things worthy of note about this circuit. First of all, you will note that the computer circuits at both ends of the transmission line are completely isolated from one another and from the transmission line. They do not even share the ground line. This is important because a ground line several miles long can carry some substantial voltages which can cause hum and loss of data as well as current damage and malfunctioning of sensitive digital circuits.

Secondly, you will note that the device as shown is a one-way link. A read switch driven by PIA-2 could be used to interrupt the loop current and a second photo isolator shown dotted could be used as a receiver by PIA-1. Obviously, both ends could not transmit simultaneously. However, the receiving end could signal the sending end of a request to transmit by opening the loop which would be sensed by the sending end during a stop bit.

HARDWARE VERSUS SOFTWARE

In the arrangements as discussed thus far, it is presumed that the data transmission and the data sensing can be done using any output port and input port with the code being sent one bit at a time and sensed one bit at a time under complete software control. Up to transmission speeds of 9600 Baud, a 6800 CPU and a 6821 PIA could keep up with this—provided they had little else to do. An 1802 CPU would give up somewhat earlier. There is, however, hardware aid available to facilitate faster data exchange and free the processor for other tasks as well.

It is obvious that the use of an 8-bit machine to 5-, 6- or 7-bit output words 1 bit at a time is a bit wasteful of the machine capabilities. For this reason, several chip manufacturers offer special purpose dedicated chips for the purpose of freeing serial communications. Basically, these devices are *serial/parallel* and *parallel/serial converters*. In the transmitting case, the processor supplies a single parallel word to the device. Depending upon the condition code, the chip interprets this as a 5-, 6- or 7-bit character. Depending upon other condition codes, the chip can add parity and start and stop bits of any of the three lengths. The word is then shifted out at a Baud rate determined by the Baud rate clock supplied to it.

There is an obvious speed up here. Only a single output instruction is required to handle the 11 bits of a full ASCII character and the chip does the parity calculation as well. When the chip is empty, it sets a flag to inform the processor that it is ready for the next character. Obviously, this could speed up the transmission by a factor of more than 11. The achivement of Baud rates as high as 500 KBaud is possible.

On receive, the chip detects the start bit, marches the data into the shift register and sets a flag when it is filled. It will also test parity and test for overflow and set flags accordingly. Here again, the potential for speedup is obvious.

Motorola calls this form of device an Asynchronous Communications Interface Adapter (ACIA). The Motorola MC6850 ACIA is addressed like memory and is initialized with a routine similar to that used to initialize a PIA. The format can be changed regarding word length, parity and stop bit length under software control. In distinction to this, the RCA CDP 1854 has lines which must be held high or low to achieve this function. This chip has the advantage when used with the 1802 that it is capable of demixing the data from the data/address bus of the 1802 without additional hardware. In other applications, the receiver and transmitter sections can be used simultaneously since a separate parallel bus is provided for both the receiver and the transmitter sections. Similar chips are available for use with other processors and some of the chip manufacturers who do not offer processors also have chips with similar features available.

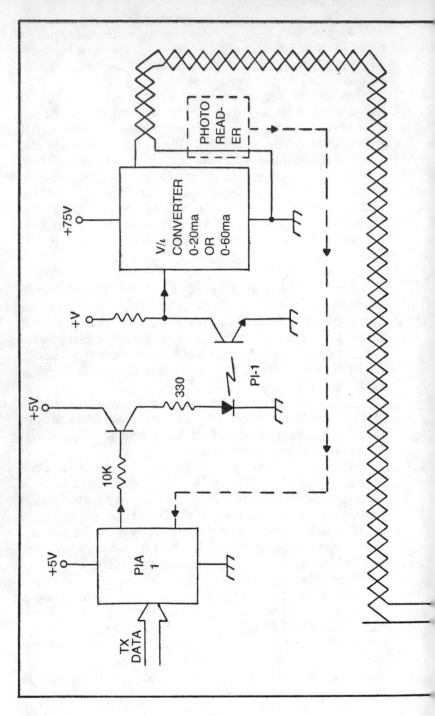

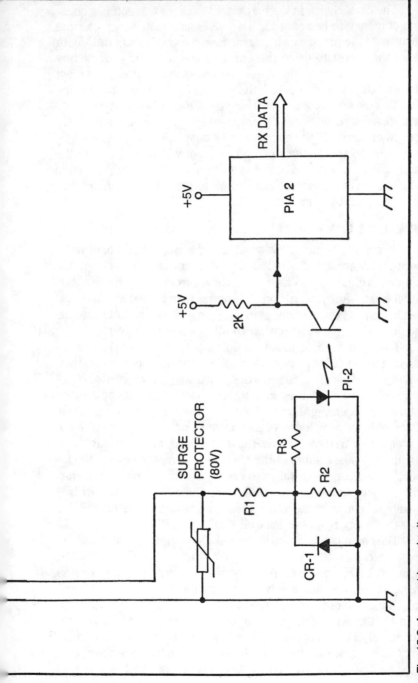

Fig. 15-2. A current loop circuit.

293

The chief choice in the hardware/software tradeoff is a question of money to be spent for hardware serialization versus time spent with the processor in performing the transmission. In both cases the power to drive the external line must be provided by external circuitry and the detection and isolation functions must also be externally provided. If the processor is not very busy at the time that the serial communication is required, money can be saved on the hardware by simply driving from an available output port. On the other hand, if the processor is busy, the simplification in software and the reduces processor load will be well worth the hardware cost. It should be noted that some of the third generation single-chip computers such as the Motorola 6801 offer ACIA features as a built-in function.

THE KANSAS CITY FORMAT

Frequently some of the small stand-along single board microcomputers are listed with the legend "record and load programs using an ordinary audio tape cassette recorder using the Kansas City format." A few words on the Kansas City format are in order both because of the usefulness in very small development systems and because of the relationship to other audio type systems.

To begin with, a small audio cassette recorder is mainly designated to record voice transmissions and perhaps some rather lo-fi music. Most of these recorders have a very powerful automatic level control and they are not equipped with a manual level control for recording. Furthermore, they will generally play back at some speed which can depart from the recording speed by 1 percent to 2 percent. Since the human ear is not particularly sensitive to phase shifts of the harmonics compared to the fundamental, no great care is taken to keep the harmonic phase constant with respect to the fundamental. In addition to this, the low frequency response of these machines is sharply truncated and the high frequency response isn't all that great either.

The combination of the strong ALC and the phase shift causes these machines to do cruel things to the shape of squarewave inputs. A 1 KHz squarewave will typically emerge as a more or less triangular wave with a few hooks on the sides near the zero crossings. In a non-return to zero code, a long string of zeros will open up the ALC and the next one will saturate the machine. Conversely a string of several 1s will sag badly in the middle to the point of approaching the zero level. Obviously, something else must be done if the code is to be preserved on the tape.

In the Kansas City Format this is done by deriving all of the code cells by counting down from a 4800 Hz block. The Kansas City format was originally formulated during a symposium sponsored by BYTE magazine in Kansas City, Missouri in November of 1975. It has the following features:

■ A logical I is recorded as eight cycles of a 2400Hz sinewave.

■ A logical 0 is recorded as four cycles of a 1200 Hz sinewave.

Note that since both of these are derived from the same clock, the transition takes place at the zero crossing with minimal transient disturbance.

■ A recorded character begins with a space or logical 0 as a start bit. This is followed by eight data bits. The cahracter is ended with two or more marks or logical Is as stop bits.

■ The interval between characters consists of an unspecified amount of time with the line in the Mark or logical — condition (in other words at 2400 Hz).

■ In the data character, the LSB is transmitted first and the MSB transmitted before the stop bits.

■ The data train is of variable length at the option of the recorder but must be preceded by at least five seconds of Marks (2400 Hz).

■ Meaningful data must not be recorded on the first 30 seconds of the tape following the clear leader.

In the realization of the KC format in the Motorola MEK-D2 kits, there were some features added which make the format easier to use for certain things.

■ At the beginning of the tape (BOT) the ASCII character "B" is transmitted after 1024 successive marks (about 30 seconds).

■ Immediately following the "B" is one byte containing the number of bytes in the program block.

■ Immediately following this is a 2-byte block containing the starting address in memory for the program. Note that is any absolute addresses are used it is necessary that the program reside at a specific address; it is not "transportable."

■ Up to 256 bytes of data are then recorded.

■ The close of the program is signaled by 25 successive marks (2400 Hz) and the ASCII character "G."

The KC format is relatively successful as a mechanism for recording and perhaps transmitting or transporting short programs of the sort that you are likely to write into the RAM of one of the development or evaluation type single-board microcomputers. The format is relatively slow. The individual bit represents either eight cycles at 2400 Hz or four cycles at 1200 Hz or 0.00333. A complete byte takes 11 bit times or 36.67 microseconds. Therefore, a 255 byte segment takes 9.35 seconds to transfer. However, note that the preamble and the post amble require something approaching a minute the Motorola configuration. The transmission rate is 300 Baud. In some of the hobby-type home computers, the loading of a truncated BASIC would take 150.19 seconds for the 4K byte program. You can plan to sit and wait a bit while the recorder churns out the program.

Despite these drawbacks, the KC format has the advantage that it can be operated with an absolute minimum of hardware or at least no special, expensive hardware. Since the modulation is entirely at two frequencies well within the voice frequency range, and since the frequencies are filtered out to be relatively pure sinewaves, the reproduction from even a fairly cheap cassette recorder is very good. The quality is also enhanced because the transitions between 0s and 1s take place at the zero crossings. Therefore, the harmonic content in minimized. This format is also suitable for transmission over the telephone lines for the same reasons. It places minimal demands upon any channel designed for voice transmission. In areas where the relatively slow data rate is not objectionable, this is a reasonably good choice.

The filtering of the squarewaves into sinewaves can be readily accomplished with a few IC packages configured into active bandpass filters in a matter of only a few square inches of board space. The hardware realization of the entire arrangement is inexpensive and non-critical.

STANDARD INTERFACES

The basic purpose of the standard interface is to ensure that two units with the standard interface will plug together. The plug on one unit will fit the socket on the other and all of the voltages will be of the right polarity and magnitude so that the units will not burn one another out and hopefully the first unit can operate the second and vice versa.

In actual practice, the user might buy several units all possessed of the same interface and usually find that they do indeed plug together and they will generally not burn one another out. However, the software that will operate one line printer or plotter will

296

not necessarily operate another from a different manufacturer even though both are advertised as having a "standard RS-232 interface" or being "IEEE-488 compatible."

Each of these standards is far too large to examine in any significant detail in this book since they each fill a small book by themselves. For the reader who will actually have to be working with one or the other of these, the only real solution is to buy the specification itself and plan to spend a fair number of evenings trying to decipher the meaning of some of the definitions.

For this book, I will have to be content to point out a few of the salient features of the individual standard and the manner in which they affect the usage with a microprocessor.

The RS-232-C Standard

The RS-232-C standard is used for interconnecting all sorts of printers, plotters, terminals and other peripheral devices to minicomputers and computers. The official title is: EIA STANDARD - Interface between Data Terminal Equipment and Data Communications Equipment Employing Serial Binary Data Interchange. August, 1969. It is available from:

Electronic Industries Association
Engineering Department
2001 Eye Street N.W.
Washington D.C. 20006

This standard is used throughout the United States and Canada. For the rest of the world, the more common standard is the CCITT-V24.

The RS -232 was originally promulgated to permit the manufacturers of peripheral equipment for use with computer to be "plug compatible" with one another. The basic idea is that items purchased from different manufacturers could simply plug into one another. A computer purchased from firm A could be plugged into a terminal from firm B, etc. To this extent the standard is a success. The plugs do fit and the voltages do not cause the units to destroy one another. However, it should be noted that no particular coding is specified in the serial data to be sent and no specific interpretation is applied to the coding sent. Therefore, the statement "RS-232C compatible" does not necessarily mean that any two devices can be simply unwrapped, plugged together and be expected to operate immediately.

A parallel can be drawn to the telephone system. The telephone companys of the world guarantee to provide a microphone capable of accepting human speech, an earphone capable of reproducing human speech and the necessary amplifiers and switching equipment to connect any two instruments together. The process of transacting business over the telephone is left entirely to the user. If you call someone in Belgium on the telephone, there is no guarantee that the person who answer the call will understand the sounds of the English language.

The interface voltage on RS-232 is bipolar. Both positive and negative voltages are used. The table that follows the various notation used to describe the state of a given line.

NOTATION	VOLTAGE ON LINE	
	$+25 > V > +3$	$-25 < V < -3$
Binary State	0	I
Signal Cindition	Space	Mark
Function	ON	OFF

The various notations are used interchangeably to describe the state of a line. The load impedance of a receiving device attached to the line will show a dc resistance between 3,000 and 7,000 ohms and the shunt capacitance measured at the interface point will be less than 2500 pf.

On the driver or transmitter end, the voltage applied to the line under open circuit conditions will not exceed 25 volts. With a proper termination, the driver will stay between 5 and 15 volts. The driver impedance will also be such that a short circuit between any two terminals will result in a current less than a half ampere.

There are a number of other items in the specifications concerning the transitions. The time being specified is not more than one millisecond or 4 percent of the signal normal duration and the voltage rate of change not exceeding 30V/microseconds. The RS-232 uses a 25 pin plug and only pins 11, 18 and 25 unassigned. The labels for the plug are shown in the Table 15-3.

One of the most obvious interface requirements involves the level shifting required to convert the bipolar signals to the TTL levels which are more standard on most processor interfaces. There are a number of chips which have been developed for this use. However, the circuit shown in Fig. 15-3 represents an im-

Table 15-3. RS-232-C Connector Pin Assignments
(Cinch Model DB-51226-1 or Equivalent).

Pin Number	Circuit	Description
1	AA	Protective Ground
2	BA	Transmitted Data
3	BB	Received Data
4	CA	Request to Send
5	CB	Clear to Send
6	CC	Data Set Ready
7	AB	Signal Ground (Common Return)
8	CF	Received Line Signal Detector
9	-	(Reserved for Data Set Testing)
10	-	(Reserved for Data Set Testing)
11		Unassigned (See section 3.23)
12	SCF	Sec. Rec'd. Line Sig. Detector
13	SCB	Sec. Clear to Send
14	SBA	Secondary Transmitted Data
15	DB	Transmission Signal Element Timing (DCE Source)
16	SBB	Secondary Received Data
17	DD	Receiver Signal Element Timing (DCE Source)
18		Unassigned
19	SCA	Secondary Request to Send
20	CD	Data Terminal Ready
21	CG	Signal Quality Detector
22	CE	Ring Indicator
23	CH/CI	Data Signal Rate Selector (DTE/DCE Source)
24	DA	Transmit Signal Elemnet Timing (DTE Source)
25		Unassigned

plementation of the transmit and receive functions using discrete components.

In the transmitter, a TTL high will cutoff Q1 which in turn cuts off Q2. A TTL low will saturate Q1 which in turn saturates Q2. Thus a TTL high will produce an output of +7.3 volts minimum and +8.64V maximum for an RS-232-c logical 0. There is a data inversion in the transmitter. A TTL low will produce an output of approximately −9 volts. The 40 ohm resistor will limit the current to 0.5 amp on an intermittant short. It will overheat on a continuous short. The data inversion can readily be accomodated by software.

The receiver does not require logical inversion since it performs the inversion as well as the level shifting function. The diode CR-1 is used to protect the base-emitter junction of Q3 from the RS-232-C logical 0 voltage which can reach +25 volts which would exceed the PIV rating of the junction. The base resistor approaches the minimum RS-232-C load and the capacitive loading is only a few pf. The RS-232 standard is recommended for cable lengths of 15 meters or less. However, longer cables can be used if attention is given to the capacitive loading.

The IEEE-48 Standard

The IEEE-488-1975 standard is somewhat different in application from the RS-232-C. Whereas the 232 is used largely in traditional computer/data processing applications, the 488 was specifically developed for the interconnection of desktop computer/calculators to laboratory instruments such as voltmeters, programmable power supplys, signal generators and data plotters. Whereas the 232 is a strictly serial data arrangement, the 488 sends data bytes and addresses in parallel and only the byte string is serial.

The 488 standard was initally conceived by the Hewlett Packard Corporation as a mechanism for automation of laboratory and production measurements employing their standard instruments and desktop computers. It was subsequently adopted by the IEEE for general usage. The rapid adoption of this standard was probably due in large measure to the position of the Hewlett Packard Corporation in the measurement and computer industry. At the time of the promulgation of the 488 standard, only Hewlett Packard was producing both a very broad line of instruments and a broad line of desktop computers and computer peripherals. The very adoption of the standard as an internal standard within Hewlett Packard made it attractive to other instrument suppliers since their instruments could be adapted to the use of Hewlett Packard computers if they matched the HPIB standard. Conversely, firms like Commodore that manufacture only computers could take advantage of the standard and use their computer to drive standard instruments. The Pet computer communicates with all peripherals via the 48 bus.

The 488 interface bus is described in detail in: IEEE Standard Digital Interface for Programmable Instrumentation IEEE Std 488-1975. It is available from:

The Institute of Electrical And Electronic Engineers
345 East 47th Street
New York, NY 10017
The bus operates at standard TTL levels with some special re-

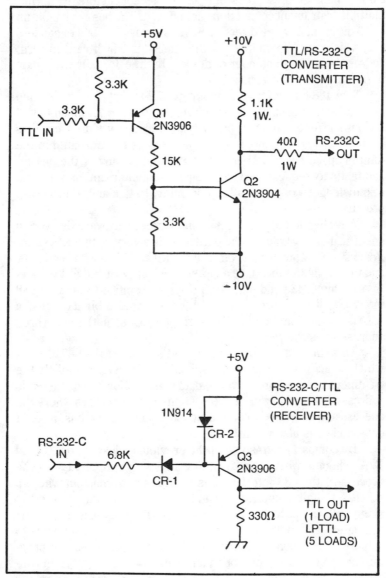

Fig. 15-3. Implementation of the transmit and receive functions using discrete components.

quirements upon the transmitters and receivers. It is limited to cables of 15 meters in general. However, it can be extended with certain precautions. The plug and socked used carries 24 pins and is of the Microribbon type. Cables in finished form are available from a number of sources and stackable connectors to permit multiple instrument connections are offered. The bus can handle up to 15 different devices directly. Several firms offer bus expanders win which one bus address is the expander which can, in turn, address some large number of devices by transforming input data into extended addresses.

The 488 bus differs also from the 232 in that it has a detailed protocol and state structure for addressing the various inhabitant of the bus and for establishing primary and secondary addresses. This protocol and arrangement is far too complex to be treated in the limited space available here. Mechanisms for any of the bus inhabitants to request service, request an interrupt, accept and acknowledge service from the computer, to talk and to listen are provided.

A realization of the 488 bus in discrete hardware or even in small scale integration at the gate level is a very complex system. Fortunately, Motorola has offered the MC68488 interface adapter and the MC3448A interface adapter which are LSI and SSI respectively. One 68488 and four 3488 chips will suffice to provide 488 interfacing to any processor with a dedicated 8-bit data bus, a READ/WRITE and an $\overline{IRQ}$ (interrupt request not) line. Three address lines are required as well.

This chip has a setup arrangement similiar to the 6821 PIA in which specific commands to specific addresses establish the treatment to be accorded to the data which follows. The 68488 is addressed as memory in a 6800 system. For processors where the address and data have to be multiplexed on the same bus, a set of data latches is also required.

By comparison to some of the previously described A/D and D/A schemes where a dedicated converter is supplied with the processor, the 488 interface bus provides a mechanism where a purchased digital multimeter can be directly plugged into the bus along with the purchased power supply and a purchased desktop computer. The multimeter can be switched from volts to ohms to amperes under software control. The power supply can be programmed to output n volts or m amperes also under program control. The user need only supply the software and connect the instruments.

Compared to the 232, the transfer of data can be faster since it is sent a byte at a time rather than a bit at a time. Furthermore, 488 compatible devices are built so that they have the capability to listen to messages addressed to them and ignore all others. The 232 devices might or might not have such provision since it is not specified.

Compared to completely dedicated control applications, the very flexibility of the 488 bus puts it at a speed disadvantage since you must specify in the command which device is to be addressed, the mode in which it is to be addressed and what it is expected to do. You must also wait for the device to acknowledge receipt of the command. By comparison, an output voltage command to a D/A is only a single word sent to a specific memory address.

Economic consideration are also significant. When the task is to monitor a changing voltage, does the monitor function get performed by a $8 A/D on the processor address bus or by a $3,450, 488-Compatible Digital Multimeter? If the device needs changes of functions such as a switch from volts to ohms to amperes, the 488 bus might make sense.

As a general rule, the 488 bus is probably worth inclusion in any general usage controller which is intended to function for a time at one task and be frequently reassigned to other tasks. For specific monitoring and control applications, the dedicated system will show cost and speed advantages in most cases.

Index

Index